US Business Cycles 1954–2020

What causes cyclical downturns that wreak havoc on our lives? Most economists will say that they result from random external shocks and that, without these, the economy would sail along beautifully. In *US Business Cycles 1954–2020*, John T. Harvey argues that overwhelming evidence points to an internal dynamic, one related to the behavior of economic agents that generates what we call a business cycle. He draws on the work of past Post Keynesian and Institutionalist scholars to create a current theory of business cycles, one that treats them as systemic and not the result of random chance. He addresses not only unemployment and bankruptcies that are the immediate consequence of the business cycle but also critical social challenges like climate change and elderly care. Examining an extensive history of US fluctuations, Harvey fills a long-standing void within the discipline by offering an alternative theory of income, employment, and price determination.

John T. Harvey is the Hal Wright Professor of Economics in the Department of Economics at Texas Christian University. He is a well-known heterodox scholar who has published extensively, including two books: *Currencies, Crises and Capital Flows* (2009) and *Contending Perspectives in Economics* (2020, 2nd edition). He has earned numerous awards for teaching and research, and his work focuses on exchange rates and business cycles.

US Business Cycles 1954–2020
Sources, Symptoms, Solutions

JOHN T. HARVEY
Texas Christian University

Shaftesbury Road, Cambridge CB2 8EA, United Kingdom

One Liberty Plaza, 20th Floor, New York, NY 10006, USA

477 Williamstown Road, Port Melbourne, VIC 3207, Australia

314–321, 3rd Floor, Plot 3, Splendor Forum, Jasola District Centre, New Delhi – 110025, India

103 Penang Road, #05–06/07, Visioncrest Commercial, Singapore 238467

Cambridge University Press is part of Cambridge University Press & Assessment, a department of the University of Cambridge.

We share the University's mission to contribute to society through the pursuit of education, learning and research at the highest international levels of excellence.

www.cambridge.org
Information on this title: www.cambridge.org/9781009693530
DOI: 10.1017/9781009693509

© John T. Harvey 2025

This publication is in copyright. Subject to statutory exception and to the provisions of relevant collective licensing agreements, no reproduction of any part may take place without the written permission of Cambridge University Press & Assessment.

When citing this work, please include a reference to the DOI 10.1017/9781009693509

First published 2025

Cover image: lvcandy / DigitalVision Vectors / Getty Images

A catalogue record for this publication is available from the British Library

A Cataloging-in-Publication data record for this book is available from the Library of Congress

ISBN 978-1-009-69352-3 Hardback
ISBN 978-1-009-69353-0 Paperback

Cambridge University Press & Assessment has no responsibility for the persistence or accuracy of URLs for external or third-party internet websites referred to in this publication and does not guarantee that any content on such websites is, or will remain, accurate or appropriate.

For EU product safety concerns, contact us at Calle de José Abascal, 56, 1°, 28003 Madrid, Spain, or email eugpsr@cambridge.org

Contents

List of Figures	*page* vii
List of Tables	ix
Preface	xi
Acknowledgments	xvii
1 Introduction: The Sorry State of Modern Macro Theory	1
2 Theoretical Foundation aka What Causes Business Cycles?	6
3 Additional Factors: Inflation, Monetary and Fiscal Policy, the Stock Market, and Secular Stagnation	35
4 US Business Cycles 1954 through 2020	53
5 Policy and Conclusions	106
Appendix: Critical Survey of Business Cycle Theories	129
References	161
Index	177

Figures

2.1	Feedback loops and the business cycle	*page* 20
2.2	Kalecki's investment-gestation period	33
A.1	Kalecki's investment-gestation period	137
A.2	Kalecki's investment-decision curve	139
A.3	Shifts in the investment-decision curve creating a cycle	140
A.4	Minsky's investment without financing	143
A.5	Minsky's investment including internal financing and borrower's risk	144
A.6	Minsky's investment with financing and borrower's and lender's risk	145
A.7	Demand for capital curve	147
A.8	The determination of the spot price	147
A.9	Complete demand for and supply of capital	148
A.10	Negative net investment	148

Tables

2.1	Preliminary evidence from US cycles US 1954Q3 to 2020Q2	page 22
2.2	Balance sheet of a representative commercial bank	25
2.3	Balance sheet immediately after loan	27
2.4	Lehman Brothers' balance sheet	29
4.1	US cycles since 1954	54
4.2	Key indicators 1954Q3 through 2020Q2 (omitting 1980Q4 through 1982Q4)	55
4.3	Key indicators Ike I Cycle	57
4.4	Key indicators Ike II Cycle	61
4.5	Key indicators Vietnam Cycle	64
4.6	Key indicators Oil Shock I Cycle	71
4.7	Key indicators Oil Shock II Cycle	75
4.8	Key indicators Volcker Cycle	79
4.9	Key indicators Desert Storm Cycle	83
4.10	Key indicators September 11 Cycle	88
4.11	Key indicators Subprime Crisis Cycle	94
4.12	Key indicators COVID Cycle	100
4.13	Contributions to GDP growth by category	101
5.1	The economy in three sectors	122
5.2	Sectoral balances in selected periods	122
A.1	Stages in Kalecki's cycle	140

Preface

WHY I WROTE THIS BOOK

This volume represents the end of a very long journey, one that began well before my first economics course. The seeds were planted in early childhood as I learned of my maternal grandparents' experiences during World War II. Initially, they were together in London. My grandfather, an Irish national, had apparently not been in England long enough to be trusted to carry a gun, so they let him join the fire service.[1] He extinguished blazes started by the Luftwaffe all through the Blitz and the V1 and V2 attacks. Meanwhile, my Nan – along with my Mum – was evacuated to the countryside. My mother, though very little, can even remember German prisoners of war working the fields (they would give the English children some of their Red Cross candy). By the end of the war, one of Granddad's brothers was buried in a military cemetery in North Africa, where he still lies. I have the telegram announcing his death to his mother (in English and Irish) on my office wall and his portrait over my desk.

Hearing these stories gave me an intense interest in military history, especially World War II in Europe. And while at first that meant reading about events like the Battle of Britain, Stalingrad, and D-Day, it later led to wanting to understand how the world came to such a brutally low point in the first place. Enter economics and the Great Depression.

Many factors contributed to Hitler's rise to power, but historians agree that one of the most critical was Germany's economic collapse (Voth 2020). It was a function of the conditions imposed by the Treaty of Versailles and, later, the

---

[1] The family joke was that, had he truly wanted to cause mayhem, the National Fire Service would have been perfect cover! "Jaysus, Mary, and Joseph, how did another fire start over there!!!" Fortunately for England, neither he nor his brothers had any such intention.

worldwide depression. John Maynard Keynes, an economist whose work is central to the rest of this volume, wrote about the fatal flaws in the former in his *Economic Consequences of the Peace* (1920). He had intimate knowledge of the treaty and the process by which it had been negotiated, as he was one of the British representatives; but such was the writing on the wall that he resigned. My attention, however, was drawn instead to the economic downturn and particularly the fact that *the Great Depression followed directly on the heels of one of the strongest expansions in history*, the Roaring Twenties. What made this transition from boom to bust possible? How could US unemployment hover around 4 percent for the latter half of the 1920s and then rise suddenly and catastrophically to double digits by 1931 and remain there – peaking at just under 25 percent – until 1941? Conditions were much worse in Germany, of course, where they added decisively to the forces contributing to the rise of nationalism, racism, and violence.

My curiosity remained unsated for quite some time, however, as answers were not readily available, at least not in the books I was reading nor the wargames with which I had become obsessed.[2] I was taken further afield by my strongly held belief that what I really wanted to do with my life was become a physicist. Taking "Honors Fundamental Physics: Heat and Light" in the fall of 1979 quickly cured me of that, but I had been so sure of this goal that I had no backup plan. I was disheartened and adrift for a while, trying to figure out what I really wanted to study. It should have been obvious, given my passion for military history and understanding the underlying causes of conflict. Fortunately, I eventually saw this and gave up on my dreams of working in the space program to become a double major in political science (focusing on international relations) and economics. Now I could finally learn how *Roaring* turned into *Depression* and furthered the rise of totalitarianism ... or so I thought.

Unfortunately, none of my undergraduate classes ever explained business cycles. I had assumed that this would be a major topic, but it was not. That said, I thoroughly enjoyed my professors and their courses, so much so that it convinced me to go to graduate school.[3] Not only was I anxious to know more, but surely there I would learn about the Great Depression and other such downturns!

Again the answer was no. When I started the program in 1983, the core macroeconomics faculty were all mainstream economists. As will be explained in Chapter 1, they do not believe that business cycles even exist. Rather, they think that the economy could stay at full employment forever, sailing happily along unless and until some external force (like COVID) knocks us off our

---

[2] These are complex board games with maps, hundreds to thousands of playing pieces, and rule books ranging from 10 to 100 pages. Playing time could be hours to days or weeks. Needless to say, I did not date much.
[3] Only later did I understand that these had been all the nonmainstream economists.

Preface   xiii

pleasant equilibrium. The Great Depression was just some weird thing that happened, and who really knows why?[4] On the one hand, I cannot deny that weird things **do** happen sometimes; on the other, because the rest of what I was learning from those same instructors seemed so out of touch with reality, I had a gnawing feeling that there was more to it.

There was one place in my graduate education where I sensed that I was getting at least the beginnings of an answer. Ironically, it was in a course that is rarely offered in economics doctoral programs today: the history of economic thought. There, you learn about the scholars who played foundational roles in our discipline: Adam Smith, David Ricardo, Karl Marx, Alfred Marshall, Carl Menger, John Maynard Keynes, and so on. In my professor's (Hans Jensen) version, we were assigned Keynes' *General Theory of Employment, Interest, and Money*, a volume written during the Great Depression and with a self-conscious understanding of the role that the economic collapse was playing in the rise of extremism across the globe (Keynes 1936). While I struggled to understand some of what Keynes was saying, and he only had one chapter on business cycles, I knew this was the right direction. I was finally getting a glimmer of light at the end of the tunnel, and I hoped to keep moving forward once I finished my doctorate and secured a position somewhere.

That somewhere turned out to be Texas Christian University, where I started work in 1987 and remain today. I was very lucky to land here, as it is a rare institution where research outside of the mainstream is rewarded. I was thus able to set about trying to learn a new economics, different from that in which I had been trained in my core macroeconomic theory courses.[5] This took very many years, most of which were occupied by writing about another interest of mine, exchange rates.[6] While I had not given up on business cycles, I simply felt too unprepared to say anything useful of my own, and so I just kept reading. Finally – fully fifteen years after I had earned my PhD and decades after I had first wondered how expansions can turn into recessions – I published an article in the area (Harvey 2002). It would be nine more years before I did another, however (Harvey 2011). I was getting there, but it was slow going.

In the meantime, I did something that I am not sure students realize us professors do: I created a class on the topic simply because I wanted to force myself to learn more about it! The first iteration was in 2004, and it was a massive undertaking. There is no decent textbook, and I was also keen to cover

---

[4] They reacted similarly to the financial crisis of 2007–2008, referring to it as a black swan event.
[5] Although it was entirely consistent with that which I had learned from my economic history and history of economics instructors – including the aforementioned Hans Jensen – all of whom were Institutionalists and not Neoclassicals.
[6] I was still studying Keynes, however, as I believed that much of his analysis of financial markets could be transferred over to currency markets. In that sense, it was still contributing to my macroeconomics re-education.

the history of US business cycles as well as the theory of what drives them. This required reading hundreds and hundreds of pages of contemporary accounts and collecting these into documents that the students could read. Fast forward twenty years and add in a sabbatical focused on learning the many theories that have been forwarded on the subject, and you get this book. Finally, after all this time, I feel as if I understand the economic event that was a major catalyst in creating the world in which my nan and granddad found themselves in 1939. In that sense, this volume is for me a huge relief and a kind of closure.

So what caused the Great Depression? Ironically, it is not covered here because my historical survey does not start until 1954 (the point at which there exists a sufficient volume of reliable data for the analysis I wish to undertake)! But, to say something very briefly and simply, there were multiple problems. First, over the 1920s, people in the US continued to move from the countryside to the cities as industry grew. This now made employment increasingly dependent on the business cycle. An economic downturn on a farm is not pleasant, especially as they became increasingly tied to farming for the market. But, their situation is much more flexible than that faced by an auto worker (especially before the New Deal programs came into effect). Furthermore, people have to eat, so there is a strong core demand for agricultural products. Not so for what most factories sell. Second and related to the first, rural communities had always enjoyed a sort of unofficial form of Social Security in the ability to absorb family members – regardless of their productivity – into the farm. We really do not need Grandma's help with the washing, but she is, after all, Grandma, and this fact alone earns her the right to sit at our table. That becomes a more difficult accommodation, however, when you have moved hundreds of miles from home to work at the Ford factory. Extended families still existed in the city, but sharing any surplus became more difficult. People were more vulnerable. Third, industrial and agricultural productivity grew by tremendous rates over the Roaring Twenties. On the one hand, this sounds wonderful as it means that we can produce – and therefore consume – more per person. On the other, it means that firms require fewer workers per unit of output. And if demand is not growing at least as fast as productivity, then unemployment rises. We can technically produce more, but will only do so if it remains profitable to hire those made redundant by the new production techniques.

Through the 1920s, demand **did** grow quickly, and any potential problems were avoided. This was because there was a massive increase in capital investment, especially in industries related to automobiles. We needed everyone to help build new factories, roads, refineries, service stations, and so on. But when those were built – and this starts to get into the issues that will be covered in great detail later – the demand for labor collapsed. At the very point when we had the ability to produce goods and services on a scale never before seen by humanity, millions were going without. *Our system is not designed to take into account the fact that the private sector's demand for workers is reluctant, tenuous, and cyclical.* That a massive collapse followed a massive boom makes

Preface xv

perfect sense once you understand what drives the system. But the rest of that story must wait for later chapters.

HOW TO USE THIS BOOK IN THE CLASSROOM

I wrote this book primarily for other economists, but always had in mind the idea that I would use it in class, too. Indeed, I have been doing so for many years as different chapters came into existence. Hence, I kept technical detail to a minimum in the main volume and offered more in-depth analysis in the appendix. With respect to what to assign, I have used every chapter in one class or another. In intermediate macroeconomics, they read Chapters 2 ("Theoretical Foundation aka What Causes Business Cycles?") and 3 ("Additional Factors: Inflation, Monetary and Fiscal Policy, the Stock Market, and Secular Stagnation") as the foundations and then 5 ("Policy and Conclusions") for policy. In my business cycles course, which has intermediate macroeconomics (though not necessarily mine) as a prerequisite, they start with the Appendix ("Critical Survey of Business Cycle Theories") and then work back to Chapters 2, 3, and 5, plus 4 ("US Business Cycles 1954 through 2020"). But I pick out chapters for use in other classes, too, for example, mine on international monetary economics. You cannot understand global capital flows and exchange rates without knowing how the macroeconomy operates, especially the financial sector. For that reason, they read Chapters 2 and 3.

And if students can read this volume, then so can lay people – and I hope they do!

Acknowledgments

No one writes a book by themselves. I first want to thank my wife, Melanie, who has not only been very supportive, but read through some sections for me as my in-house representative noneconomist. My apologies to her for how bad some of the early versions of Chapter 3 were! Thanks, too, to the many students who let me know things like, "You say 'the former' and 'the latter' too much and I get confused!" I am also grateful to the staff at Cambridge (particularly Robert Dreesen and Sable Gravesandy) and the anonymous readers whose suggestions greatly improved the volume. Thanks to Mum and Dad, as well, for their example – see you on Thursday when I stop by to take out your garbage!

As I approach retirement, I am reminded of the many professors who touched my life, most of whom are no longer with us but remain in my heart. I am so thankful to them. They were, in the economics department at the University of Tennessee, Bill Cole (1931–2011), Hans Jensen (1919–2008), Anne Mayhew (1936), and Terry Neale (1925–2004); and in political science, Vernon Iredell (1929–1995) and Thomas Ungs (1928). I loved your classes and stopping by your offices to chat!

Last, as I look at our world faced with so many challenges, I cannot help but think of our daughters, Meg, and Alex. It will be up to them and their contemporaries to solve the many problems earlier generations have left them. I hope Chapter 5 is something of a guide, it certainly gives me hope, as does the fact that young people today strike me as more compassionate, intelligent, and driven than any others I have experienced going back to my own youth. It is said that in an age of dragons, you should raise dragon slayers. I think we have done just that.

I

Introduction
The Sorry State of Modern Macro Theory

Recessions are to the entrepreneur like droughts are to the farmer: You can work from sunup to sundown and do everything just right and still face ruin. This was the case after the financial crisis of 2007–2008, when roughly 1.8 million small businesses – virtually none of which had any connection whatsoever to the underlying forces leading to the collapse – failed between December 2008 and December 2010 (Weltman 2023). Who knows how many of these were owned by families who had put their personal finances on the line, hoping that their enthusiasm and hard work would be sufficient to turn a profit. They were not. Workers, too, are subject to these same ill fortunes. In December 2007, the date marked by the National Bureau of Economic Research as the start of the financial crisis recession, unemployment was 7.6 million. By its official end in June 2009, it was 14.7 million (finally peaking at 15.4 million in October 2009). Once again, they were innocent of the actions that brought them economic, social, and psychological hardship.

What causes the cyclical downturns that can wreak havoc on our lives? That is the central question asked – and answered – by this volume. Most economists will say that they are the result of random external shocks and that without these, the economy would sail along beautifully. Take, for example, this quote from Dr. Christina Romer, one-time Chair of President Barack Obama's Council of Economic Advisors: "Just as there is no regularity in the timing of business cycles, there is no reason why cycles have to occur at all. The prevailing view among economists is that there is a level of economic activity, often referred to as full employment, at which the economy could stay forever. (Romer 2008)" We are only knocked off of this happy equilibrium by chance events. None of these, according to mainstream economics (aka Neoclassicism or orthodoxy), occurs in a manner that creates a recognizable pattern.

To be fair, there are of course random, non-economic factors that can have a serious impact on the economy. COVID certainly proved that. I will argue, however, that the overwhelming weight of evidence points toward the conclusion that *there exists an internal dynamic, one related to the behavior of economic agents, that generates what we call a business cycle*. Expansions create the conditions that cause recession and vice versa. Whatever fate may then throw at us is on top of this.

The reason Neoclassical economics has failed to recognize this is because their theories and models have become increasingly divorced from reality. Indeed, Nobel Laureate Paul Romer (no relation to Christina) – himself a mainstream economist – calls ours the era of "Post-Real" economics (Romer 2016: 4). In his words, "In the last three decades, the methods and conclusions of macroeconomics have deteriorated to the point that much of the work in this area no longer qualifies as scientific research" (Romer 2016: 1).[1] I think this is an understatement and, given the importance of economic theory to our lives, a crime.

Fortunately, orthodoxy is not the only game in town. There exists a deep and insightful literature reaching back over a century. Wesley Clair Mitchell (1874–1948), for example, an Institutionalist economist who was one of the founders of the National Bureau of Economic Research (the private-sector think tank that still officially dates business cycles in the US), did brilliant, path-breaking work on the subject that pointed to real-world phenomena such as systemic fluctuations of profits and input costs as the culprits.[2] Today, however, his efforts are all but forgotten; and when they are not, he is criticized by the mainstream for having "eschewed theory in favor of meticulous empirical investigation" (Williamson 1996: 391).[3] This is code for Mitchell not having expressed the "complexities and interdependencies of the real world in a maze of pretentious and unhelpful symbols" (Keynes 1936: 298). In other words, he did not produce pages of equations and proofs. Instead, he focused on real-world data and their fluctuations over the course of actual business cycles.

The nature of the mainstream dismissal of his work is typical of what Romer describes in his critique, and it neatly illustrates one of the primary obstacles to useful economics: an obsession with complex mathematics *regardless of the light they shed on the question at hand*. Some have argued that this is a function of the discipline's "masculinist bias," wherein the author's real goal is to prove their (usually "his," given how white-male dominated our discipline is) superiority over their colleagues/opponents (Nelson 1995). "If you can't

---

[1] I happened to be on a panel at the US Naval War College with Dr. Romer between his writing of the article cited above and his winning of the Nobel Prize. He said that he received some extremely negative feedback after posting this piece to his web page. It was telling, however, that the focus of the comments was not any fault in his logic, but the fact that he dared say anything bad about our revered intellectual ancestors.

[2] Put briefly, Institutionalists are followers of the economist Thorstein Veblen (1857–1929). Mitchell was, in fact, one of Veblen's students.

[3] Which is impossible, of course, as theory determines which variables you include in your empirical study.

1 Introduction: The Sorry State of Modern Macro Theory

understand my model, then clearly I'm smarter than you." That by itself is disturbing, but it leads to further problems: "With enough math, an author can be confident that most readers will never figure out where a FWUTV (fact with unknown truth value) is buried. A discussant or referee cannot say that an identification assumption is not credible if they cannot figure out what it is and are too embarrassed to ask. (Romer 2016: 15)" In other words, not only is there a strong tendency to prefer complexity over relevance as a form of posturing, but this has also had the effect of causing the peer-review process – so vital to the maintenance of scientific standards – to break down.

There is nothing wrong with mathematics, of course. It is an essential shorthand and one of the things that attracted me, a former physics major, to the discipline. But, to give the extended passage from which the above Keynes quote is drawn:

The object of our analysis is, not to provide a machine, or method of blind manipulation, which will furnish an infallible answer, but to provide ourselves with an organised and orderly method of thinking out particular problems; and, after we have reached a provisional conclusion by isolating the complicating factors one by one, we then have to go back on ourselves and allow, as well as we can, for the probable interactions of the factors amongst themselves. This is the nature of economic thinking. Any other way of applying our formal principles of thought (without which, however, we shall be lost in the wood) will lead us into error. It is a great fault of symbolic pseudo-mathematical methods of formalising a system of economic analysis, such as we shall set down in section vi of this chapter, that they expressly assume strict independence between the factors involved and lose all their cogency and authority if this hypothesis is disallowed; whereas, in ordinary discourse, where we are not blindly manipulating but know all the time what we are doing and what the words mean, we can keep "at the back of our heads" the necessary reserves and qualifications and the adjustments which we shall have to make later on, in a way in which we cannot keep complicated partial differentials "at the back" of several pages of algebra which assume that they all vanish. *Too large a proportion of recent "mathematical" economics are merely concoctions, as imprecise as the initial assumptions they rest on, which allow the author to lose sight of the complexities and interdependencies of the real world in a maze of pretentious and unhelpful symbols.* (emphasis added; Keynes 1936: 297–8)

Mitchell's work is an excellent example of someone following Keynes' advice (albeit before he actually gave it!). It will be one of the foundations – along with that of John Maynard Keynes, Michal Kalecki, Hyman Minsky, and Paul Davidson – of the theory forwarded in this volume.

Note that disappointment in existing macroeconomic theory is not limited to professional economists such as Romer or non-mainstream ones like myself. Its state is so abysmal that even their own PhD students avoid it:

In the interviews, macro received highly negative marks across schools. A typical comment was the following: "The general perspective of the micro students is that the macro courses are pretty worthless, and we don't see why we have to do it, because we don't see what is taught as a plausible description of the economy. It's not that macroeconomic questions are inherently uninteresting; it is just that the models presented in the courses are not up to the job of explaining what is happening. There's just a lot of math, and we can't see the purpose of it." (Colander 2005: 180)

These students are not afraid of the math, per se, as the entire discipline has become increasingly mathematically oriented. Rather, their lack of enthusiasm is a function of the fact that "the macro that is taught to the students in the core has lost touch with both policy and empirical evidence" (Colander 2005: 196).

Hence, mainstream macroeconomics stands before us today bleeding from a series of largely self-inflicted wounds. To start, in the post–World War II period they essentially declared the business cycle dead, focusing instead on growth (Backhouse 2017). It was their opinion that Keynesian – as opposed to Keynes', there is a big difference – policy had developed means of fine-tuning the economy such that any fluctuations that occurred were the result of shocks or errors. As you will see in Chapter 4, which offers a history of US business cycles, it is very difficult to defend such a position. Only someone already wearing those blinders could have interpreted the events that way. Furthermore, in such an environment, the business cycle theories that did emerge – particularly Real Business Cycles – were based on the premise that there was no cycle! This was the dead end about which Paul Romer was so upset. And Neoclassicism became increasingly insular. A combination of factors allowed them to build barriers to entry against other schools of thought both at the stage at which we train new economists and once they gain employment. The journal ranking system that has emerged is probably the most egregious of these. In addition, classes at both the undergraduate and graduate levels have de-emphasized lessons that offer context to the theories we put forward (see Harvey 2020a pp. 8–54 for an extensive discussion of these last two issues). Last, the very tools of analysis embraced by Neoclassicism makes it extremely difficult for them to explain real-world macroeconomic fluctuations (Harvey 2020b).

Things have reached the point that some PhD programs have even asked whether or not it is worth continuing to include macroeconomics as a core part of the curriculum (Colander 2005: 195–6). This means making it optional for budding economists to study such concepts as unemployment, inflation, interest rates, expansions, recessions, monetary policy, fiscal policy, and GDP growth. I wonder what members of the general public would think of this state of affairs, wherein most of the factors that have a direct impact on their quality of life are treated as "electives?"[4] Policy makers, too, have had second thoughts regarding the utility of Neoclassical macro models (Giles 2017).

For all these reasons and more, this volume puts forward yet another business cycle theory. To offer a brief preview, the argument will be made that developments during the upturn cause the downturn. In particular, the environment in which entrepreneurs make decisions, the relationship between their

---

[4] For other critiques of mainstream economics, see Harvey 2020a, Harvey 2020b, and Keen 2011.

investment spending and profits, and the relative ease with which we can add to our stock of physical capital combine to create a situation in which the expansion witnesses a saturation of the market for physical capital, a fall in investment (and therefore profits), and a panicked reaction to the latter on the part of entrepreneurs. This happens time and time again because it is built into the system.

This does not mean that we are forced to live with the consequences, however. There exist policies, in particular those associated with the Job Guarantee, that can not only insulate us from the damaging effects of recession but at the same time deliver a more experienced and skilled workforce and address many of the social problems we face today (including, especially, climate change). And it's easily affordable (although in a very real sense, we cannot afford not to do it regardless of the "cost"). That will be the subject of Chapter 5. Before that, a basic theory of business cycles will be laid out (Chapter 2), additional factors added (Chapter 3), and a history of US cycles from 1954 to 2020 offered (Chapter 4). After Chapter 5, there is an appendix showing more sophisticated versions of the models upon which the volume is based.

It is my sincere hope that the reader – economist or otherwise – finds the analyses presented here to be logical, reasonable, firmly grounded in the real world, and, in the end, hopeful.

2

Theoretical Foundation aka What Causes Business Cycles?

As a first step, some basic concepts will be reviewed. This will be kept brief, however, as there is already a lengthy appendix in which more detail is offered regarding the models and theories referenced in this book. It includes explanations of the nonmainstream approaches developed by Wesley Clair Mitchell, John Maynard Keynes, Michal Kalecki, Hyman Minsky, and Paul Davidson. It also covers the following mainstream theories: interest-rate-driven cycles, Stop-Go cycles, the monetarist approach, real business cycles, and Austrian business cycle theory.

2.1 TYPES OF CYCLES

First on the agenda is determining what is meant by business "cycle" in this volume. This is particularly important because, as suggested in the Chapter 1, mainstream economists claim one does not exist. Looking again to Christina Romer: "In many ways the term *business cycle* is misleading. 'Cycle' seems to imply that there is some regularity in the timing and duration of upswings and downswings in economic activity. Most economists, however, believe otherwise. Booms and recessions occur at irregular intervals and last for varying lengths of time (Romer 2008)."

To be fair, the last sentence is factually correct. Since World War II, for example, we have witnessed the following extremes:

- longest expansion = 128 months (post-Financial Crisis of 2007–2008 expansion that ended with the onset of COVID);
- shortest expansion = 12 months (upturn before the Volcker Recession);
- longest recession = 18 months (recession following the Financial Crisis of 2007–2008);
- shortest recession = 2 months (COVID recession).

2.1 Types of Cycles

But the implicit – and false – assumption being made in Romer's denial of any cycle regularity is that economic events should parallel celestial ones. Unless there is a reason to believe that economic downturns are somehow linked to the Earth's position during its annual rotation around the sun, there should be no reason that business cycles are seasonal.[1] We should not, for example, expect that recessions always last some specific number of months. Nor is there a reason to think that an expansion or recession should equal X number of Earthly rotations around our local star. One cannot deny the existence of a business cycle simply on the basis that the components thereof do not exhibit a correspondence to timing we derived from the duration of events in our solar system (years, months, weeks, days, hours, etc.).

Instead, economic activities follow economic – not celestial – logical processes. What those processes are will covered at length later in this chapter. In the meantime, however, I will offer two lines of defense in favor of the existence of a business cycle. First and most simplistically, a cycle is merely a series of events that repeat in the same order. Given that the business cycle is composed of only two events – expansion and recession – they must logically follow one another. By this definition there *is* a business cycle and it is only in this sense that modern mainstream economics recognizes one. Even then, they prefer the term "economic fluctuation" as it is more consistent with their view that, in the absence of policy errors or external shocks, the economy could stay in a state of perpetual boom (Romer 2008). For them, any cyclicality is trivial, the result of the phenomenon in question having only two possible states (one of which, according to them, we could potentially stay in forever).

As has already been made clear, however, that is not the position taken here. The reason I and other Institutionalist and Post Keynesian authors call this a business *cycle* is that, despite its irregularity as compared to celestial events like the Earth's orbit around the sun, *the conditions created by one stage lead directly and inevitably to the next*. Recession follows expansion not simply because there are only two states of the world, but because the expansion sows the seeds of recession and vice versa. A business cycle exists and it is far from trivial.

That said, scholars who recognize this have come from a variety of perspectives. There are those, for instance, who have argued that very long-term cycles exist, too, manifesting themselves over periods of a half century of more. Often called Kondratiev waves after Nikolai Kondratiev, an early proponent, these and other types are argued to be driven by a wide range of different phenomena (Wallerstein 1999). Joseph Schumpeter's approach is one of the most famous, suggesting that innovation is the main factor (Bellofiore 1999). When an innovation occurs, it could have effects well outside of its own industry. It may also lead to creative destruction, whereby some sectors are outcompeted into

---

[1] There is, of course, annual seasonality to some economic processes, but they cannot explain the multiyear business cycles we witness.

virtual or complete nonexistence. However, eventually the market matures and the innovation itself becomes ripe for destruction. This occurs over and over and is not necessarily exogenous, as one might imagine. Instead, entrepreneurs are assumed to be constantly striving to come up with new concepts, markets, inventions, processes, etc. Hence, while we may not be able to predict the timing of key innovations, we can – in Schumpeter's view – rest assured that they will happen. And these will create recognizable cycles.

These will not, however, be among the varieties studied in this chapter. Instead, we will assume that innovations are not playing any significant role in the transition from expansion to recession and back and that, rather, problems arise even in a static environment because entrepreneurs saturate the market for physical investment which lowers profits in an unexpected manner (much more about this later in the chapter). This is not to confirm or deny the existence of the longer-term cycles so much as focus on different phenomena. If in the real world innovations have an impact on economic outcomes, then this is included in Chapter 4 – just not in the context of any long-term cycles.

2.2 AN INSTITUTIONALIST/POST KEYNESIAN BUSINESS CYCLE THEORY

An explanation of the course of the US economy from 1954 to 2020 requires an underlying theory. While there are several candidates within the Neoclassical camp, none offers sufficient insight into the workings of a modern financial capitalist economy to be of use in explaining real-world economic fluctuations. For that reason, what follows is drawn exclusively from the Institutionalist and Post Keynesian traditions, where the emphasis is on building models that take into account as much of the actual structure and institutions of macroeconomies as possible. This, of course, must be balanced against the need to simplify in order to make the models manageable; but if a simplification causes a model to generate significantly a-historical predictions, then the cost exceeds the benefit.

Institutionalists and Post Keynesians have made a number of important and unique contributions to business cycle theory, including Wesley Claire Mitchell's pathbreaking empirical work, John Maynard Keynes' uncertainty-based revolution, Michal Kalecki's mathematical formalizations, Hyman Minsky's financial instability hypothesis, and Paul Davidson's modeling of the capital-formation process. Rather than employ these en masse, I have drawn selectively from them in order to create a synthesis that I believe best reflects the empirical realities of the US business cycle 1954–2020. For those who are interested in the specific individual contributions of these scholars, more detail may be found in the appendix that appears after Chapter 5.

First and foremost in terms of the theoretical underpinning of this volume, it will be argued that business cycles are endogenously generated. The conditions of economic expansion create the forces that lead to recession and vice versa.

2.2 An Institutionalist-Post Keynesian Theory

As explained earlier, nearly all mainstream models of the business cycle assume instead that fluctuations in the level of economic activity are entirely exogenous and largely random or the result of policy errors. While it is of course true that external events and errors can play a decisive role, I would argue that the Institutionalist and Post Keynesian economists cited above showed decisively that the system itself is unstable and prone to breakdown.

Second and again in contrast to economic orthodoxy, the role of the financial sector will be highlighted. Many of the mainstream's mea culpas after the Financial Crisis of 2007–2008 included open admissions regarding the low level of importance they placed on such factors (Harvey 2020b). A postcrisis paper coauthored by Neoclassicals Brian Eggertsson and Paul Krugman, the latter a Nobel Laureate, is representative:

> Given the prominence of debt in popular discussion of our current economic difficulties and the long tradition of invoking debt as a key factor in major economic contractions, one might have expected debt to be at the heart of most mainstream macroeconomic models – especially the analysis of monetary and fiscal policy. Perhaps somewhat surprisingly, however, *it is quite common to abstract altogether from this feature of the economy* (emphasis added; Eggertsson and Krugman 2012: 1470–1).

Unfortunately and despite the clear implication that their paper is going to be different, they then go on to account for debt in a manner that fatally misrepresents the actual mechanisms and consequences of real-world financial relations. Not surprisingly, you cannot predict a financial crisis by using a model that doesn't have a realistic financial sector. That mistake will not be made here.

Last before diving into the model specifics, an implicit assumption underlying this volume is that unemployment is an unnecessary evil. The belief at the Federal Reserve that there exists a tradeoff between unemployment and inflation whereby we need to increase the former in order to control the latter is patently false. As will be explained at length in the Chapter 3, the causes of rising prices are many and complex and none of them suggests that the solution is to intentionally reduce the level of economic activity. Furthermore, not only is there no silver lining to unemployment, it creates many other social problems on top of the joblessness itself (Tcherneva 2017). It is immoral to have the productive capacity to meet everyone's basic needs (and well above that), and yet have millions who are unable to find gainful employment. And it hurts even those who have jobs and incomes.

A recession is a sustained decline in the growth rate of economic activity, usually measured as real gross domestic product (GDP). According to mainstream economics, these declines need never occur because the economy can stay at full employment forever. Unfortunately, this is simply not true. There is a systemic tendency in capitalist economies for economic activity to not just slow, but reverse direction. *The upturn creates the conditions that cause the downturn.* The quick and dirty reason is that physical (not financial) investment spending – which drives the expansion – slows as firms reach targeted levels of capacity (targets based on their forecast of future demand for whatever the finished investment will produce). The fall in spending leads to a fall in profits, which disappoints entrepreneurs' otherwise optimistic expectations. Because it is safer not to spend than to spend, they then cut back even more and this causes an extended downturn, that is, a recession. Compounding matters is the fact that during the expansion, the financial sector will have been creating liquidity for the nonfinancial sector and thereby engaging in acts that tend to make their solvency increasingly dependent on the continuation of the upturn. Once the latter has ended, financial institutions may fail or at least be far more cautious in terms of their willingness to back projects. Liquidity may dry up to the point that firms find it difficult to fund even everyday operations, let alone physical investment projects.

The story does not end there, however. Over the course of the recession, capital equipment wears out, becomes obsolete, or proves less profitable for other reasons. Initially, firms simply allow capacity to decline, preferring not to undertake significant expenditures during a recession. But eventually, depreciation will reach the point that firms are forced to replace capital. In addition, the bad memories of the downturn fade and financial institutions' portfolios recover to the point that they are willing and able to lend again. All this leads to a jump in investment spending, which in turn raises profits and thus encourages other firms to follow suit. A new expansion thereby begins. The details underlying this sequence are laid out below.

2.2.1 Injection and Leakages

The first step in dissecting the business cycle is understanding how GDP is determined. GDP is total market value of all goods and services produced within the US in a specific time period, normally one year. Since in order to have a market value it must have sold, GDP also represents total sales. And because that transaction created income for the seller, GDP is also total income. This means that in a closed system, total sales equal total income which equals the total dollar value of all goods and services in question. Indeed, these are all simply different sides of each individual transaction. Meanwhile, *real* GDP is inflation-adjusted GDP.

GDP has four components: consumption expenditures (C), physical investment expenditures (I), government expenditures (G), and net exports (X-M, or exports minus imports).[2] In 2023, US GDP was \$27.4 trillion (current dollars), of which C = \$18.6 trillion, I = \$4.8 trillion, G = \$4.7 trillion, and X-M = –\$0.8 trillion (Economic Report of the President). Given these magnitudes, one might imagine that consumption is the driver of economic activity.

---

[2] One may wonder how there can be a negative component of GDP. This is because C, I, and G include foreign transactions that must be netted out. If they did not, then M would be completely unnecessary, and all components would be positive.

2.2 An Institutionalist-Post Keynesian Theory

This is not true, however, as it generally follows fluctuations in GDP rather than leads them. In other words, consumption rises because GDP (which, recall, is also total income) rises and not the other way around. There can be exceptions, but these are rare. In general and despite its overall size, consumption is generally passive.

This is also true of imports as they are just consumption again, but of foreign goods and services. It is not true, however, of investment, government spending, and exports. None of these depends directly on current levels of domestic income (and, therefore, current levels of GDP) such as consumption and imports do. The government can raise spending even if the economy is in deep recession, as we saw with the COVID relief programs; exports are a function of foreigners' income, not ours; and investment is funded by liquidity created by the financial sector, a process independent of any savings left over from household income (a point that will be explained in detail later). This means that government spending, physical investment spending, and exports can all be causal: They can rise (or fall) first and thereby create a rise (or fall) in GDP. These are, as a whole, called *injections*, because they inject new income into the economy.

Despite their relatively small size, the impact of injections is magnified by the fact that when someone receives new income, they spend some portion of it and thereby create more income for someone else. For example, when the government issued $1,200 checks to struggling Americans in the first COVID summer of 2020, this represented $1,200 of new income for each of those individuals. If a recipient spent, say, $1,000 of it, then, another $1,000 of income has been created; and if that person spends $800 of the $1,000, then another $800 of income has been created; and so on. It is by this multiplier process that investment, government spending, and exports drive GDP and exert an influence out of proportion to their size.

Balanced against these injections but playing a much more passive role are what economists call leakages. These are tax revenues, saving, and the aforementioned imports. Because they represent a leakage from the domestic income stream, each of these has the effect of lowering GDP as they rise. Generally speaking, however, leakages change *in response to* a change in GDP, rather than the other way around. For example, when we are in recession and GDP is falling, so will the government's tax revenues, the amount people can save, and how much we can afford to import. The opposite is true in an expansion. It is possible, if less common, for a leakage to change first. When the government raises tax rates, this will raise tax revenues even without there being a larger tax base from rising GDP; if people decide to become more thrifty, this raises savings even at the same level of income; and if foreign goods and services become more attractive to us, this raises imports independent of other factors.

The relationship between injections and leakages is a key one in the determination of GDP and is easily understood in the context of a bucket of water (GDP), a garden hose (injections), and a hole in the bucket (leakages).

Injections raise GDP, much like water from a hose raises the water level in a bucket; leakages lower GDP, just as a hole in the bucket would do to the water held therein. In both the economy and the bucket of water, the injections and leakages seek the point where they are equal. If water from the hose is filling the bucket faster than the hole is emptying it, the water level will rise until the pressure is such that the leakages become equal to the injections and the water level stabilizes; and if water from the hose is filling the bucket more slowly than the hole is emptying it, the water level will fall until the pressure is such that the leakages become equal to the injections. In the same manner, when investment plus government spending plus exports are greater than saving plus taxes plus imports, GDP rises until they are equal (by raising the last three, since they are all positive functions of GDP); and when injections are lower than leakages, GDP falls until they are equal.

2.2.2 The Key Injection: Physical Investment Spending

Returning to the business cycle, since leakages tend to be passive, the answer to what causes economic fluctuations must lie in the behavior of the injections. This is indeed the case. However, the blame is not spread equally across all three because one of them is far more volatile than the other two. Exports tend to change relatively slowly because they are mostly dependent on the incomes of our trading partners, which in turn are generally fairly stable.[3] Government spending can rise or fall quite suddenly in response to economic crises like those associated with COVID and the Financial Crisis of 2007–2008; but even with that, its average inflation-adjusted rate of change from 1948 to 2020 is still *one-third* that of the real culprit: physical investment spending. Over that period, government spending tended to change around 4.6% from quarter to quarter, while the same number for investment spending is 14.6% (each measured in real terms and as an annualized rate of change).[4] In other words, from one three-month period to the next, the US economy witnessed a 14.6% annualized rise or fall in investment spending *just on average*. Of the 292 quarters from 1948 to 2020, the range of fluctuation was larger than 20% during 75 quarters, larger than 30% during 39 quarters, and larger than 40% during 20 quarters. In addition, over one-third of those quarterly growth rates represented not just changes, but outright reversals in direction relative to the immediately previous one (i.e., positive growth to negative growth, or vice versa).

---

[3] In addition, at least for the US, net exports is a relatively small number.
[4] It is common to express quarterly growth data in annual terms. In other words, quarterly GDP growth rates, for example, are shown as the percentage change in GDP that *would have occurred* had the economy grown (or contracted) at this same rate for an entire year. It is similar to showing a baseball pitcher's performance as how many runs he *would have allowed* over a nine-inning game, regardless of how long he actually pitched. A nine-inning game is considered a standard length in baseball, just as one year is considered a standard length in aggregate macroeconomic statistics.

2.2 An Institutionalist-Post Keynesian Theory

These are substantial changes in magnitude and often trajectory of something to which Paul Romer believes economists should be paying more attention: "the actions that people take" (Romer 2016: 4). They are not random events but homo sapiens behavior that can be explained in the context of the system in which they are operating, the constraints they face, and the environment in which they make forecasts.

Before proceeding, a clarification may be necessary with respect to what is meant by investment. First and as should already be clear, it is not financial investment and so has nothing directly to do with stocks or bonds or other securities or derivatives. It is physical investment. Second, this includes both (1) fixed investment and (2) inventory adjustment. The former means anything a firm uses to produce its output but which does not become part of its output (for example, a factory, a computer, a hammer, or an office paperclip), plus residential investment (both new construction and maintenance). It does not include raw materials since they become part of what the firm sells. Fixed investment can only be positive or zero. Inventory adjustment, on the other hand, can be negative if inventories are run down. It is counted under investment because it is not otherwise counted under GDP (as it has not yet sold), yet is a fluctuation that affected the economy.[5]

Inventory adjustment is a very small percentage of overall investment, generally no more than 5 percent. However, it is not only extremely volatile, but it can be an indicator of future trends. Unintended inventory accumulation, for example, which in the short run is a boon to economic activity, may cause firms to cut back on production in the future (and vice versa). It will therefore be a frequent topic of discussion in Chapter 4, despite its small size. Residential investment is generally about 20 percent of total, although this can vary. In the run up to the Financial Crisis of 2007–2008, for example, (and for obvious reasons, that is, the housing boom), it averaged just over 30 percent. This means that most investment (seventy to 75 percent) is nonresidential fixed.

Gross investment is the total amount of investment spending (of every variety) in a given period. It is composed of two parts: investment aimed at replacing existing capacity (replacement investment) and investment that increases total capacity (net investment). Note that, theoretically, net investment could be negative. This would occur if gross investment were insufficient to replace even the depreciating capital, let alone build any new. This would be analogous to a restauranteur deciding to both not build any new restaurants and not bother to maintain all of her existing ones. Her total capacity would shrink. Realistically speaking, however, this does not happen at the macro level (although we came close to negative net investment after the Financial Crisis of 2007–2008 and the COVID recession). Over the period covered in Chapter 4 (1954Q3 through 2020Q2), net investment averaged 45.5% of gross, while replacement was

---

[5] For an easily accessible breakdown of the components of investment, see: www.amosweb.com/cgi-bin/awb_nav.pl?s=wpd&c=dsp&k=gross+private+domestic+investment.

54.5%. Not surprisingly and consistent with the analysis presented later in this chapter, net investment tends to be smallest during recession and next-smallest during the first year of expansion. The investment that does occur during those two periods is mostly for replacement.

2.2.3 Uncertainty, Animal Spirits, and Forecasts

Returning to the explanation of the importance of investment spending in creating cyclical fluctuations, its volatility is rooted in the manner in which entrepreneurs generate forecasts. Investment spending changes rapidly because agents' expectations of future profit change rapidly. Understanding why this is so requires adding several more elements to the story. To begin, consider the very high cost of most projects. This is a weighty factor in and of itself and will almost surely require a business loan or other sources of financing (which is one of the reasons why it is so important to include consideration of the financial sector in any business cycle theory). This also means a long-term commitment since repayment will not be possible overnight. Furthermore, unlike a financial investment, it is almost impossible to change horses midstream. You can sell shares of McDonald's one minute and use the proceeds to buy WalMart stock the next, but converting a restaurant into retail sales space would be time consuming and expensive. In short, the physical investment decision is a weighty one with very long-term consequences.

However, balanced against these negatives is the possibility of profit from the new investment once it comes on line. When these prospects win out in the mind of the entrepreneur, investment spending rises; when they do not, it falls. And since the negatives are largely constant (investment is always an expensive and practically irreversible long-term commitment), it must – as already suggested – be changes in the forecasts themselves that create the sudden changes in investment spending.

In considering this question, Keynes thought it particularly important to understand first that the investment decision is made in an environment of *uncertainty* rather than *risk*.[6] He further believed that mainstream economics had overlooked this important distinction and, because they imagined forecasts as being made under *risk*, they condemned their investment theories to irrelevance. Under *risk*, agents know all possible future outcomes and the odds of each one. That is the situation one faces in a casino when playing roulette: You know every possible result and its likelihood, you just don't know for certain where the ball will settle. You therefore try to select the option that promises the best average payoff. Analogously, what if an entrepreneur were faced with three opportunities, each costing $400 and with the following possible outcomes and probabilities (assume alternate outcomes to be $0)?

---

[6] "Uncertainty" and "risk" will be italicized throughout this discussion as a reminder to the reader that their common connotations should not be employed and that instead they are being defined as Keynes specified (as will be explained later).

2.2 An Institutionalist-Post Keynesian Theory

- Investment A: 60% chance of $1,000 (expected value of 60% × $1,000 = $600)
- Investment B: 40% chance of $2,000 (expected value of 40% × $2,000 = $800)
- Investment C: 10% change of $2,500 (expected value of 10% × $2,500 = $250)

Because the entrepreneur knows all the possible outcomes and the odds of each one, she would clearly choose B, the one with the highest average payoff (note that C, on average, actually leads to a loss of $150 since it cost $400).

Now say she was unsuccessful but is presented with these opportunities again – what will she choose? B, of course. And if she failed once again? B. It does not matter how many times she loses, how others act, or what rumors she hears, under *risk* she will always choose the alternative that she *knows* with mathematical certainty has the highest expected value. She has all the information necessary to build a conclusive argument: B is best, period. Furthermore, she may be disappointed and reach a point where she can no longer raise the funds for another try, but she never really panics over which of the three options to take next. *She is never led to question the entire foundation of the forecast that led to her choice.* She was just unlucky.

Decision making in an environment of *risk* therefore generates very stable behavior. Because this is decidedly not what we witness from investment – the single most volatile component of GDP – Keynes suggested an alternative: *uncertainty*. Under *uncertainty*, agents do not know all the possible outcomes or their odds and, as will be shown below, such a world is much more frightening, and realistic, than a *risky* one.

Consider the following (which, for ease of comparison, is identical to the above save for the fact that B no longer has a known likelihood):

- Investment A: 60% chance of $1,000 (expected value of 60% × $1,000 = $600)
- Investment B: ??% chance of $2,000 (expected value of ??% × $2,000 = $??)
- Investment C: 10% change of $2,500 (expected value of 10% × $2,500 = $250)

Now which choice to make? First off, Keynes is not arguing (as is often suggested) that agents act irrationally. They use what information they have as best they can. Hence, she will not choose C since is it clearly inferior to A. But then A or B? To make that choice, she will have to try her best to fill in the missing data for B. The fact that she is operating in an environment of *uncertainty* means that she will never know enough to come up with the true value that would then allow her to generate a conclusive argument, but she must try.[7] Worse still, in

---

[7] Assuming a *true* value even exists. Do real-world events have likelihoods, or are they binary – either they happen or they do not – and likelihoods are simply reflections of our attempts to

a more realistic scenario, she would almost certainly be forced to do this for *all* (or nearly all) the values in A, B, or C.

Whatever she determines, she will be faced with the fact that while A offers the more certain outcome, the payoff in B is double that of A. Perhaps she initially selects A because of her greater confidence in her prediction; let us say that she does so and she loses. Now what choice does she make for her second go? Maybe A again, or maybe B's higher payoff beckons (particularly as she just played and lost). Suddenly and in stark contrast to the scenario under *risk*, behavior from one time period to the next – even in this extremely simple example – is no longer predictable. Past outcomes now affect her future choices and others' actions interest her. Although this played no role in the earlier example, under this scenario she is keen to discover how other entrepreneurs choosing A versus B fared. She will also want to know who didn't play at all and what rumors are circulating. *Uncertainty* creates a very different world, one in which her overall level of nervous excitement and anxiety is bound to be higher so that the decision maker may fluctuate between what Keynes called errors of optimism and errors of pessimism. She will doubt herself – did I do the right thing? – in a manner that she never does under *risk*.

It is important to make clear that by this definition, different degrees of *uncertainty* do not exist. It is binary: either the environment in which a decision is being made is *uncertain* or it is not; either one lacks sufficient information to make an expected value calculation of every single possible future outcome, or one does not. And in the case of the economy, the environment is most definitely *uncertain*. Given this, one may reasonably ask a more fundamental question: why, given the difficulties created by *uncertainty*, would anyone undertake an investment at all? Surely the high cost, irreversibility, and long time commitment would win out every time versus a forecast of future profitability that is built on an inconclusive foundation. Indeed it would, Keynes argued, were it not for animal spirits, or the "spontaneous urge to action rather than inaction" (Keynes 1936: 161). This is what allows the decision maker to act even when it is impossible to choose by simply comparing "the outcome of a weighted average of quantitative benefits multiplied by quantitative probabilities" (Keynes 1936: 161).

Animal spirits are also binary: either homo sapiens exhibit a tendency toward action rather than inaction, or they do not. Animal spirits cannot, therefore, be strong or weak. Note that this is not a universally accepted interpretation of Keynes' meaning. Indeed, it conflicts with his own usage, as shown here: "Thus if the animal spirits are dimmed and the spontaneous optimism falters, leaving

---

predict them with necessarily limited information and cognitive abilities? Napoleon won a decisive victory at the Battle of Austerlitz – were there, in nature and independent of human attempts to forecast the outcome, "odds" that he would win? No, likelihoods are opinions and not derived from nature. This adds yet another nail in the coffin of the *risk* approach: outside of trivial events such as dice rolls, agents cannot *know* values that do not exist.

2.2 An Institutionalist-Post Keynesian Theory

us to depend on nothing but a mathematical expectation, enterprise will fade and die; – though fears of loss may have a basis no more reasonable than hopes of profit had before (Keynes 1936: 162)."

The fact that they can be "dimmed" implies that, in Keynes' mind, there were more than two states. I would argue, however, that (a) this is not useful, (b) another and better concept already exists for what he is actually describing, and (c) his use of animal spirits as both a dichotomous and continuous state is one of the reasons why the term has created confusion. Instead, in this volume it will be forecast confidence and forecast optimism that may wax and wane, while *uncertainty* and animal spirits simply exist. Fortunately, Keynes used these two former concepts, as well (though not always by those names), and in a manner consistent with the general connotations so that no unique definitions need to be kept in the back of the reader's mind.

To clarify the roles of forecast confidence and forecast optimism, reconsider the original three choices (each with a cost of $400) listed above, but this time with italics to signify what these values are in real life, that is, forecasts and not known values:

- Investment A: *60%* chance of *$1,000* (expected value of *60%* × *$1,000* = *$600*)
- Investment B: *40%* chance of *$2,000* (expected value of *40%* × *$2,000* = *$800*)
- Investment C: *10%* change of *$2,500* (expected value of *10%* × *$2,500* = *$250*)

These are the predictions generated by our representative entrepreneur: she thinks Investment A might on average generate $600, Investment B $800, and Investment C $250 – but she cannot be sure because she operates in an environment of *uncertainty*. There is always doubt and the only reason she is willing to act is because she imbued with animal spirits.

To make a choice, it will be necessary for her to balance both her relative optimism and confidence. In terms of the former, the numbers above suggest that she is most optimistic about Investment B (then A, then C). But, what if she is more confident regarding the calculations associated with Investment A? Which should she choose? In fact, she might even consider Investment C (despite its low payout versus cost) if we add yet another layer of realism and allow for a range of forecast outcomes rather than a single value. This is a world that creates angst in a way that *risk* does not. She must repeatedly review, reevaluate, and reconsider the data and forecasts and she will never be able to formulate a conclusive argument regarding which choice she should make. "About these matters there is no scientific basis on which to form any calculable probability whatever. We simply do not know" (Keynes 1937a: 214).

Particularly important in this world is the manner in which agents react to outcomes that differ from what they expected. Positive surprises may increase both optimism and confidence and encourage an emerging boom. Negative ones, however – because the investment decision is an expensive and practically irreversible long-term commitment – hit much harder. As will be shown below, their impact on optimism and especially confidence can be enough to turn an erstwhile strong expansion into a panic and collapse. This will play a key role in the discussion to follow.

Keynes, incidentally, clearly recognized the importance of confidence when others did not: "The state of long-term expectation, upon which our decisions are based, does not solely depend, therefore, on the most probable forecast we can make. It also depends on the confidence with which we make this forecast – on how highly we rate the likelihood of our best forecast turning out quite wrong (Keynes 1936: 148)."

And:

The *state of confidence*, as they term it, is a matter to which practical men always pay the closest and most anxious attention. But economists have not analysed it carefully and have been content, as a rule, to discuss it in general terms. In particular it has not been made clear that its relevance to economic problems comes in through its important influence on the schedule of the marginal efficiency of capital ("marginal efficiency of capital" can be understood as analogous to the Investment A, B, C choices above; Keynes 1936: 148–9).

Particularly relevant to this volume is the following from his chapter on the trade cycle:

Let us recur to what happens at the crisis. So long as the boom was continuing, much of the new investment showed a not unsatisfactory current yield. The disillusion comes because *doubts* suddenly arise concerning the reliability of the prospective yield, perhaps because the current yield shows signs of falling off, as the stock of newly produced durable goods steadily increases ... Once *doubt* begins it spreads rapidly (emphases added; Keynes 1936: 317).

Doubt does not exist in a *risky* world, something that mainstream economics has entirely missed.

2.2.4 The Investment Decision

Given this background, the investment decision can be understood as follows:

1. entrepreneurs first generate forecasts, which they must do regardless of the existence or nonexistence of *uncertainty*;
2. because *uncertainty* does exist, however, those forecasts cannot take the form of mathematically objective expected-value calculations and entrepreneurs will therefore not be able to form conclusive arguments;
3. the presence of animal spirits in homo sapiens is the reason they do not then immediately stop and are instead willing to continue their deliberations – animal spirits are thus a necessary but not sufficient condition for investment to occur;

2.2 An Institutionalist-Post Keynesian Theory

4. agents must now fill in the missing data as best they can;
5. investment then occurs if and only if the following two tests are passed:
   a. Investment forecast optimism: those calculations must be sufficiently high to generate at least one worthwhile project; and
   b. Investment forecast confidence: agents must have sufficient confidence in that forecast to be willing to commit to it.

Understanding step 5 requires further explanation and some new terminology. In this context, it is important to note that Investment Forecast Optimism and Investment Forecast Confidence are not the same as firms' Overall Forecast Optimism and Overall Forecast Confidence. The former reference firms' position with respect to adding new capital, while the latter apply to overall operations. Businesses may, for example, feel very optimistic about the upcoming quarter's total profits (high Overall Forecast Optimism) but have no desire to undertake any new investment projects (low Investment Forecast Optimism) – you can believe that your existing restaurant is going to do really well but have no desire to build a new one. There is a relationship, but it is not one-to-one.

Consider the following (wherein optimism will be directly modeled in the equations but the role of confidence will be added in discussion):

$$Opt_t = f(\pi_{t-1}) \atop + \tag{2.1}$$

$$IOpt_t = f(Opt_t, Gap_t) \atop + \quad\quad + \tag{2.2}$$

$$I_t = f(IOpt_t) \atop + \tag{2.3}$$

$$\pi_t = f(I_t) \atop + \tag{2.4}$$

$$Gap_t = f(I_{t-1}) \atop - \tag{2.5}$$

where Opt_t is Overall Forecast Optimism (measured as expected overall profits), $IOpt_t$ is Investment Forecast Optimism (measured as profits expected from new investment), I_t is investment, π_t is overall profits, and Gap_t is firms' target level for the stock of physical capital (e.g., how many restaurants they believe would be profitable in the current environment) minus their actual level (total number of restaurants actually in operation).[8] In other words, Gap_t is how much more they think they can profitably add to capital. Eq. (2.1) implies that agents use adaptive expectations in forecasting such that they believe that time

---

[8] There is no effort here to distinguish between profits in a given period (say, 2000Q2) and the discounted present value of all future profits. I am for simplicity, assuming that these will vary together.

period t will look like time period ($t-1$). High realized profits in 2000Q1, for example, will lead to an optimistic forecast of profits for 2000Q2. This specification is consistent with the work of Keynes and Kalecki and is supported by system dynamics research (Kalecki 1937: 84; Keynes 1936: 148; Sterman 2000: 631–60). People will of course try to take other factors into account when forecasting, but generally speaking it is safe to say that they expect things to remain the same or nearly so.

$IOpt_t$ would most certainly be affected by Opt_t, just as shown in Eq. (2.2). But, there is an additional consideration and one that plays a key role in creating the business cycle: $IOpt_t$ is also affected by how much capital firms have already built. Firms have an implicit or explicit target in mind when adding to their physical capacity because they know that the market for whatever their capital will produce is limited. The closer firms already are to that target, the less optimistic they will be regarding how profitable further additions would be regardless of their Opt_t. Gap_t can therefore lower $IOpt_t$ sufficiently for investment spending (Eq. (2.3)) in period t to be very limited despite a high Opt_t. *This is precisely what happens in late expansion, which then sets the stage for the recession.*

The key relationships are illustrated in Figure 2.1. Note the existence of two feedback loops, one positive and one negative. The former is on the left and links Opt_t, $IOpt_t$, I_t, and π_t. Starting with investment, Eq. (2.3) argues that is it a direct function of entrepreneurs' optimistic expectations of profit from investment ($IOpt_t$). There are other factors driving investment, of course, but this is by far the most significant (Harvey 2022). Eq. (2.4) and the diagram specify investment as the major determinant of actual profits (if for no other reason than rising investment stimulates the macroeconomy though, as will be shown later, there is actually a much stronger and more direct relationship than this). Lagged profits directly affect agents' overall optimism with respect to current profits (Opt_t) and that optimism is one of two factors determining investment forecast optimism ($IOpt_t$).

This completes the positive-feedback loop. Were that the only factor, one could expect investment to continually increase over time and for the economy to be in a perpetual state of boom. It is not, however, for at the same time that investment is contributing to current profits, it is closing the gap between the stock of physical capital that entrepreneurs believe will be profitable given

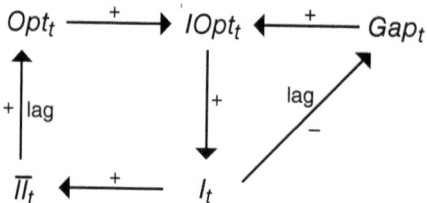

FIGURE 2.1 Feedback loops and the business cycle

2.2 An Institutionalist-Post Keynesian Theory

current market conditions and that in existence (i.e., Gap_t in Eq. (2.5); the lag in the equation and figure is a function of the fact that time passes between breaking ground on a project, construction, and the capital finally coming online). The smaller Gap_t becomes, the lower $IOpt_t$ will be regardless of Opt_t.

Whether or not we are in expansion or recession at any given point in time thus depends in part on which cycle is dominant. In the early stages of the upturn, the positive feedback loop is more powerful since Gap_t will be quite large given entrepreneurs' earlier reluctance to invest over the course of the recession. With Gap_t as a positive contributor at this stage, investment creates profit which raises forecast optimism (both varieties) which raises investment once again – the positive-feedback loop in Figure 2.1. Some of this will come as a welcome surprise, especially in early expansion. This will boost both optimism and confidence. However, as time passes and the upturn matures, Gap_t decreases. Its impact will eventually outweigh that of Opt_t in the determination of $IOpt_t$. This is so because at the extreme, were $Gap_t = 0$, then $IOpt_t = 0$ regardless of the size of Opt_t. No actual or expected volume of overall profit is sufficient to induce the entrepreneur to invest if she is convinced that she already has sufficient capacity to meet consumer demand. She may eventually reconsider her conception of the latter, but this would still enter via a change in Gap_t and not Opt_t.

Note the important implication here that recessions are NOT initiated by a falling overall profit optimism. Indeed, the fact that investment – and therefore profits – may be falling while overall optimism is still high is a key factor in the downturn as it creates a very unpleasant surprise. This is what makes possible the catastrophic collapses in investment we witness in the real world as both optimism and confidence are attacked.

When the disillusion comes, this expectation is replaced by a contrary 'error of pessimism', with the result that the investments, which would in fact yield 2 per cent in conditions of full employment, are expected to yield less than nothing; and the resulting collapse of new investment then leads to a state of unemployment in which the investments, which would have yielded 2 per cent in conditions of full employment, in fact yield less than nothing (Keynes 1936: 321–2).

And as Keynes' writes regarding expectation formation in an environment of *uncertainty*:

In particular, being based on so flimsy a foundation, it is subject to sudden and violent changes. The practice of calmness and immobility, of certainty and security, suddenly breaks down. New fears and hopes will, without warning, take charge of human conduct. The forces of disillusion may suddenly impose a new conventional basis of valuation. (Keynes 1937a: 214–5).

Because it is safer not to spend than to spend, investment grinds to a halt.

Without this (e.g., in a *risky* world), once firms have reached target levels of capacity, they might thereafter simply continue to invest at whatever rate is necessary to replace depreciation. While this may well be at a slower rate than was experienced earlier in the expansion, it could – barring exogenous shocks – continue forever with the economy in a state of semi-boom. We would not witness a cycle, but rather, after a period of adjustment, a perpetual steady state – just as Neoclassicism predicts.

2.3 PRELIMINARY EVIDENCE

While great deal more will be said in Chapter 4 regarding how well this theory fits the US experience, a brief preview is offered here. There have been ten recessions since 1954. If we count early expansion as one year and late expansion as one year, then all but two had a distinct early, mid, and late period, then a recession.[9] This leaves us with eight. The story told so far suggests that over those cycles, we should see a big jump in profits in early expansion (the pleasant surprise) that is caused by a resurgence in investment; positive but not unexpected profit growth then occurs in mid expansion as investment continues to grow; and finally a decline in profits in late expansion (the unpleasant surprise) as firms reach targeted capacity. The recession follows.

Table 2.1 provides evidence of this for the US from 1954Q3 to 2020Q2. Profits are averages for annualized rates of change of inflation-adjusted corporate after-tax profits (FRED database); investment data are averages of annualized rates of change of inflation-adjusted investment spending (FRED database); and optimism is represented by the Purchasing Managers' Index (PMI; Institute for Supply Management). With respect to the last, it is a widely regarded proxy for business expectations. The PMI is calculated by asking purchasing managers at various manufacturing firms a short list of very simple questions that amount to: "Were more orders placed this month than last month? Yes, no, or no change?" These are then aggregated and weighted. When the resulting index is above fifty, this indicates that purchasing managers saw an increase; when it is below fifty, this indicates a decrease. While these are not forecasts, per se, they are the result of forecasts because those

TABLE 2.1 *Preliminary evidence from US cycles US 1954Q3 to 2020Q2*

Stage	Profit growth (%)	Investment growth (%)	Optimism
Early expansion	5.75	18.3	55.4
Mid expansion	2.66	7.3	55.8
Late expansion	−0.45	1.2	52.2
Recession	−4.09	−17.8	43.5

[9] The exceptions are the expansions that occurred before the May 1960 to Feb 1961 and Aug 1981 to Nov 1982 recessions, each of which was too short to be divided without redefining the length of the early and late periods.

2.3 Preliminary Evidence

doing the purchasing will have been asked to buy more materials if and only if other managers at the same firm expected demand for their final products to increase. Indeed, in many respects this is better than the forecast data one usually encounters where respondents are simply asked what they expect the future to bring. Who knows how much effort is expended in coming up with these predictions? But in this case, these are expectations upon which agents took action: they placed orders with purchasing managers.

These data are just as expected. Profits grow fastest in early expansion because that is when investment is recovering – indeed, it is booming. This comes as a pleasant surprise to firms, boosting confidence and optimism. But was it a surprise given that the PMI was 55.4? Yes, because it is necessary to recall that > 50 simply means "better." They expected profit growth to be better than the –4.09% they were experiencing during recession. Hence, even a slower rate of contraction would have been deemed an improvement. Instead, 5.75% is faster than in any other stage of the cycle and it comes as a very welcome surprise.[10]

This leads to mid expansion which witnesses solid investment and profit growth and an expectation that conditions will continue to improve (PMI = 55.8). But they will not. Investment spending rapidly decelerates in late expansion as firms reach targeted capacity, which leads to negative profit growth. Because this occurs when firms are still forecasting higher profits (at PMI 52.2), this creates the negative surprise that causes investment – and profits – to collapse. The error of optimism is replaced by the error of pessimism.

One apparent inconsistency here is the fact that investment growth in late expansion is – while very slow – still positive. Why is this so and how can this be reconciled with the negative growth under profits? In response to the first question, investment in the late expansion before the recession caused by 1973 OPEC oil embargo grew at a very strong 11.28%. Omitting that one cycle causes average investment growth in late expansion to become negative, which is consistent with the underlying theory. However, even though the embargo was clearly an exogenous event and in that sense could be justifiably dropped from the data, it is a questionable practice to omit observations simply because they do not support the hypothesis. Hence, it remains in Table 2.1 and the late-expansion growth rate of investment is, while small, positive.

Why, then, is profit growth negative? The answer is that, over the course of an economic expansion, government spending – one of the three injections – will tend to decline (as fewer people qualify for unemployment insurance and income assistance) and tax revenues (a leakage) will rise (as more people are working and higher incomes raise the effective tax rate). As evidence of this, consider the data below showing the federal government's surplus as a percentage of GDP (negative numbers are deficits and hence have an expansionary effect on the economy; FRED database):

---

[10] Empirical studies using a more complex representation of this phenomenon have shown tremendous support for the hypothesis (see Harvey 2022 and Harvey and Pham 2024).

-4.87%   early expansion
-3.30%   mid expansion
-1.93%   late expansion
-5.10%   recession

The offsetting effect of government deficits is weakest precisely when investment growth is decelerating. It therefore contributes to the downturn.

Though I would rank it second to fluctuations in investment spending, this is nevertheless a significant factor and one about which Institutionalist and Post Keynesian authors have raised alarms during the evolution of previous cycles. Wynn Godley's warnings (issued through the *Levy Economics Institute*) are particularly noteworthy. Often presented in the context of the sectoral-balances approach he pioneered, the most famous of these was perhaps the one issued near the end of the 1990s expansion (part of the September 11 cycle discussed in Chapter 4). While mainstream economics was boasting of a New Economy and government and private-sector forecasts were predicting a continuation of happy days, Godley's paper took "issue with these optimistic views, although it recognizes that the US economy may well enjoy another good year or two" (Godley 1999: 3). Key to his analysis was his conclusion that the government's restrictive fiscal stance, which at the time of his writing promised to become even moreso, would create negative forces that "cannot forever be more than offset by increasingly extravagant private spending" (Godley 1999: 3). He was dead on and, consistent with his prediction, the expansion ended in March 2001.

One may wonder why the systemically contracting fiscal stimulus has been the focus of so much Institutionalist and Post Keynesian attention if it is actually changes in investment spending that are the main culprit. The reason is that we can change the pattern currently inherent to government spending with the stroke of a pen. That is not the case with entrepreneurs' behavior. This is a key point about which much more will be said in Chapters 3 and 4 and especially 5.

One more factor in addition to falling investment and government deficits is the increase in imports that one can expect to occur over the course of expansion (something Godley also mentioned in his 1999 piece). One of the most robust results in empirical economics is the high income elasticity of import demand functions (Sawyer and Sprinkle 1996). The data for the US from 1950 to 2020 are consist with this. During all but the last year of every expansion, real GDP grew by an average of 4.82%; during the last year it grew by 2.41%; and during recessions that number was -3.73%. If imports are relatively income elastic, then we should expect the analogous numbers to larger – and indeed they are. Inflation-adjusted imports grew by 10.07% in all but the last year of expansions, 3.86% in the last year, and -10.22% during recessions. Of course, it is possible that in some cases this may be offset by export growth, but that is dependent on the contemporaneous situation in US trading partners.

2.4 FINANCING PHYSICAL INVESTMENT

The systemic factor is a negative one in terms of its effect on profits. In sum, this means that investment, government budget balance, and net exports all operate to chip away at the strength of any economic expansion.

2.4 FINANCING PHYSICAL INVESTMENT

The above represents the core argument in this volume, but not the only leg thereof. The next element to consider is financing. Investment is expensive. This is why Keynes argued that "banks hold the key position in the transition from a lower to a higher scale of activity" (Keynes 1937b: 668). It doesn't matter how clever or sound your business plan is, if you cannot get a loan officer to agree (or financial investors to float your stock or bond sale) then it will never see the light of day. In this context, the financial sector must:

1. be capable of providing sufficient funding to support investment and other forms of spending; and
2. practice portfolio management policies that encourage financial sector stability, especially in terms of making reasonably accurate evaluations of the credit worthiness of borrowers.

While financial institutions generally excel at the former, problems with the latter contribute to the instability of an already unstable system.

In spite of both popular and professional opinion to the contrary, the money banks loan out is not dependent on the current volume of saving. That view is based on the false premise that what banks do is essentially loan out deposits. Models based on this assumption argue that when savings rise, this induces banks to lower interest rates in order to loan out those funds. The lower interest rates are then assumed to cause increased borrowing for investment. Hence, saving causes investment in this conceptualization of the financial market. However, in reality not only is investment notoriously unreceptive to changes in the cost of borrowing (Sharpe and Suarez 2013), but banks and other financial institutions *can create money with a keystroke*, something that is both conducive to economic growth and a source of instability.

To see this, consider first the balance sheet of a representative commercial bank (Table 2.2).

TABLE 2.2 *Balance sheet of a representative commercial bank*

Assets (millions)	Liabilities (millions)
$60 T bills	$200 checking
$160 loans	$10 borrowed funds
$20 cash reserves	$30 net worth
Total $240 million	Total $240 million

Assets are items that add value to the bank while liabilities represent their obligations. *Net worth* shows the value of assets remaining were all liabilities to be simultaneously settled. In the US, if this number becomes negative then the bank would be insolvent and is forced to close.

Assets can take a number of forms which typically offer rates of return inverse to their relative safety. Cash (under *Reserves*) is default-proof, but earns nothing (this is no longer true as the Federal Reserve now pays interest on reserves, but was true for the period covered by Chapter 4 and will be assumed here); US government treasury bills (*T Bills*) are among the safest assets on the planet and consequently promise a very low rate of return; and while *Loans* will be the bank's biggest money maker, they also carry the greatest risk since it is possible that the debtor does not repay. Under liabilities, banks owe depositors whatever they have in their checking accounts (*Checking*) and the bank borrows money (*Borrowed Funds*), too, in their case from other banks, individuals and businesses, and the Federal Reserve.

Note first that there is insufficient money in the vault (*Reserves*) to meet demand were all the bank's customers to draw on their checking accounts simultaneously. This would be the result if there were a bank run and this could force the bank into insolvency. However, despite the fact that this often the story told to economics students as the primary source of instability in the financial system, such an eventuality is extremely unlikely. This is not simply because deposits are now insured by the Federal Deposit Insurance Corporation, but because standard operating procedure at the Federal Reserve requires them to supply reserves whenever the system runs short.[11]

For example, consider what happens when a bank makes a loan. Even if banks are required to keep, say, 10 percent of deposits in reserve (the rule before its suspension in March 2020), maintaining this is little more than an afterthought.[12] Imagine that an entrepreneur approaches the above bank with a very promising project that will require a loan of $10 million. Since loans are the biggest source of income for the bank, the loan officer will want to accept this application before the entrepreneur decides to go to one of their competitors. She will therefore adjust the bank's balance sheet as shown in Table 2.3 (italicized numbers are changes from above).

Loans have risen by $10 million and so has checking. The latter occurred because the manner in which the bank extended the loan was by creating a checking account in the amount of $10 million – from thin air – for the entrepreneur in question. All of this is perfectly legal and routine for banks, who

---

[11] Note that this means to the system, not necessarily to individual banks.
[12] This story is based on the assumption that the Federal Reserve requires banks to maintain a certain percentage of total deposits in reserve. As of March 15, 2020, this requirement was suspended. However, this was not the case for the period covered by this volume. In the end, it does not really make much difference – which is part of the reason it was suspended. More on this later.

2.4 Financing Physical Investment

TABLE 2.3 *Balance sheet immediately after loan*

Assets (millions)	Liabilities (millions)
$60 T bills	$210 checking
$170 loans	$10 borrowed funds
$20 reserves	$30 net worth
Total $250 million	Total $250 million

have the power to create brand new money.[13] It is estimated that something on the order of 97% of all our money was created by this process (Werner 2014: 71). Commercial banks (as opposed to investment banks – more on them momentarily) can certainly loan out your savings, but the majority of what they do is create credit, or promises to pay. It is akin to the bank signing (on your behalf) an IOU, however with their reputation to back it. An IOU requires no cash – indeed, it was because you had none that it was created.

I will expand on this later, but the important thing now is to address the unresolved issue in the above balance sheet: the fact that the bank no longer holds 10 percent of deposits in reserve. Before the rule's suspension (which, to reiterate, covers the entire period discussed in Chapter 4), they had fourteen days to comply so that it did not represent a realistic obstacle on the day that the loan officer acted to secure the promising loan. Once they do decide to address the shortfall, the first place they will look is the federal funds market, where those banks finding themselves with excess reserves would loan them overnight to those facing a shortage. Such a solution would appear on the balance sheet as an addition of $1 million to both *Reserves* (under assets) and *Borrowed Funds* (under liabilities), causing both assets and liabilities to increase to $251 million. However, the more interesting and important scenario is one where the entire system is short, as might be the case during an economic expansion. *The fact that the Federal Reserve targets interest rates all but obligates them to supply the missing reserves since failing to do so would drive up rates.* They would accomplish this by purchasing Treasury bills, which would affect the balance sheet by lowering *T Bills* by $1 million and raising *Reserves* by the same amount – total assets and liabilities would remain at $250 million. In short, given the conditions under which modern banking takes place, maintenance of sufficient reserves is therefore almost a nonissue – indeed, so much so that the Federal Reserve suspended the rule entirely at the outbreak of COVID (and with no timetable or intent to bring it back).

Returning to the suggestion at the beginning of this section that the financial system must both provide liquidity and decide which borrowers are the most creditworthy, the above discussion indicates that they can accomplish the former with ease. An economy emerging from a deep recession does not need to

---

[13] As do many other institutions since the repeal of Glass–Steagall – the key is the legal right to accept deposits. This also allows them to *create* deposits.

wait for sufficient savings to accumulate for the banking sector to be able to channel those funds to firms for physical investment projects. Were that true then recovery would be doubly difficult. Instead, new credit money can be created practically at will by the private sector, with any system-wide shortfalls in reserves being made good by Federal Reserve intervention that is automatic and not discretionary given their commitment to hit interest-rate targets. If they do not act when there is a net shortage of reserves (by buying Treasury Bills), interest rates would rise as institutions competed for the scarce funds; and if they do not act when there is an excess (by selling Treasury Bills), then interest rates would fall. The bottom line is that, in terms of fulfilling its first assigned task of providing sufficient funding for investment and other forms of spending, the system is fully capable of doing so. That is not a worry.

However, managing assets in a manner that contributes to system stability is more problematic. Unfortunately, over the course of an upturn financial institutions tend to create increasingly fragile portfolios. This means that just as investment spending starts to tail off in late expansion, causing the rate of growth of firms' profits to decelerate or even turn negative, the financial system is at its most vulnerable. The key here is net worth and its relationship to the institution's assets. Recall Table 2.2.

The net worth-to-asset (or capital-to-asset) ratio is $30/$240 = 12.5%. This means that the bank's assets can depreciate by no more than a 12.5% before it becomes insolvent. And while the *Reserves* and *T Bills* are safe, the *Loans* – the place where the bank really makes its money – are not. Defaults and write offs of $30 million or more would cause the bank to fail. Now examine what happened on Table 2.3 (after they extended the new $10 million loan).

TABLE 2.2 *Balance sheet of a representative commercial bank*

Assets (millions)	Liabilities (millions)
$60 T bills	$200 checking
$160 loans	$10 borrowed funds
$20 cash reserves	$30 net worth
Total $240 million	Total $240 million

TABLE 2.3 *Balance sheet immediately after loan*

Assets (millions)	Liabilities (millions)
$60 T bills	$210 checking
$170 loans	$10 borrowed funds
$20 reserves	$30 net worth
Total $250 million	Total $250 million

2.4 Financing Physical Investment

The capital to asset ratio has fallen from 12.5% ($30/$240) to 12% ($30/$250). Granted, this bank has yet to address its shortfall in reserves, but doing so by selling Treasury Bills still leaves it at 12% (*T Bills* falls by $1 million while *Reserves* rises by the same amount, leaving total assets unchanged), while borrowing on the fed funds market actually makes things worse (*Borrowed Funds* and *Reserves* rise by $1 million, as does total assets, so the ratio falls to $30/$251 or 11.95%). *In short, every new loan – the very thing the bank must target in order to earn higher profits and which will represent an increasingly large percentage of their assets over the course of an expansion – lowers the capital-to-asset ratio and makes them more vulnerable to a downturn.* In addition, bankers also operate in that same environment of *uncertainty* as those they serve meaning that they, too, are subject to euphoria and panic and are dependent on animal spirits to overcome any misgivings. Add to all this the fact that Hyman Minsky argued that over the course of expansions, agents come to view their levels of caution regarding debt as excessive (Minsky 2008). During the good times, both borrowers and lenders decide that they have been too careful and have missed out on profit opportunities – and so they borrow and lend more. Stability thereby creates instability.

Even financial institutions like investment banks that do not normally take deposits (and therefore cannot create money) face such problems.[14] Operating in the higher end of the market, they deal primarily with other large financial institutions and with corporations requiring advice, brokering, and other services related to funding operations. This simplified version of Lehman Brothers position in May 2008 offers an example of their operations (they declared bankruptcy in September 2008) (Table 2.4).[15]

Roughly speaking, *Fin (Financial) Instruments Owned* counts assets such as securities and derivatives; *Collateralized Agreements* represents loans in exchange for temporary ownership of customer financial assets (the customer sells the asset

TABLE 2.4 *Lehman Brothers' balance sheet*

Assets (millions)		Liabilities (millions)	
Cash	$20,000	Short-term borrowing	$175,000
Fin instruments owned	$270,000	Long-term borrowing	$130,000
Collateralized agreements	$300,000	Collateralized financing	$210,000
Receivables	$40,000	Payables	$100,000
Other assets	$14,000	Net worth	$29,000
TOTAL	$644,000	TOTAL	$644,000

[14] Note that since the repeal of Glass–Steagall, there is no longer a clear legal distinction between commercial banking and other types of financial institutions. However, that does not affect the current discussion.

[15] For a more complete breakdown, see pages 56 and 57 of Ball 2016.

to Lehman, then repurchases it later); *Receivables* is money owed to Lehman for various services; and *Other Assets* includes things like property. Under liabilities, *Short-* and *Long-term Borrowing* are unsecured loans (the former for under one year and the latter for over one year; roughly 80% of the *Short-term Borrowing* is Lehman taking short positions in the market, having sold an asset but not yet purchased it); *Collateralized Financing* is the reverse of *Collateralized Agreements* (it is Lehman who is selling securities on the agreement to repurchase them later); and *Payables* is money Lehman owes for various services.

At this point in time, Lehman's capital-to-asset ratio was 4.5%.[16] During the Financial Crisis of 2007–2008, the stock market lost over 20% of its value in just a single week. Even if this only affected *Financial Instruments Owned* and none of the other asset categories in the above portfolio, this is more than enough to make Lehman insolvent (20% of $270 billion is $54 billion, the loss of which leave them with a net worth of -$25 billion). Hence, financial institutions with portfolios that include a significant volume of assets traded on exchanges are also vulnerable – in many ways more so, for while loan write offs tend to occur incrementally and presumably with some notice, the value of tradeable financial assets can change in moments.[17] Thus, regardless of whether waves of investment are funded via loans or other instruments such as new issues of stock, economic expansions create portfolios increasingly dependent on the continuation of the upturn – an upturn that will inevitably run out of steam.

Not that the financial sector is in a constant in a state of chaos. As Keynes wrote (where the state of long-term expectation is that which would govern the financial investment decision):

We should not conclude from this that everything depends on waves of irrational psychology. On the contrary, the state of long-term expectation is often steady, and, even when it is not, the other factors exert their compensating effects. We are merely reminding ourselves that human decisions affecting the future, whether personal or political or economic, cannot depend on strict mathematical expectation, since the basis for making such calculations does not exist; and that it is our innate urge to activity which makes the wheels go round, our rational selves choosing between the alternatives as best we are able, calculating where we can, but often falling back for our motive on whim or sentiment or chance (Keynes 1936: 162–3).

This description is much more consistent with what we observe in the real world: periods of relative stability punctuated by episodes of volatility, euphoria, panic, boom, and bust. These are not black swan events, they are generated systemically.

---

[16] In reality, various types of assets are given different weights based on their relative safety. For example, cash would receive a higher weight than treasury bills, which would receive a higher weight than stocks. Such a level of detail is not necessary here.

[17] This is also why Glass–Steagall had prohibited commercial banks from owning stocks. The goal was to ensure that those institutions holding the savings of the American people did not take excessive risks.

2.5 ADDITIONAL FACTORS

The above is sufficient to build the endogenous business cycle story suggested at the opening of Section 2.2. There, it was argued that the recession occurs because physical investment spending slows as firms reach targeted levels of capacity. This leads to a fall in profits, which disappoints entrepreneurs' otherwise optimistic expectations. In an environment of *uncertainty* rather than *risk*, disappointment can weigh heavily and cause even further cut backs, generating an extended downturn. Because the financial sector (also operating in an environment of *uncertainty*) will have been creating liquidity for the nonfinancial sector during the expansion at the same time they have become less risk-averse, they will have lowered their net worth-to-asset ratios and have thereby made their solvency increasingly dependent on the continuation of the upturn. Once the latter has ended, the liquidity-creating function of the financial sector will be impaired, possibly to the point that even everyday operations are difficult to fund.

Over the course of the recession, however, capital equipment wears out, becomes obsolete, or proves less profitable for other reasons. At first, firms may resist repairs and replacement given the depressed state of the economy. Eventually, however, depreciation reaches the point that firms are forced to replace capital. In addition, the pessimism bred by the downturn fades and financial institutions' portfolios recover to the point that they are willing and able to lend again. This leads to a jump in investment spending, which in turn raises profits and, in the environment of *uncertainty*, boosts forecast optimism and confidence and leads other firms to follow suit. A new expansion begins.

Institutionalist and Post Keynesian authors have identified other factors, too, that are related to the business cycle. As these elements play visible roles in those to be covered later in the volume, they will be added to the basic model. They are:

- interest rates
- differential price movements
- gestation period
- principle of increasing risk

Each will be explained in turn.

While interest rates play the central role in many mainstream explanations of the business cycle (as exogenous, policy-related causes of recession), they are generally minor factors in Institutionalist/Post Keynesian analyses. That said, the possibility that rising levels of economic activity may push borrowing costs up is conceded. Mitchell writes, for example, that during the upturn stress may emerge from:

the accumulating tension of the investment and money markets. The supply of funds available at the old rates of interest for the purchase of bonds, for lending on mortgages, and the like, fails to keep pace with the rapidly swelling demand. It becomes difficult to negotiate new issues of securities except on onerous terms, and men of affairs complain of the "scarcity of capital." Nor does the supply of bank loans grow fast enough to keep up with the demand (Mitchell 1913: 573).[18]

However, while he raises this as a potential complication, his argument is based more heavily on the existence differential price movements and their impact on firm profits (more on that in a moment). Keynes, meanwhile, writes:

Now, we have been accustomed in explaining the 'crisis' to lay stress on the rising tendency of the rate of interest under the influence of the increased demand for money both for trade and speculative purposes. At times this factor may certainly play an aggravating and, occasionally perhaps, an initiating part. But I suggest that a more typical, and often the predominant, explanation of the crisis is, not primarily a rise in the rate of interest, but a sudden collapse in the marginal efficiency of capital (his "collapse in the marginal efficiency of capital" is akin to the panic discussed above; Keynes 1936: 315).

He further believes that rates are more likely to rise *after* the downturn due to the sudden increase in liquidity preference (i.e., the rush to cash and other more liquid assets – note that central banks often act quickly to offset this in the real world so we do not witness the increase in rates that might otherwise occur). One can find similar sentiments in the works of other Institutionalist/Post Keynesian scholars. The bottom line is that interest rates and other borrowing costs may well rise over the course of the expansion and could on occasion be the trigger for the turn, but in general they represent complicating rather than root causes. While they should not be ignored and they will not be in the coming chapters, they play only a secondary and sometimes tertiary role. Again, this is in stark contrast to Neoclassical theory.

A more significant factor is the fact that during an expansion, the magnitude and timing of price movements can vary in a manner that – marginally at first but eventually with considerable power – erodes profits. To Mitchell at least, this was key. The general idea is that over the course of the boom, all prices are pushed up: final sales, financing, raw materials, capital goods, labor, and overhead. Profits, Mitchell's primary focal point, are positively correlated with the first and negatively with the rest. His empirical research indicated that there was a tendency for financing, raw materials, and capital goods prices to rise faster than those for final sales, thus depressing profits. However, also evident was the fact that the pressure on labor and overhead costs lagged considerably. Particularly because of their relatively large weight compared to the other categories, he concluded that in early to mid expansion profits rose, thereby encouraging even more investment. Mitchell explains,

In the great majority of enterprises, larger profits result from these divergent price fluctuations coupled with the greater physical volume of sales. For, while the prices of raw materials and of wares bought for resale usually, and the prices of bank loans often, rise

---

[18] Note that the US was on the gold standard when he wrote this.

2.5 Additional Factors

faster than selling prices, the prices of labor lag far behind, and the prices which make up supplementary costs are mainly stereotyped for a time by old agreements regarding salaries, leases, and bonds (Mitchell 1913: 572).

Eventually labor and overhead agreements would expire, leading to rising costs sufficient to depress profits. As this occurs, Mitchell argues that this causes a significant shift in priorities as "the problem of making profits on current transactions, is subordinated to the more vital problem of maintaining solvency" (Mitchell 1913: 576). The economy therefore shifts into recession until these very same differential rate of change of prices works in reverse to stimulate economic recovery.

While not as central in his analysis, Keynes does mention the impact of prices on profits, particularly as related to the cost of capital goods. But his belief was that optimistic expectations would tend to offset the rising cost of production (Keynes 1936: 315). Nicholas Kaldor also includes this as a factor creating drag on the expansion (Kaldor 1940: 81), as does Minsky (Minsky 2008). In any event and for whichever set of reasons, data presented in Chapter 4 will show that there is a great deal of evidence to support the claim that profits fall in late expansion – before the onset of recession – regardless of the underlying reason.

Kalecki's analysis of the business cycle adds two additional factors to consider: The gestation period necessary for investment spending to produce a capital good and the principle of increasing risk. The former is meant to remind us that while breaking ground for the new factory did not begin until June, the decision to do so undoubtedly took place months before this. This is important because it highlights the fact that investment spending in June is almost certainly not a reflection of entrepreneurial expectations that same month, but of what they had forecast well before. Thus, to understand the conditions that determined the volume of investment in June, we must reach back to, say, January.

Given that increases in investment lead to increases in profits, stages 2, 2′, and 2″ in Figure 2.2 are periods of rising income for investors. Because Kalecki assumed, along with Keynes, that "the facts of the existing situation enter, in a sense disproportionately, into the formation of our long-term expectations" (Kalecki 1937: 84, quoting Keynes 1936: 148), he suggested that the agents witnessing the rising profit at stages 2, 2′, and 2″ will believe that this will continue and they will be induced to invest even more (López and Assous

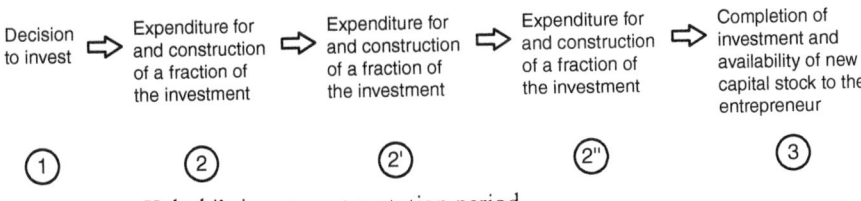

FIGURE 2.2 Kalecki's investment-gestation period

2010: 93–4). Balanced against this is the fact that at the same time, firms throughout the economy are also reaching stage 3, thereby lowering profits and consequently depressing expectations (Kalecki 1937: 89). Hence, Figure 2.2 illustrates two opposing forces at work (similar to those in Figure 2.1), the relative weights of which determine the current stage of the business cycle. When stages 2, 2′ and 2″ dominate, we expand because investment spending creates profits; if, however, firms reaching stage 3 decide not to start a new project, investment and profits decline.

Earlier, it was argued that firms will eventually stop investing because they will reach a point where they think that existing capacity is sufficient to meet demand. Kalecki didn't approach it quite that way. And without that element, why would investment ever decline? If greater investment leads to greater profits, which spurs on more investment, why won't firms continuously start new projects after reaching stage 3? Kalecki argued that the relevant constraint was related to the fact that:

The rate of risk of every investment is greater the larger is this investment. If the entrepreneur builds up a factory he incurs a certain risk of unprofitable business, and these losses, if any, will be more significant for him the greater proportion the investment considered bears to his wealth. But besides this, in "sacrificing" his reserves (consisting of deposits or securities) or taking credits, he exhausts his "sources of capital," and if he should need this "capital" in the future he may be obliged to borrow at a high rate of interest because he has overdrawn the amount of credit considered by his creditors as "normal." Thus both these aspects of risk incurred by investment shot that the rate of risk must grow with the amount invested (Kalecki 1937: 84–5).

This, then, is the counter to the otherwise positive feedback loop leading to larger and larger levels of investment spending: the principle of increasing risk. This can be added to the factors contributing to the business cycle.

2.6 CONCLUSIONS

While additional factors will be introduced in Chapter 3, the above represents the core theory on which the explanations in Chapter 4 will be based. Note that it has not been argued here that the cause of recession is overinvestment, or the building of productive capacity the output from which would not be in demand even if the economy were at full employment. This is of course possible and perhaps even likely on the micro level, something Keynes referred to as "misdirected" investment (Keynes General Theory chapter 22). In general, however, and in stark contrast to theories like those of the Austrians, Keynes believed that it was more likely that the nature of the business cycle was such that investment tended to stop – because of disappointed expectations rather than overbuilding – *before* society had exhausted all of the productive investments available (Keynes 1936: 323).

3

Additional Factors

Inflation, Monetary and Fiscal Policy, the Stock Market, and Secular Stagnation

Chapter 2 offers a business cycle theory based on the assumption that events that occur during the upturn lead directly to the downturn. In other words, in a market economy, expansions sow the seeds of recession. While that will be the major focus of Chapter 4, there are other factors to consider, too. Chief are inflation, monetary and fiscal policy, the stock market, and secular stagnation. These will be explained below, especially any role they may play in the business cycle.

3.1 INFLATION

Standard operating procedure at the Federal Reserve is to increase interest rates as an economic upturn matures. This is because they believe that economic expansions create inflationary pressures and that these are serious problems. They therefore act to reduce the level of economic activity by raising interest rates. It is for this reason that inflation, or the threat thereof, is often invoked as an indirect cause of recession: it triggers the Federal Reserve into causing one. This is precisely what Neoclassical economist Rudiger Dornbusch had in mind when he wrote, "None of the U.S. expansions of the past 40 years died in bed of old age; every one was murdered by the Federal Reserve" (quoted in Temin 1998: 1).

Of course, in his school of thought, recessions are always caused by an external event. In their view, full employment is the default state of the macroeconomy and can be maintained indefinitely. It is therefore necessary for them to identify an external source like Federal Reserve policy. Not only is that not the perspective forwarded in this volume, but, except at extremes, interest rates are not a particularly efficient means of slowing economic activity (fiscal policy is far more effective). And even if they were, there is no logical reason to believe that inducing recession is an effective response to inflation.

More fundamentally, in some instances inflation plays a positive role. On those occasions, we should not try to stop it at all because it is sending appropriate signals to entrepreneurs. And when that's not true, raising interest rates does not help. Because confusion regarding the causes and effects of inflation are so widespread, a lengthy explanation follows.

The first point to be made is that inflation is always concentrated in certain sectors, not spread equally over the entire economy. There may be contagion effects such as rising prices in one area causing costs and therefore prices to rise in another; but when inflation is, say, 5 percent, that does not mean that all prices are rising simultaneously by that same degree. Some rise more, some rise less, and some may even fall. This may seem rather obvious, but policy is rarely designed to take this into account. A forced recession by the Federal Reserve, for example, does not focus on certain markets but "attacks" the entire economy at once. Consider the situation in the 1970s and early 1980s. The source of the inflation was obvious: the OPEC oil embargo.[1] Despite this fact, the Paul-Volcker Federal Reserve saw fit to raise interest rates to historic levels and cause what was at the time the worst recession since the Great Depression.[2] It is difficult to see how unemployment of over 10 percent was addressing the real issue. Instead, it surely made things worse for most Americans who were already paying much higher energy prices and now had to do so with lower (or no) incomes as well.[3] *Inflation must be viewed as sectoral and not economy-wide if it is to be understood and addressed.*

A second issue this raises is the relative impact of inflation. Because it is sectoral and not universal, not everyone suffers by the same degree – indeed, some gain! Returning to the OPEC example, those who were involved in the oil and gas industry clearly benefitted. Although they, too, paid higher prices for groceries, entertainment, housing, etc. (because energy price increases bled into other sectors), the prices that directly contributed to their incomes rose far more than those they paid. The Bureau of Labor Statistics' inflation numbers for 1974 support this. While consumer price inflation was 11%, everyone wasn't 11% worse off. Gasoline prices, for example, rose by 35.3 percent. Hence, the prices determining the incomes of those in the petroleum industry rose over three times as much as those they paid. *The bottom line is that inflation redistributes income.*

---

[1] In July 1973, three months before the invasion of Israel, a barrel of oil sold for $3.56 (West Texas Intermediate, all data from Federal Reserve Bank of St. Louis). By the same date the next year, it was $10.11. In July 1980, it was $39.50.

[2] As suggested above, interest rates can have an effect at extreme levels.

[3] Their logic, incidentally, was that prices were rising due to "inflationary expectations:" people expected inflation, so workers built that into their wage demands and firms into their pricing, which created a self-fulfilling prophecy. The central bank's goal was to beat these expectations out of the private sector. Unfortunately for future inflationary episodes, this was hailed as a success because inflation did come down a few years thereafter. However, in reality this was a side effect of the Iran–Iraq War and the fact that it reduced OPEC's monopoly power (Rubin 2003).

3.1 Inflation

That said, the redistribution of income resulting from (or causing) inflation is not necessarily without benefits. If someone comes up with a wonderful new invention or innovation that is in high demand, they too will become wealthy at others' expense – but in that case the others will have acted voluntarily and are presumably pleased to pay for whatever the item may be. This can still be inflationary, however, particularly if the extra demand it creates causes bottlenecks and rising costs of production in other sectors. Continuing to use oil as the example, if a miraculous cancer-curing drug were developed that required large quantities of oil during the manufacturing process, this could be every bit as inflationary as the OPEC embargo, and it would redistribute income in a similar manner (but this time also to the drug manufacturer). Again, however, this redistribution would be voluntary and the result of an otherwise positive development.

There's another reason to believe that not all inflation is bad. If demand for the cancer-curing drug is high and it creates tremendous profits for the seller, then this both induces the seller to find a means of increasing supply and attracts others to the industry. An increased supply of the drug is precisely what consumers wanted. This is an example of the market working well (ignoring for purposes of this example the moral question of whether or not we would want to leave the distribution of such an important drug entirely to the private sector). *Rising prices are one of the means by which consumers can get producers to do what they want, that is, to sell more of the products they most desire.*

This discussion suggests that we should adopt a more nuanced approach to inflation. Rather than following our current policy of treating it all as identical and then inducing an economy-wide recession to "solve" it, five questions should be asked:

1. Cause: What was the immediate cause of the price increase(s)?
2. Locus: Where is the inflation concentrated and how is it spreading?
3. Winners and losers: Who, if anyone, is benefitting from a net redistribution of income caused by the inflation and at whose expense (bearing in mind that the latter may be entirely voluntary)?
4. Impact: What incentives are being created by the rising prices and are vulnerable segments of the population being affected?
5. Policy response: Is a policy response necessary and, if so, how it should be targeted?

Before generalizing on these observations, some examples may be useful.

3.1.1 Inflation Examples

Example 1: Housing Boom Driven by Demographic Trends
Say there is a housing boom driven by demographic (rather than speculative) trends and that it has led to an increase in housing prices and bottlenecks in

the markets for bricks, lumber, and related building materials. As housing is a component of the consumer price index (about one-third), inflation accelerates.

1. Cause: Population rising faster than housing supply.
2. Locus: The inflation is centered in residential real estate, with contagion into the building-materials industry.
3. Winners and losers: The primary beneficiaries will be those selling real estate and building materials; the source of their higher incomes will be home buyers.
4. Impact: Rising residential real estate prices will encourage more home building and increased production of the requisite materials; low-income households and individuals may be disproportionately impacted.
5. Policy response: No policy response is necessary. Consumers' demand for more housing has bid up prices, which will lead to an increase in the supply of housing. The market is doing exactly what it is supposed to do and what consumers want. If it is determined that any particularly vulnerable groups are being affected, then *focused* action should be taken. The government has at its disposal a range of options, from subsidies to builders or buyers to reductions in permit costs. Note, however, that there is absolutely no logical role for the Federal Reserve's standard operating procedure of an increase in interest rates aimed at lowering the level of economic activity. While it may lower prices since people would not have the income to buy a house, this is the same outcome (i.e., a shortage) without the positive impact of rising prices creating an incentive to produce more.

Example 2: Housing Boom Driven by Speculative Activity

If the housing boom is driven instead by speculative activity – individuals and businesses buying up homes solely in the hope that they can turn around and sell them at a profit – then the story is a little different. It still leads to rising housing prices and bottlenecks in the markets for bricks, lumber, and related building materials, but with complications.

1. Cause: Demand from speculative purchases of homes.
2. Locus: The inflation is centered in residential real estate, with contagion into the building-materials industry.
3. Winners and losers: The primary beneficiaries will be those selling real estate – *including those who had purchased homes with no intention of living in them* – and building materials; the source of their higher incomes will be home buyers and other speculators.
4. Impact: Rising residential real estate prices will encourage more home building and increased production of the requisite materials; low-income households and individuals might be disproportionately impacted. The rising prices may also encourage more speculation.
5. Policy response: In the previous example, the rising prices and consequent incentive to build more homes were generally welcome because there was

3.1 Inflation

a legitimate social need for more housing. In this case, however, the homes being held by speculators – up to one in three in some real-world instances – stand empty and serve no real purpose other than as a vehicle for capital gain (Texas McCombs 2021). A multitude of other such vehicles already exist so that there is no need to link one to a basic need like shelter. In addition, the existence of speculative buyers means that even those who are able to secure housing must pay a higher price. The government should introduce measures to limit speculation in a market that serves such an essential purpose. Note that, once again, there is absolutely no logical reason to increase interest rates in an attempt to lower the level of economic activity.

Example 3: Rising Chip Costs Due to Supply Chain Issues
This example is drawn from one of the problems arising during COVID. A decrease in the supply of computer chips caused a spike in the cost of chips and products using these chips (JP Morgan 2023). While the overall rate of inflation remained fairly low for most of this period, this was only due to other sectors being severely depressed by the pandemic. It still represents a route by which the overall price level could rise (and later in COVID this is precisely what happened as additional pressures emerged).

1. Cause: Quarantines, social distancing, illnesses, and deaths resulting from COVID led to reduced supplies.
2. Locus: Chip prices rose, which caused the prices of products using chips to rise as well.
3. Winners and losers: This requires additional explanation but allows for the introduction of a new concept. The issue is this. Say that the COVID-related production problems caused the quantity of chips to fall by 25 percent. Clearly those who want to buy chips as a component in their manufacturing process are worse off, as will be their customers, because the lower quantity supplied will bid up the price. But what about those selling the chips? It depends. If the prices rise by more than 25 percent, then their revenues will actually increase; on the other hand, if prices rise by less than 25 percent, then their revenues will fall. The related economic concept is called "price elasticity of demand." If price rises >25 percent, then the demand for that product is said to have been relatively *inelastic* (consumers were less willing to stop buying the product and thus bid up the price even more than the reduction in quantity); if price rises less than the reduction in quantity, demand is categorized as relatively *elastic* (consumers were less willing to pay the higher prices and so the prices didn't rise proportionally). Thus, in this case, it depends on the price elasticity of demand for computer chips, and although there will still be redistributional effects, they are more complicated. It is entirely possible for everyone to be worse off (though not necessarily to the same degree – some will undoubtedly suffer more than others). Note, incidentally, that the reason OPEC and the petroleum industry benefitted from

the embargo was that the demand for oil was extremely inelastic. Their revenues rose significantly.
4. Impact: This creates an incentive to manufacture more chips and may attract others to the industry (while chip consumers may try to substitute away from them).
5. Policy response: When the source of the inflation is a natural event like a pandemic, or a hurricane or war, policy must focus on overcoming whatever obstacles have been placed in the way of production. This may prove to be very difficult. The best defense against COVID, for example, was always going to be vaccination and herd immunity. Until this occurred, however, bringing workers back into the factory to make chips was going to be problematic. The remaining logical course of action for the government was to do all it could to make research and subsequent availability of a vaccine as simple and cheap as possible, which is precisely what they did. What this drives home again is that inflation must be understood sectorally. It has to be attacked at its source, and broad-based policies are necessarily going to be ineffective and probably counterproductive. One thing we definitely do not want to do in this example is follow standard practice at central banks and try to reduce the level of economic activity. It would only add salt to the wound.

Example 4: Rising Food Costs Due to Geopolitical Unrest

A hot topic at the time of this writing is the inflation stemming from the Russian invasion of Ukraine, which began February 24, 2022. As both countries are major sources of grain and fertilizer, this has led to worldwide food price increases (Welsh 2024). The Federal Reserve has tried to control the inflation by increasing interest rates, which is, of course, futile (and a policy that contributed to the collapse of the seventh-largest bank in the US; Bivens 2023).

1. Cause: Russian invasion of Ukraine interrupting food production and supply.
2. Locus: Food.
3. Winners and losers: As in the COVID-chip example, the question of winners and losers here depends on the price elasticity of demand. It is perhaps safe to say in this instance, however, that everyone loses given that there is simply less food.
4. Impact: Higher food prices create an incentive to increase production outside of Russia and Ukraine.
5. Policy response: As with the previous example, there is no easy solution here. Ending the war and resuming production is obviously the best way to lower food prices. Barring that, however, it simply takes time to shift to new, and likely still more expensive, sources. What the Federal Reserve actually did, however, was raise interest rates in order to lower the overall level of demand. This in no way addresses the real problem – a food shortage – and, in fact, makes things worse.

3.1 Inflation

The preceding discussion should give the reader a much stronger sense of how inflation really operates and the manner in which it should be addressed. With that foundation laid, we can now move beyond individual scenarios and offer some generalizations regarding six different types of inflation: demand-pull, demand-pull in the labor market, cost-push/market power, cost-push/supply shock, speculative, and currency depreciation. After a basic description, the same format will be used as above.

3.1.2 Demand-Pull Inflation

When prices are bid up because demand is outstripping producers' ability to supply, this is demand-pull inflation. Like any kind of inflation, however, it must be considered sectorally. Even when the economy as a whole is growing at a rapid pace, it is not the case that the increase in demand is spread over every market evenly. It may be automobiles, appliances, entertainment, houses (as in example 1), or whatever else consumers desire.

1. Cause: Rising consumer demand for some good or service.
2. Locus: The industry in which rising consumer demand is concentrated.
3. Winners and losers: Those selling the goods and services most in demand by consumers will earn more income; that new income will have been supplied by those purchasing the goods and services in question.
4. Impact: Suppliers will be induced to increase production, and others will be attracted to the industry.
5. Policy response: The incentives being created by the rising prices will lead to the outcome desired by consumers. There is therefore no need for a policy response unless some vulnerable group is being affected, and there is definitely no need to reduce the overall level of demand in the macroeconomy. An exceptional circumstance was created by the full-employment economy in the World War II. In that event, not only were incomes rising, but there were fewer consumer goods to be had since resources were reserved for the war economy. As rising prices would not lead to an increase in the production of the goods and services most in demand, a broad-based approach was justifiable. Taxes were raised and bonds were sold to lower consumer spending. In general, however, carefully targeted policies are necessary.

3.1.3 Demand-Pull/Labor Market Inflation

A special case of the demand-pull inflation phenomenon is when the bottlenecks make themselves felt in the labor market. If firms find it difficult to hire as many employees as they would like at the current wage, those wages will be bid up. Workers in these industries would no doubt argue that this makes perfect economic sense: if there is an excess demand for their services, why should they not earn more? This is indeed the argument we have made when we have experienced an increase in the demand for gasoline in the summer, heating oil in the winter, ceiling fans, and smaller cars after the OPEC-induced energy crisis, medical alcohol after COVID, and so on. Why should it be any different when the commodity is labor? And yet it *is* treated differently, for the Federal Reserve reacts negatively to pressures in the labor market and will attempt to dampen the demand by raising interest rates and lowering the level of economic activity.

This makes no sense, particularly given the increasing income inequality we have experienced over the past forty to fifty years. That our middle class is disappearing is not even terribly controversial anymore, with both parties citing it as a policy concern in the last several presidential elections. Not only is allowing price of labor to be bid up precisely what we would allow if this were a share of stock, but it would address the income distribution concern as well.

1. Cause: Labor shortage.
2. Locus: The industry in which consumer demand is concentrated (this would again be sectoral, with possible contagion effects).
3. Winners and losers: Workers in the industry in question win at the expense of business owners and their customers.
4. Impact: Rising wages would attract more workers – which is, of course, precisely what businesses wanted. Sectoral prices would almost certainly rise, too, just as they would if any other cost went up.
5. Policy response: None is necessary unless the price increases resulting from rising wages are causing hardship for vulnerable segments of the population. As always, carefully targeted policies are the logical choice rather than an economy-wide recession. Wage and price controls may be justified under exceptional circumstances, and the provision of low-cost training to address the labor shortage might also be an option. In general, however, wages should be allowed to increase.

3.1.4 Cost-Push/Market Power Inflation

Research suggests that many industries in our economy have become increasingly monopolistic (or, more properly, oligopolistic, meaning a few rather than just one) over the past forty to fifty years (De Loecker, Eeckhout, and Unger 2020.). What this means is that firms in those industries do not face as much competition due to the barriers to entry they have erected and they are therefore able to raise prices – even with no change in demand – in order to generate higher profits. They cannot do so entirely without consequence, as the quantity of their sales will almost certainly decline; but, in markets with relatively inelastic demand, they can nevertheless enjoy higher revenues over a wide range of prices. Examples of oligopolistic industries include health care, mass media, airlines, and wireless carriers.

3.1 Inflation

1. Cause: Exercise of market power.
2. Locus: Industry in which oligopolistic power is being exercised.
3. Winners and losers: Firms in that oligopolistic industry win at the expense of their customers.
4. Impact: Reduction of supply and increase in cost of the products sold in the oligopolistic industry; but, because of the barriers to entry, this occurs without the positive effect of inducing firms to produce more and attracting other firms to that sector.
5. Policy response: An economy-wide recession may reduce prices somewhat as consumers are less able to buy the goods and services sold by the oligopolist, but the latter is bound to suffer much less than the owners, managers, and workers in more competitive industries. This was the case when the Federal Reserve induced recession in order to address OPEC's oligopoly power. The average consumer was hurt far more than the oil exporters. Instead, policy must be aimed directly at the industry in question with the goal of eliminating or at least reducing its market power. This may involve breaking up the industry or regulating it.

3.1.5 Cost-Push/Supply Shock Inflation

Another means by which prices may rise is as a result of a decidedly noneconomic phenomenon, such as a weather event, a pandemic, or a war. Any one of these can interrupt the supply of a variety of products. Or the impact may be in terms of rising costs due to rebuilding after a disaster, as with tornadoes and the consequent destruction of homes and businesses.

1. Cause: Supply shock.
2. Locus: The sector in which the supply shock has affected the economy.
3. Winners and losers: As suggested in examples 3 and 4 above (chip prices during COVID and food prices during the Russia–Ukraine war), there is the possibility that no one wins, as this depends in part on the relevant price elasticities of demand. However, it is not unusual for some groups to benefit, for instance, the construction industry when rebuilding is required. This would be at the expense of their customers.
4. Impact: The rising prices will induce firms to increase supply and may attract others to the industry.
5. Policy response: Any policy response should focus on overcoming the specific difficulties created by the supply shock. Reducing the level of economic activity would be counterproductive and add to the woes created by the shock.

3.1.6 Speculative Inflation

Speculative pressures can contribute to inflation via two main channels: direct speculation and as a side effect of asset market speculation. The first is like that described in example 2 (housing speculation). If individuals and businesses buy up a specific item (such as homes, gaming systems, or hand sanitizer) with the sole goal of reselling it later at a higher price, this clearly raises the price of that item. The second form occurs when futures for that item are sold on an exchange. Changes in the futures price can affect current production decisions in the nonfinancial economy. This occurs on occasion in the petroleum industry, for example. When speculation in oil futures bids up their price, oil producers interpret this as a signal to slow current production in favor of the future (Senate 2006). This then drives up the spot price, causing inflation. The rising spot price may consequently serve to convince speculators that they had been correct to forecast a price increase, leading them to buy more futures.

1. Cause: Direct or indirect speculation.
2. Locus: Industry in which the speculation is occurring.
3. Winners and losers: The primary beneficiaries will be those selling the product whose price is driven up by the speculation, including those who never intended to consume the item in question and only bought in the hopes of earning a quick profit. This would be at the expense of end users of those products.
4. Impact: In the case of direct speculation, the impact is the encouragement of more production of the good in question. Unfortunately, the activities of the speculators mean that the social goal of supplying the goods to the final consumer is at least partially frustrated. For indirect speculation through the futures market, the impact is more complex and will include both incentives to increase production and signals that lead to a reduction.
5. Policy response: Keynes wrote in the General Theory, "Speculators may do no harm as bubbles on a steady stream of enterprise. But the position is serious when enterprise becomes the bubble on a whirlpool of speculation" (Keynes 1936: 159). That lesson is relevant here. Some speculation is not terribly harmful. However, when it is playing the predominant role in driving prices, then we are approaching Keynes' casino and "the job is likely to be ill-done" (Keynes 1936: 159). In that event, the government must introduce measures to limit speculation.

3.1.7 Currency Depreciation Inflation

When a currency depreciates for whatever reason, this makes imports more expensive. If those imports are not necessities or if there are readily available (if somewhat more expensive) substitutes, the impact need not be that great. If that is not the case, however, then it can be quite substantial. This is true even if the domestic export sector experiences a boom because of the decline (in foreign currency terms) in the prices of the products they sell.

1. Cause: Domestic currency depreciation.
2. Locus: Import sectors.

3.1 Inflation

3. Winners and losers: In order to gauge the impact of currency depreciation on income distribution, a slightly different approach is necessary. The complication is that there are three prices: the foreign currency price of the product in question, the exchange rate, and the domestic currency price. For example, say that the US imports rice from Mexico and that the peso price of a 100-weight bag is 800 pesos and the exchange rate is 20 pesos/dollar. That makes the domestic price $40 (for convenience, ignore any other costs such as transportation, and import duties). Now let the dollar depreciate to 10 pesos/dollar. There are reasons to believe that the peso price of 800 pesos per 100-weight bag would be little affected by this. Mexican rice producers are dependent on an array of costs in their domestic market, plus they are competing with other foodstuffs at home. That would put the dollar price (given the new exchange rate of 10 pesos/dollar) at $80: US importers of Mexican rice find themselves owing twice as much in dollars as before, despite the fact that the peso price is unchanged. Who does this help, and who does it hurt? Part of this, once again, depends on the price elasticity of demand. If US consumers happily substitute away from rice in favor of other starchy foods, then the rice importers are stuck absorbing most of the dollar price change themselves (as they will only be able to raise the dollar price moderately, which will lower their profits), plus quantities sold will fall. On the other hand, if people in the US are unwilling to part with rice (as might more realistically be the case with oil, for example), then there will only be a small reduction in sales and the increased costs can be passed on to the consumer. Profits could actually rise.
4. Impact: Theoretically, production of the goods and services in the now-expensive import sectors would be encouraged, but the situation is more complicated when it is across currencies. Adding to the uncertainty is the fact that currency prices are extremely volatile and driven primarily by speculative financial capital flows. Hence, they do not have a strong connection to the prices in the goods and services market that consumer price inflation reflects.
5. Policy response: This is a question of exchange rate policy rather than domestic macroeconomy management and will therefore not be pursued here. Harvey 2009 offers an extensive treatment, including a theory of exchange rate determination, a history of US currency movements, and policy recommendations. Foremost among the last is the reduction and control of international financial capital flows.

3.1.8 Inflation Summary

This yields six different varieties of inflation:

> Demand-pull inflation: Prices are bid up because demand is outstripping producers' ability to supply;

- Demand-pull inflation/labor market: A special case of the demand-pull inflation phenomenon wherein the bottlenecks make themselves felt in the labor market;
- Cost-push inflation/market power: Rising costs (translated into profits) due to firms' exercise of market power;
- Cost-push inflation/supply shock: Rising costs due to a noneconomic phenomenon (e.g., war, weather event, pandemic, natural disaster);
- Speculative: Rising prices due to a good or service being the direct target of speculative demand or because the value of an asset derivative of that good or service is being bid up;
- Currency depreciation: The increase in the price of imports due to a loss in the value of domestic currency.

In each case, it is evident that inflation is a phenomenon that must absolutely be understood sectorally and with the beneficiary of the process in mind. Sometimes, no policy response at all is required. Market economies are dynamic and price changes in response to various pressures are commonplace. Depending on the circumstances, these changes can contribute to the consumer price index in a manner that causes it to rise. But, assuming that cost-push factors or speculation are not to blame, this should be allowed to play out. Prices are signals to entrepreneurs, and rising prices generally mean rising profits. Firms will be attracted to the affected industries and output will rise – which is precisely what consumers wanted. Other than in circumstances like the full-employment, consumer-goods-scarce economy of World War II, reducing the overall level of economic activity is never useful or effective – quite the opposite. And in those instances where intervention is warranted – for example, when a vulnerable group is disproportionately affected – it must be specifically targeted.

3.2 MONETARY POLICY

Your typical economics textbook tells you that monetary policy involves central bank manipulations of the money supply. The Federal Reserve increases the money supply by buying US Treasury Bills from the public and lowers it by selling them. They can also loan money to banks via the discount window, and they can change how much money banks can lend by altering the required reserve ratio (back when one existed). But, as explained in Chapter 2, in reality central banks have very little direct control over the money supply. This is in part simply because they choose instead to target interest rates, or the price of money. You can hold either the price or quantity of a good constant, but not both. Hence, the intro econ story is false not only because "money" is difficult to define in the first place, but central banks elect to target interest rates.

Their goal in setting interest rates is to stimulate employment and constrain inflation. The standard operating procedure at the Federal Reserve is to keep interest rates low when unemployment is high and raise them when inflation is

3.2 Monetary Policy

accelerating. When unemployment *and* inflation are high, the latter is generally thought to be the bigger problem (or at least the one that must be tackled first, as "inflationary expectations" must be attacked), and so interest rates are raised. The folly of this approach was discussed at length above and will not be repeated here. In short, there is little reason to keep interest rates high other than to guarantee some minimum rate of return to those on fixed incomes (which can be accomplished more directly) or to make the cost of borrowing sufficiently high to discourage speculation (which can also be accomplished via different and more effective means). We should in general keep interest rates low (Galbraith 2023).

An area where central banks can play a critical role, however, is regulation. As shown in the Chapter 2, there are reasons to believe that the financial sector is prone to systemic instability. Margins of safety are reduced over the course of expansions, and increased loan activity necessarily reduces the capital-to-asset ratio. In addition, institutions have the incentive and means to disguise questionable investments until it is too late to rescue the position. This would not be such a problem were the only consequences borne by those putting their firms' portfolio in jeopardy, but this is not the case. The opening paragraph of this volume offered a rough overview of the extremely high costs paid for those having nothing to do with the Financial Crisis of 2007–2008. For these reasons, it is absolutely vital that the Federal Reserve actively monitor the health of financial institutions and be willing to both enforce existing rules and exercise discretionary power when innovating companies develop means of bypassing existing laws and guidelines. *This should be job #1 of the central bank*, followed by a low-interest rate policy aimed at increasing growth (and total abandonment of their inflation-watchdog role).

One final note regarding monetary policy: money growth cannot cause inflation! This is so despite the related aphorism that has become conventional wisdom well outside of economics classrooms and journals. But it is impossible. To understand this, consider the story that is usually told, one repeated in Milton Friedman's classic treatment (Friedman 1969: 1–50). In it, the central bank decides to print more money in order to stimulate the macroeconomy. People take this new money and go out to spend it. However, since the economy can only produce so many goods and services at a given point in time, this just bids up prices. Money growth causes inflation.

There are, however, several key unstated premises without which the story collapses. First, it is assumed that the economy is already at full employment. Were we not at such a point, then the influx of new cash would actually cause the economy to expand and new jobs and output would be created. But instead, the increase in the money supply makes "no additional productive capacity available" (Friedman 1969: 6). We are already at our maximum. Therefore, the central bank in Friedman's article is engaging in expansionary monetary policy *despite the fact that we already at full employment*. It is certainly possible that such a policy error could be committed, but it seems unlikely that this would be a routine event.

Even more problematic is the fact that the central bank cannot make anyone wealthier. In Friedman's paper, expansionary monetary policy is proxied by a helicopter flying over and dropping out new cash, "which is, of course, hastily collected by members of the community" (Friedman 1969: 4–5). The problem is that this is actually fiscal policy, not monetary. The Federal Reserve can only change the form in which wealth is held. If, for example, the Federal Reserve engages in an open market operation and buys a Treasury bill from an individual for $100, that individual is no richer than before: they simply traded a $100 Treasury bill for $100 cash. For Friedman's helicopter pilot to mimic this, it would be necessary for her to land, sneak into people's homes, and leave a crisp, new $100 bill in place of an equivalently valued asset.

If that is so, however, an essential element of Friedman's original argument no longer follows. There, he argued,

> If every individual simply decided to hold on to the extra cash, nothing else would happen. Prices would remain what they were before, and income would remain at $10,000 per year ... But this is not the way people would behave. *Nothing has occurred to make the holding of cash more attractive than it was before*, given our assumption that everyone is convinced the helicopter miracle will not be repeated (emphasis added; Friedman 1969: 5).

This is not true if the recipient of $100 cash simultaneously lost a $100 asset. There is, therefore, every reason to believe that they would simply save the new cash and, as a consequence, no inflation would result (or they may attempt to buy another financial asset, which affects prices there and not in the market for goods and services).

Although the above is enough to ground Friedman's helicopter, there is another leg of the argument to consider: those making the money-growth-causes-inflation argument insist that the Federal Reserve can increase the money supply without the cooperation of the public (see, for example, Batten 1981). In other words, new money can be forced on people. The more scholarly version of this is to say that the money supply can be increased beyond the demand for money. Again, however, it can be demonstrated that this premise does not hold up, for it is impossible for the Federal Reserve to increase the money supply if no one is willing to sell a Treasury Bill. Unless a member of the public wants to accept new money, it cannot come into existence. The supply of money is like the supply of haircuts: without a simultaneous demand, it cannot be created. Monetary policy cannot create an excess supply of money.

There are so many holes in Friedman's argument that it is difficult to understand why it has become gospel to so many. Perhaps it is because helicopter analogy is so quick and easy to understand, while following the real story requires much more institutional and theoretical background. Or it may be that it has a strong appeal to those who already believe that the government is irresponsible and should be straightjacketed when it comes to economic policy.

The fact that it is still taught in most economics classrooms (including mine many years ago) cannot help. The irony is that a ready and reasonable candidate for government-created inflation already exists: fiscal policy. If the economy is at full employment (as it was during World War II), then any additional fiscal stimulus would, indeed, be inflationary (as it was during World War II). But monetary policy is not.

3.3 FISCAL POLICY

Fiscal policy is related to government spending and taxation. Unlike monetary policy, its impact is very direct and significant. Fiscal policy can be divided between automatic stabilizers and discretionary intervention. The former refers to the fact that during an economic downturn, tax revenues fall (since people lose jobs and have no income) and spending on unemployment and income support programs rises. This fiscal stimulus keeps recessions from being as severe. Because such changes in taxes and spending do not require deliberation on the part of the president and Congress, they are automatic; because they act countercyclically, they are stabilizers.

Discretionary policy requires deliberation that automatic stabilizers do not, but can be more specifically targeted to the problem at hand. The American Recovery and Reinvestment Act of 2009 was passed in response to the downturn caused by the Financial Crisis 2007–2008, while the Coronavirus Aid, Relief, and Economic Security Act of 2020 was enacted in order to ease the burden on households and firms of the global pandemic. However, such efforts necessarily entail a time lag between the onset of the problem and the actual implementation of relief programs. This lag is affected by the fact that it is necessary to first estimate the size of the downturn, then devise policy to address it, and finally to debate and pass the legislation. Still, the impact is substantial.

In terms of the magnitude, the key is not so much the government spending (which is an injection) as the difference between that and the level of taxation (a leakage). Though there is some stimulative effect when the two are equal because the private sector may have saved some portion of the taxed income while the government will spend it all, generally speaking, government deficit spending is required if the aim is to expand the current level of economic activity by any significant amount. Indeed, this will later be described as the only logical means of addressing the problems created by the business cycle. Nor is deficit spending problematic, particularly for the US. Money does not grow on trees, but it does grow on keyboards. The US government can and does create money out of thin air all the time. This is precisely what they did to finance World War II and, more recently, the checks sent out to families after COVID. For these reasons, it is impossible for the US to default on its debt. This will be explained at length in Chapter 5, where it will be shown to be a key element in addressing economic instability.

3.4 FINANCIAL MARKETS: TRADEABLE SECURITIES

There has already been some discussion of financial markets in the Chapter 2 when covering banks, their ability to create money, and the importance of capital-to-asset ratios in financial institutions. What has not been mentioned are securities, or tradeable financial instruments used to raise funds. Stocks, bonds, and derivatives garner a great deal of attention, and they capture the imagination of the public. It is often implied by the press that even daily fluctuations in stock prices reflect important economic events. The truth is more nuanced.

The first important point to make is that the overwhelming majority of trades on any given day are secondary, such that the asset issuer sees none of the proceeds. They earned those on the initial sale and they are only concerned with subsequent trades insofar as these affect their credit rating, the efficacy of further initial offerings, or the security of the management team's jobs. Otherwise, asset prices represent continuous revisions of the value of the asset issuer by financial market participants. How accurate are those revisions? Clearly not sufficiently so as to prevent booms, busts, and financial crises. The problem is that forecasts in market for tradeable securities are affected every bit as much by *uncertainty* as those guiding the physical investment decisions discussed in Chapter 2. Recall that *uncertainty* was one of the key factors contributing to physical investment spending being the most volatile component of GDP. Now add to this the fact that those involved in buying stocks and bonds do not have to worry that the decisions they make are practically irreversible and represent long-term time commitments. Instead, individual market participants operate under the false illusion that if things go south, they can always quickly unload any bad decisions – unless, of course, everyone else is thinking the same thing. Agents are therefore far more willing to buy and sell on basis of scant information (see, for example, Baker and Wurgler 2007). It is for these reasons that stock prices are even more volatile than physical investment spending.

That said, not that many people are affected by price fluctuations, at least not directly. Although 53% of Americans owned stock in 2019, 70% of the value was held by families in the top 10% of incomes (Smart 2021). There are nevertheless serious indirect effects, as shown by the Financial Crisis of 2007–2008. A collapse in stock prices can place the financial firms discussed in Chapter 2 in a difficult place with respect to capital-to-asset ratios and funding may therefore be hard to come by. This reduces spending and employment across the economy. And, rightly or wrongly, people view the market for tradeable securities as a faithful representation of the current state of the economy. Hence, a collapse in the stock market brings down sentiment elsewhere, even if those places were otherwise totally unaffected by the bust. Suffice it to say that for purposes of this volume, financial markets are extremely important in terms of funding (as explained in Chapter 2), but the segment that focuses on tradeable securities tends to have an impact in excess of its practical importance. Impact the economy it does, however, and so it will be mentioned on occasion in Chapter 4.

3.5 SECULAR STAGNATION

Another issue that will arise in Chapter 4 is secular stagnation, or the decline in the average rate of growth over time. There are a number of theories regarding why this has occurred. Mainstream economist Robert Gordon has suggested that we should never have expected growth to be steady in the first place; instead, it occurs in spurts (Gordon 2016). "The economic revolution of 1870 to 1970 was unique," he writes, and has not been maintained because we face strong headwinds (Gordon 2016: 72). Included among these are income inequality, the slowing rate of educational attainment, the aging population and retirement of the baby boomers, and the rising government debt/income ratio (Gordon 2016: 72). Except with respect to his last point, it is unlikely that many nonmainstream economists would disagree with him except in detail. Indeed, Institutionalist Wallace Peterson's argument is similar in many respects (particularly on the pivotal role of the disappearance of the middle class), except that it calls for a strong government response – involving a great deal of spending – as a cure (Peterson 1994).

More closely related to discussion in Chapter 2 is the stagnation theory forwarded by Institutionalist/Post Keynesian scholars Harold Vatter and John Walker (Wray 2008). Recall that physical investment spending is the key driving force in economic expansion and that – because it is relatively easy to build – it has a tendency to trail off and eventually collapse. Vatter and Walker look to a longer-term implication of this process: successive net increases in investment over cycles will lead to successive net increases in capacity and productivity. This increase in the ability to supply relative to demand will make it progressively more difficult to generate enough of the latter to reach full employment. Unless other sources of demand increase to compensate, overall growth will decline over time – as it has. For this reason, Vatter and Walker argued "that government spending would have to grow at a pace that exceeds GDP growth in order to avoid stagnation" (Wray 2008: 155). Indeed, it would need to grow during both the expansion and then especially in the recession as a sort of offsetting ratchet effect.

Another factor that has accompanied stagnating growth rates is the emergence of money-manager capitalism. If the desired rates of return are no longer available on real investments, then capitalists must turn to financial ones. However, if real returns are falling, then so are financial ones. Only by adjusting your portfolio to take on more risk can this be avoided. Unfortunately, "By focusing on riskier segments of the credit market and/or using more leverage in their financial strategies, money managers have promoted the use of leverage in the rest of the economy, increased systemic financial fragility, and ultimately generated financial instability (Tymoigne 2022: 333)." We can, according to this, expect to witness stagnation accompanied by financial bubbles, which are then popped by financial crises. This will be especially evident in the discussion of the Financial Crisis of 2007–2008.

4

US Business Cycles 1954 through 2020

With the basic theory laid out, this chapter will now analyze the ten cycles (defined as an expansion followed by a recession) since 1954. This start date was selected because it is the beginning of the first expansion for which all of the data to be presented are available. Table 4.1 offers a summary of the periods to be studied, with the dates corresponding to those assigned by the National Bureau of Economic Research (NBER). While months are clearly more precise, the corresponding quarters are included because data limitations were such that some of the most important indicators were only available at that frequency. Note that each cycle has been given a descriptive name. These are intended only to give an easy means of referencing them and a sense of their historical context (with the chronological focus being on the recession part of the cycle rather than the expansion). The names are not meant to indicate the major cause of the cycle over that period (though sometimes they do).[1] Note that all growth data are annualized and inflation adjusted unless otherwise specified.

As explained in Chapter 2, the approach adopted in this volume rejects the mainstream view that economies tend to remain at full employment unless subjected to an external shock. Rather and consistent with the work of Institutionalist and Post Keynesian economists like Davidson, Kalecki, Keynes, Minsky, and Mitchell, it is maintained that business cycles are endogenously generated, that is, that expansions create the conditions that lead to recession. External shocks can of course lead to an economic downturn, but they are unnecessary. The system is already prone to breakdown and there is no reason to expect it to create a job for everyone who would like to work.

---

[1] Generally speaking and for obvious reasons, the length of each recession or expansion in quarters is roughly 1/3 that of their length in months. However, one may note that the COVID recession is marked as lasting both two months and two quarters. This is the official NBER dating and is not an error.

TABLE 4.1 *US cycles since 1954*

Cycle	Expansion	Recession
Ike I	Jun 1954 ... Aug 1957 (39 months) 1954Q3 ... 1957Q3 (13 quarters)	Sep 1957 ... Apr 1958 (8 months) 1957Q4 ... 1958Q2 (3 quarters)
Ike II	May 1958 ... Apr 1960 (24 months) 1958Q3 ... 1960Q2 (8 quarters)	May 1960 ... Feb 1961 (10 months) 1960Q3 ... 1961Q1 (3 quarters)
Vietnam	Mar 1961 ... Dec 1969 (106 months) 1961Q2 ... 1969Q4 (35 quarters)	Jan 1970 ... Nov 1970 (11 months) 1970Q1 ... 1970Q4 (4 quarters)
Oil shock I	Dec 1970 ... Nov 1973 (36 months) 1971Q1 ... 1973Q4 (12 quarters)	Dec 1973 ... Mar 1975 (16 months) 1974Q1 ... 1975Q1 (5 quarters)
Oil shock II	Apr 1975 ... Jan 1980 (58 months) 1975Q2 ... 1980Q1 (20 quarters)	Feb 1980 ... Jul 1980 (6 months) 1980Q2 ... 1980Q3 (2 quarters)
Volcker	Aug 1980 ... Jul 1981 (12 months) 1980Q4 ... 1981Q3 (4 quarters)	Aug 1981 ... Nov 1982 (16 months) 1981Q4 ... 1982Q4 (5 quarters)
Desert storm	Dec 1982 ... Jul 1990 (92 months) 1983Q1 ... 1990Q3 (31 quarters)	Aug 1990 ... Mar 1991 (8 months) 1990Q4 ... 1991Q1 (2 quarters)
Sept 11	Apr 1991 ... Mar 2001 (120 months) 1991Q2 ... 2001Q1 (40 quarters)	Apr 2001 ... Nov 2001 (8 months) 2001Q2 ... 2001Q4 (3 quarters)
Subprime crisis	Dec 2001 ... Dec 2007 (73 months) 2002Q1 ... 2007Q4 (24 quarters)	Jan 2008 ... Jun 2009 (18 months) 2008Q1 ... 2009Q2 (6 quarters)
COVID	Jul 2009 ... Feb 2020 (128 months) 2009Q3 ... 2019Q4 (42 quarters)	Mar 2020 ... Apr 2020 (2 months) 2020Q1 ... 2020Q2 (2 quarters)

The reason is directly related to fluctuations in physical investment spending. Investment drives the expansion, but then slows as firms reach targeted levels of capacity. Since investment is highly correlated with profits, the latter also falls which in turn disappoints erstwhile optimistic entrepreneurs. In an environment of *fundamental uncertainty*, this can lead to overreaction, panic, and a further decline in investment spending. This is compounded by the fact that during the expansion, the financial sector will have been creating liquidity for the nonfinancial sector and thereby engaging in acts that tend to make their solvency increasingly dependent on the continuation of the upturn. Once the latter has ended, financial institutions may fail or at least be far more cautious in terms of their willingness to back projects. Liquidity may dry up to the point that firms find it difficult to fund even everyday operations, let alone physical investment projects. On top of all this, government automatic stabilizers will have been operating in reverse, cutting spending and raising effective tax rates. Other factors will be referenced below as necessary, but this is the core theory.

4 US Business Cycles 1954 through 2020

TABLE 4.2 *Key indicators 1954Q3 through 2020Q2 (omitting 1980Q4 through 1982Q4)*

	Unemp	GDP	Inv	π	PMI	Gov't	Int	CPI
Early-to-mid expansion	5.91	4.82	12.56	3.413	56.57	−3.062	5.80	2.94
Last year of expansion	4.61	2.41	1.18	−0.676	52.09	−1.678	7.94	4.97
Recession	6.40	−3.73	−16.88	−4.029	43.72	−4.555	7.25	3.92

Key: Unemp = unemployment rate; GDP = inflation-adjusted GDP growth; Inv = inflation-adjusted growth physical investment spending; π = inflation-adjusted growth of corporate after-tax profits; PMI = Purchasing Managers' Index; Gov't = federal government surplus as a percentage of GDP (negative indicates a deficit); Int = Prime interest rate; CPI = consumer price inflation.[2]

Each section will be organized as follows. It will open with a table like that above (Table 4.2), summarizing key data over the cycle in question. For consistency of interpretation, the indicators included on these opening tables remain the same throughout the chapter. Note that they are divided into "Early-to-mid exp," "Last year of exp," and "Recession," rather than simply "Expansion" and "Recession." This is done so that the emergence of recessionary forces during the expansion can be isolated (this was not done for the Volcker cycle as it only lasted a year in total – it is omitted from averages in Table 4.2). While there is no a priori reason to believe that the seeds of the downturn are always visible over precisely that length of time, allowing this period to vary by cycle might lead to the temptation to make adjustments that bias the analysis toward confirming the hypothesis. For this reason and because empirical testing offers support for this period, one year is used throughout as the span over which we might expect to see the first signs of a slow down emerging (Harvey 2022: 252).

Table 4.2 shows the averages for all the cycles studied (except the Volcker one for reasons explained above). The first column shows unemployment percentages which, as one would expect, are lowest at the close of an expansion and highest during the recession. GDP, measured as the inflation-adjusted annualized rate of change, is the first indication that there may be something to the endogenous business cycle story, for in the last year it drops to exactly half of what it was in early-to-mid expansion. Even more significant given the explanation offered in Chapter 2 is the massive collapse in late expansion of Inv (inflation-adjusted annualized rate of change of investment spending). It was argued there that this was the key driver of the endogenous business cycle and that it would decelerate significantly and perhaps even fall in late expansion as firms reached capacity targets and slowed capital expenditures. It does precisely this (actually turning negative one-third of the time). According to

---

[2] All data from FRED database except PMI, from Institute for Supply Management.

Chapter 2, what was most important was the impact of the decline in investment on profits. That, too, is evident in Table 4.2, where inflation-adjusted growth of corporate after tax profits (π) turns negative in late expansion.

But Chapter 2 said more than this. It was also argued that the fall in profits would be unexpected. Here, again, Table 4.2 offers evidence consistent with this hypothesis, as shown by the behavior in the PMI, or Purchasing Managers' Index, column. As explained in Chapter 2, the PMI is a widely regarded proxy for business expectations. When it is above 50, firms expect business to improve; when it is below 50, they expect deterioration. With respect to the table, while it is evident that expectations are somewhat tempered in late expansion (with PMI falling from 56.57 to 52.09), *they are nevertheless still optimistic*. Firms expect conditions to continue improve. However, in stark contrast to this, profits actually fall. This is the trigger that, in an environment of *uncertainty*, causes those doing the investing to shift from an error of optimism to an error of pessimism. PMI then falls to an average of 43.72.

Another important factor is the systemic change that occurs in government deficit spending over the business cycle. In Chapter 3, it was noted that (a) fiscal policy is far more effective than monetary policy, (b) deficit spending, in particular, is a powerful driver of economic activity, and (c) because of the manner in which we have programmed taxation and income support spending, government deficits tend to automatically fall as the economy grows. This is so because as incomes rise and unemployment falls, tax revenues increase and government spending on things like unemployment insurance, food stamps, and welfare declines. What this means is that in late expansion – precisely when the economy could use a significant boost from additional government deficit spending – that spending actually falls. This contention is supported by the data in Table 4.2, where Gov't is the federal government's surplus as a percentage of GDP (negative numbers are deficits and hence have an expansionary effect on the economy). Over the course of the expansion and leading into the last year thereof, that measure falls to almost one-half of its earlier size. In short, the stimulative effect of both private sector physical investment and government deficit spending falls in late expansion. The fact that the programmed pattern of government spending is not inevitable and could be reversed is addressed at length in Chapter 5. Data for interest rates (Int) and inflation (CPI) are included for reference.

After the introductory table and an indication of the relevant presidential administrations over the cycle, the dominant factors driving the expansion are considered. Background for this discussion is derived primarily from the *Economic Report of the President*, supplemented by the *Survey of Current Business* and the *Federal Reserve Bulletin*. Particular note will be made of any emerging issues related to the theory put forward in Chapter 2 and to important external factors (like the OPEC oil embargo or COVID) that may be contributing to the end of the expansion. The recession is then explained and summary notes are offered.

4.1 IKE I CYCLE

Expansion: Jun 1954 ... Aug 1957 (39 months); 1954Q3 ... 1957Q3 (13 quarters)

Recession: Sep 1957 ... Apr 1958 (8 months); 1957Q4 ... 1958Q2 (3 quarters)

TABLE 4.3 *Key indicators Ike I Cycle*

	Unemp	GDP	Inv	π	PMI	Gov't	Int	CPI
Early-to-mid expansion	4.56	4.51	12.33	3.25	59.50	0.213	3.30	0.69
Last year of expansion	4.08	3.10	−0.15	−0.73	48.48	0.546	4.08	3.48
Recession	6.2	−3.80	−19.87	−7.20	40.64	−2.059	4.07	3.13

Key: Unemp = unemployment rate; GDP = inflation-adjusted GDP growth; Inv = inflation-adjusted growth physical investment spending; π = inflation-adjusted growth of corporate after-tax profits; PMI = Purchasing Managers' Index; Gov't = federal government surplus as a percentage of GDP (negative indicates a deficit); Int = Prime interest rate; CPI = consumer price inflation.

Relevant Presidential Administrations
- Dwight David Eisenhower (R): January 20, 1953 to January 20, 1961

4.1.1 Early-to-Mid Expansion: 1954Q3 through 1956Q3

The expansion of the cycle just before this one was incredibly strong with unemployment as low as 2.6% (1953Q2) and real GDP growth rates as high as 13.8% (1952Q4). However, the end of the Korean War (July 1953) and reductions in business inventories – which, recall, manifest themselves as a decline in physical investment spending – conspired to bring on a recession lasting from 1953Q3 through 1954Q2. However, by spring 1954, inventories were run back down to target levels and the adjustment process ended, leading to a recovery in physical investment spending. Indeed, the period 1954Q3 through 1955Q2 witnessed quarterly increases in inflation-adjusted investment of 21%, 19%, 46%, and 27%. At the same time, though, and as a consequence of the end of the Korean War and the shift to a smaller, Cold War military, government spending went from a slight deficit to a surplus (*Survey of Current Business* Oct 1957b:5). With the government draining income from the private sector, the latter was increasingly dependent on the trend in private-sector spending.

That said, real GDP did exhibit positive if shrinking growth throughout 1955. Part of that growth may be attributed to the fact that the increases in income experienced during the expansion were evenly distributed, leading to a strong surge in consumption. In addition, production had shifted toward consumer goods now that the war was over. Without consumption's contribution to GDP growth, 1955Q4 would almost certainly have seen very moderate, if not negative, real GDP growth. The *Economic Report of the President* for 1956 (covering year 1955) traced their prosperity to the following:

> the unexpectedly large upsurge of population in the past decade, the continued growth of scientific knowledge, the onrush of technology, the rapid obsolescence of what is sometimes regarded as fixed capital, the recent development of long-range investment planning by industry, the improved control over inventories, the intensified pace of business competition, the wide diffusion of well-being among people, their insistent and growing desire to earn more and live better, the development of mass markets to match mass production, the rebuilding of Western Europe, the general recognition of government's responsibility in helping to maintain a stable prosperity, and the growing understanding that public policy must protect economic incentives if enterprise, innovation, and investment are to flourish (*Economic Report of the President* 1956: 6).

We should take some of this with a grain of salt because, while generally reliable in terms of the facts, figures, and trends reported, what actually reaches the pages of the *Economic Report of the President* can be affected by the philosophy of the party occupying the White House and the prevailing political atmosphere. In this case, the Cold War certainly altered the tone of the report. That said, there is no question that the optimistic tone displayed above reflected the attitude of the day. For example, the PMI averaged 63 over 1955. The only subsequent period with a significantly higher rate was (ironically) that immediately before the OPEC oil embargo in 1973. The *Economic Report of the President* also notes that "The expansion itself has been carried through by private citizens" (*Economic Report of the President* 1956: 8). This, too, appears to be well-founded since, at the same time, "Between the second quarter of 1954 and the last quarter of 1955, the annual rate of Federal spending on goods and services was reduced by about 3 billion dollars" (*Economic Report of the President* 1956: 8). In other words, the contribution of the public sector was declining (as mentioned above). If there was going to be positive growth, it had to come from the private sector.

This was not to continue, however, with the first problems emerging in 1956. There was a substantial decline in consumption, attributable in part to a decline in purchases of automobiles and homes (*Economic Report of the President* 1957: 24). Indeed, after a sharp increase in consumer durables spending in early 1955, this declined over the rest of the expansion. As a consequence and without substantial contributions from investment or government spending, two of the four quarters of 1956 – the first and third – witnessed negative GDP growth. Fourth quarter, however, was resurgent, with an annualized rate of increase of 6.7 percent. This was despite the continued weak performance of investment and government spending and was caused by a sudden jump in net exports and, once again, consumption, as durables spending recovered.

4.1 Ike I Cycle

4.1.2 Final Year of Expansion: 1956Q4 through 1957Q3

Eventually, however, the continued decline in investment combined with the government's efforts to maintain a surplus made themselves felt. In addition, the *Economic Report of the President* reported that businesses were already experiencing a squeeze in terms of financing even in 1956. It goes on to explain:

> Two circumstances were primarily responsible for the strong demand of business concerns for external funds. First, the internal funds available to corporations in the form of retained earnings and depreciation charges grew at a slower rate than plant and equipment expenditures and inventory investment. A small decline in retained earnings, which occurred because of higher dividend payments, was more than offset by rising depreciation charges but not sufficiently to finance the increased expenditure requirements. Second, as the year progressed, business concerns found it increasingly difficult to finance expenditures by further reductions in their holdings of liquid assets (*Economic Report of the President* 1957: 35).

This eventually abated somewhat but, more significantly and as predicted in Chapter 2, firms were reaching targeted capacities. Earlier in the expansion, the increase in investment had been spectacular:

> from the first quarter of 1955 to the third quarter of 1957 was of boom proportions, amounting to almost 50 percent. The gains in some industries were particularly large. Railroads more than doubled their capital outlays. Expenditures by manufacturers of durable goods increased by nearly 75 percent. New business was placed with producers of capital goods at such a pace that, even with production at capacity limits, backlogs of unfilled orders became extremely large. The pressure of demand in this sector of the economy was further increased as manufacturers of investment goods and their suppliers expanded their working inventories (*Economic Report of the President* 1958: 12).

However, in the second half of 1956, unfilled orders of producers of investment goods rose more slowly and by the end of the year the major expansive influence of investment spending had subsided (*Economic Report of the President* 1958: 12).

Again as predicted in Chapter 2, this led to a stagnation in profits. This was actually most significant in the quarter before the last year of the expansion (1956Q3), when inflation-adjusted corporate profits fell by almost 5 percent. As the same time, the PMI was still above fifty, though marginally so. Still, even at fifty and thereby implying the expectation of business as usual, a fall in profits is an unpleasant surprise. The PMI then recovered slightly over the next two quarters (the first half of the last year of the expansion) before dropping to an average of forty-five for the following two. Contemporary accounts reflect some optimism that the downturn would be just a bump in the road, but this turned out not to be the case.

4.1.3 Recession: 1957Q4 through 1958Q2

The decline in physical investment spending was quite dramatic during the three quarter downturn at −27%, −24%, and −8%. This is consistent with contemporary accounts: "By the end of 1957, these early signs were confirmed by lower expenditures of business concerns on machinery, equipment, and new facilities" (*Economic Report of the President* 1959: 10). In addition, "Throughout most of 1957, financing for expansion programs was becoming more costly" (*Economic Report of the President* 1959: 10–11) and "Compared with the record outlays of $37 billion in 1957, businessmen plan to spend $32 billion in the current year, reduction of 13 percent" (*Survey of Current Business* Mar 1958: 2). Lacking significant support from either government spending (which did finally go into deficit, but only after the fact) or net exports, real GDP contracted by 4% and 10% before recovering somewhat in the last quarter of the recession (by +2.7%).

4.1.4 Further Observations

This cycle appears to have been very much in the mode of that explained in Chapter 2. Government spending was relatively neutral throughout the expansion (increasing an average of 2.6% per quarter in real terms) and interest rates remained very low (the CPI deflated three-month Treasury bill went from 1.47% in Early-to-mid expansion to –0.65% over the last year). Particularly given President Eisenhower's fiscal conservatism, the private sector was left to be the primary driver of economic activity (May 1990). Investment increased at a brisk pace over early-to-mid expansion. At this same time, profits had increased nicely and business optimism remained high. Indebtedness was rising, however, something that drew comment from contemporary observers (*Survey of Current Business* Jan 1957a: 2). In addition, pressure was clearly increasing on the relative price of investment goods, where the rate of price increase had accelerated every quarter from 1954Q3 through 1955Q4 (not actually reaching its peak until 1956Q4).

According to Mainstream theory, without some external shock or the influence of monetary or fiscal policy, this expansion should have continued indefinitely. It did not. Table 4.4 shows that the transition from Early-to-mid expansion to late expansion for this cycle matched quite well with Institutionalist/Post Keynesian predictions: consumption was falling as a percentage of GDP, investment was declining, the relative price of investment goods was increasing, and, not surprisingly, the rate of increase of realized profits was slipping. Throughout this, however, average business expectations had become neutral but not negative (at 49.68, or roughly 50). The collapse of investment accelerated through the recession and was the subject of frequent discussion in the *Survey of Current Business*, for example, "Business spending for plant and equipment, having accounted for a near-record fraction of the national output in 1956 and 1957, has fallen almost $4 billion at annual rates since last summer" (*Survey of Current Business* May 1958a: 5).

4.2 IKE II CYCLE

Expansion: May 1958 ... Apr 1960 (24 months); 1958Q3 ... 1960Q2 (8 quarters)

Recession: May 1960 ... Feb 1961 (10 months); 1960Q3 ... 1961Q1 (3 quarters)

TABLE 4.4 *Key indicators Ike II Cycle*

	Unem	GDP	Inv	π	PMI	Gov't	Int	CPI
Early-to-mid expansion	6.15	9.13	32.93	9.47	62.93	−1.179	3.96	0.40
Last year of expansion	5.30	2.15	1.15	−2.51	51.44	0.308	4.92	1.83
Recession	6.20	−0.10	−9.23	−3.58	45.32	−0.179	4.59	1.20

Key: Unemp = unemployment rate; GDP = inflation-adjusted GDP growth; Inv = inflation-adjusted growth physical investment spending; π = inflation-adjusted growth of corporate after-tax profits; PMI = Purchasing Managers' Index; Gov't = federal government surplus as a percentage of GDP (negative indicates a deficit); Int = Prime interest rate; CPI = consumer price inflation.

Relevant Presidential Administrations
- Dwight D. Eisenhower (R): January 20, 1953 to January 20, 1961
- John F. Kennedy (D): January 20, 1961 to November 22, 1963

4.2.1 Early-to-Mid Expansion: 1958Q3 through 1959Q2

Once recovery came in 1958Q3, it was extremely strong with consecutive quarterly rates of real GDP growth of 9.6%, 9.7%, 7.9%, and 9.3%. Not surprisingly in the context of the theory forwarded in this volume, the contemporaneous rates of investment growth were 34%, 39%, 24%, and 35%. This was thought to be related to "the need for more or for improved facilities ... Throughout the economy, increased competitive pressures and rising costs intensified the search for more efficient production techniques" (*Economic Report of the President* 1959: 22). In addition, another component of physical investment spending, housing, contributed significantly, especially as the weather became more conducive to building. Finally, some firms initially allowed inventories to decline, then replenished them later and thus added to investment spending. Also adding to GDP growth was the fact that there was a slight government budget deficit over most of the period. This was in part due to an increase in spending resulting from "agricultural price support programs and higher Government pay scales" (*Economic Report of the President* 1959: 22). Consumption, especially on durables, was also resurgent.

4.2.2 Final Year of Expansion: 1959Q3 through 1960Q2

Unfortunately, the rapid pace of investment reversed course in 1959Q3 with a decline of 23 percent. A major factor was an exogenous one: a strike in the steel industry (recall that Institutionalist/Post Keynesian theory does not dispute the point made by Neoclassicals that external forces can play a role, only that it is unnecessary – there is already a systemic cycle). In fact, some of the earlier unusually strong growth may be attributed to firms placing anticipatory orders for steel and accumulating inventories for fear of the work stoppage that did eventually occur. Hence, inventories were run down thereafter, lowering physical investment spending. By 1959Q4, the impact of the strike appears to have dissipated (*Survey of Current Business* Aug 1960a: 7). Nevertheless, it also seems to have had a negative impact on employment and profits through the end of the year. Interestingly, while the PMI fell in response to these events, it remained well above 50.

Thus, when 1960 opened, there was some sense that a downturn had been avoided. Investment continued to rise as firms sought to replenish inventories now that the steel strike was over. But this only lasted one quarter: "In the second half of the year, expenditures on business plant and equipment, as shown in the Securities and Exchange Commission – Department of Commerce survey, began to decline, reflecting adequate productive capacity, diminishing profits, and a slowing down in the growth of demand" (*Economic Report of the President* 1961: 2–3). Investment and profits fell in 1960Q2 by 32% and 7%. Despite support from consumption and a slight government deficit, this marked the end of the expansion (for a contemporary discussion of business investment trends see *Survey of Current Business* Dec 1960b: 4–5).

4.2.3 Recession: 1960Q3 through 1961Q1

Inventory reduction continued throughout the end of 1960, leading to consecutive contractions in investment from 1960Q2 through 1960Q4. By early 1961, however, and despite continued weakness in consumer durables spending, inventory accumulation picked up again and the economy emerged from recession, although this was not immediately obvious (*Survey of Current Business* Mar 1961).

4.2.4 Further Observations

The Ike II cycle, too, was driven by fluctuations in investment, although this time also affected by a major strike. While government spending barely changed over the entire expansion, interest rates did move more significantly than they had in the previous two cycles. The nominal three-month Treasury bill started the expansion at 1.68% and rose to 4.23% in the second-to-last quarter, before dropping to 3.87% just before the recession (real rates moved similarly). However, with one exception (1959Q3), investment continued its strong growth despite the rising cost of financing. It was not until 1960Q2, when interest rates (real and nominal) were actually falling, that investment

4.2 Ike II Cycle

moved into a significant decline – due, of course, to events in the steel industry. This coincided with a rapid deceleration in realized profits but still very optimistic numbers from the PMI. Note the inconsistency of real-world events with the Neoclassical theory that interest rates play the central role.

Over the recession, real investment spending shrank by an average of 17 percent per quarter. As reported in the third quarter of the downturn:

> Business investment has tended to ease off recently and modest reductions in plant and equipment expenditures are scheduled through the first quarter of 1961 ... The reductions that have taken place stem mainly from the declines in sales and profits in many industries since the spring; sales, moreover, have not come up to earlier expectations (*Survey of Current Business* Dec 1960b: 4).

One last item of note regarding the Ike II recession relates to the ultimately failed presidential campaign of Richard Nixon. It has been argued that, in contrast to what is predicted by the political business cycle wherein the incumbent party pursues expansionary policies during election years, the Eisenhower administration continued to be fiscally conservative (Weatherford 1987). This was in spite of the obvious slowdown in economic activity and it is possible that this contributed to John F. Kennedy's victory. It has been further suggested that this more than just a function of Eisenhower's personal and political budgetary philosophy, but also a reflection of his dislike for Nixon (Frank 2013). All that said, the data are not entirely consistent with the contention that the budget's stance was a contractionary one (May 1990). We are thus left without a clear story to tell. Still, it serves as a reminder that there is a connection between politics and the economy.

4.3 VIETNAM CYCLE

Expansion: Mar 1961 ... Dec 1969 (106 months); 1961Q2 ... 1969Q4 (35 quarters)

Recession: Jan 1970 ... Nov 1970 (11 months); 1970Q1 ... 1970Q4 (4 quarters)

TABLE 4.5 *Key indicators Vietnam Cycle*

	Unemp	GDP	Inv	π	PMI	Gov't	Int	CPI
Early-to-mid expansion	4.78	5.30	8.79	1.98	57.04	−0.568	5.03	2.26
Last year of expansion	3.50	2.10	3.48	−3.34	54.85	−0.190	7.95	5.85
Recession	5.00	−0.13	−5.85	−3.27	46.23	−3.098	7.91	5.60

Key: Unemp = unemployment rate; GDP = inflation-adjusted GDP growth; Inv = inflation-adjusted growth physical investment spending; π = inflation-adjusted growth of corporate after-tax profits; PMI = Purchasing Managers' Index; Gov't = federal government surplus as a percentage of GDP (negative indicates a deficit); Int = Prime interest rate; CPI = consumer price inflation.

Relevant Presidential Administrations
- John F. Kennedy (D): January 20, 1961 to November 22, 1963
- Lyndon Baines Johnson (D): November 22, 1963 to January 20, 1969
- Richard M. Nixon (R): January 20, 1969 to August 9, 1974

4.3.1 Early-to-Mid Expansion: 1961Q2 through 1968Q4

The opening of the recovery in second quarter 1961 was quite strong and this continued for the first year. While the Kennedy administration argued that "Government fiscal and monetary policies contributed strongly to the favorable economic developments of the past year," the data suggest otherwise (*Economic Report of the President* 1962: 39). The average rate of real investment spending from 1961Q2 through 1962Q1 was 24% (as compared to −15% over the previous year). Consumption followed, driven by a significant increase in the demand for automobiles, which lead to consecutive rates of real GDP growth of 7%, 7.9%, 8.1%, and 7.3% starting in 1961Q2. Despite all this, unemployment did not respond as robustly as one might expect. The rate from 1955 through 1957 had averaged just over 4%; while it dropped quickly in the first year of recovery (from 7% to 5.6%), further gains proved difficult to achieve for some time. In an era when the Employment Act of 1946 was taken seriously, this was a cause for concern:

Despite the gains of the past 2 years, the economy has not yet regained full use of its labor and capital resources. Moreover, the progress made during the current recovery was most rapid in 1961; although advances continued throughout 1962, the rate of expansion was markedly slower. The forces responsible for slowing the expansion in 1962 threaten to

4.3 Vietnam Cycle

prolong the period of economic slack. As 1963 begins, too many workers remain without jobs; too many machines continue idle; too much output goes unrealized as our economy runs below its potential. The challenge and the opportunity for the American economy are to move from this situation of continuing slack to one which calls forth the full participation of a rapidly growing labor force and the introduction of fruitful technological developments. It is in this setting of promising change that we must consider our commitment to the goals of the Employment Act (*Economic Report of the President* 1963: 9).[3]

This was further complicated by the fact that the expansion had slowed considerably by the end of 1962. A stock market decline in second quarter may have contributed and it is true that the PMI fell from 61 in first quarter to 50 in third; however the market recovered and the Index was back to 54 by fourth quarter. A no doubt more important reason for the slowdown was the 11% decline in real investment spending in 1962Q4 (real GDP growth was a meager 1.3%). The reasons for this were the subject of some discussion, with the administration reaching the following conclusion:

With respect to both fixed investment and inventory investment, in short, the disappointing 1962 performance was a reflection of inadequate demand – not only of a current inadequacy but of one that had been accumulating for half a decade. By the end of 1962, it was plain that businessmen had become conditioned to appraise future expansion cautiously and were slow to extend their commitments beyond near-term needs. Business investment had taken on a character that was likely – in the absence of strong expansionary forces elsewhere in the economy – to cause the economy to stabilize at less-than-full employment levels more or less indefinitely. Plainly, a decisive upward adjustment in the economy's underlying expansionary forces was needed, and it is this the President's 1963 tax program is designed to supply (*Economic Report of the President* 1963: 17–8).

As the last sentence suggests, the government was particularly concerned that their fiscal stance might become a drag on growth. They further commented, "The Administration was resolved to avoid repeating the premature and abrupt swing of 1959 toward restrictive budgetary policy" (*Economic Report of the President* 1963: 18). This led to a series of measures including both corporate and personal tax cuts and spending programs. The full impact of these were not felt until after Kennedy's assassination (partly because this reduced opposition to the measures from more conservative elements in Congress), but they appear to have had the desired effect. Consider, for example, the fact that the federal budget balance as a percentage of GDP averaged −0.63% (in deficit) in the first year of the Ike I expansion to 0.74% (in surplus) for the remainder; in Ike II, those same numbers were −1.18% to 0.31%. Just as the administration worried, that same trend started to emerge in the

---

[3] Note already the consistency with the secular stagnation theory of Vatter and Walker discussed at the end of chapter 3. Without increasing demand out of proportion to the increases in the ability to supply, the economy falters.

1960s, with the opening year of the expansion showing a federal budget balance of −0.44%. By 1962Q2, however, this had turned to a surplus and was therefore a cause for concern and the reason for the Kennedy administration's shift in policy.

Note that while the emergent pattern of budget surpluses as the economy recovered was in part simply a function of the operation of the automatic stabilizers, there was also a tendency in Ike I and Ike II (as there will be again later) to target at least smaller deficits as a sign of good government. That it is not will be a major topic of discussion in Chapter 5. In any event, the Kennedy administration's desire to avoid the mistakes of the past meant that by 1964 – and before spending for the Vietnam War had really accelerated – the federal budget balance as a percentage of GDP had returned to −0.44 percent once again. As hoped, unemployment trended down for the entire year.

Before returning to the narrative, it is worth considering the success of the Kennedy administration's strategy in using government spending to offset the decline in private-sector spending. The result was that this became the longest postwar expansion in history to that point. Again, this is even before the increase in spending attributable to the war and it takes us though only the fifteenth quarter of a thirty-five quarter expansion wherein unemployment reached a low of 3.4 percent. *Were government policy designed to automatically make such changes in stance without it being necessary to design and debate new directions (that even then required the tragic death of a president for passage), then this could be the norm rather than the exception.*[4]

The Gulf of Tonkin incident in August 1964 changed the environment by ratcheting up US involvement in Vietnam. Save for the first two quarters of 1965 (when increases in investment spending were more than sufficient to sustain the upturn), the US budget never again goes into surplus until the beginning of the last year of the expansion (1969). Also significant in terms of the government's impact on the economy was Lyndon Johnson's Great Society Program. "The legislation included the Civil Rights Act, food stamp legislation, the Economic Opportunity Act, and programs for mass transportation passed in 1964. In 1965 there was Medicare and Medicaid, the Elementary and Secondary Education Act. the Higher Education Act, and the Public Works and Economic Development Act (Brown-Collier 1998: 260)."

The year 1965 was witness to the long-expected sustained decline in unemployment, dropping to 4 percent by December. When government spending and investment weren't enough to drive growth, consumer spending – especially in durables – kept the momentum going (*Economic Report of the President 1966*: 35; *Survey of Current Business* Jan 1967).

While unemployment dipped below 4 percent and continued down in 1966, this might well have been the beginning of a recession were it not for the

---

[4] It has been remarked, too, that under Kennedy, "For the first time, a president took explicit responsibility for the nation's economic performance" (Murphy 2004: 153).

4.3 Vietnam Cycle

increasingly negative budget balance of the federal government. In fact, the Index of Leading Indicators suggested that there was about to be a downturn (Harris and Jamroz 1976: 168). The triggering of this signal can probably be traced to investment spending which, after a large increase in 1966Q1, turned negative for two quarters before a slight increase in 1966Q4, followed by two more quarters of quite significant negative growth in 1967Q1 and 1967Q2. But, what made the signal false was the fact that the government's budget deficit grew progressively larger through that exact same period, keeping the rate of growth of real GDP positive: "Total Government purchases in the second quarter were again a major stimulus to economic activity" (*Survey of Current Business* Jul 1967: 2).

Contemporary accounts link the private-sector spending slowdown to contractionary monetary policy in the form of higher interest rates. Instead, the data for this period are more consistent with the hypotheses forwarded in this volume whereby factors other than interest play the key role. The PMI, for example, remained comfortably above fifty for all of 1966. In the end, credit tightening and especially the saturation of the market for physical capital were key: "Thus, it appears that capacity, after an investment expansion that has lasted more than 5 years and has outpaced all previously recorded capital goods booms, has at least temporarily caught up with immediate overall requirements (*Survey of Current Business* Dec 1966: 7)."

Profits naturally fell along with investment, in stark contrast to a PMI that was sixty. This same pattern continued through the end of 1966, suggesting that without the rising government budget deficit this might have been the last year of the expansion due to the contrast between entrepreneurs' expectations and what actually transpired. The first two quarters of 1967 were witness to PMI numbers less than fifty, large negative rates of growth of investment spending (−9.5% and −13.7%), and continued declines in inflation-adjusted corporate after-tax profits – just as one would expect in a recession. Therefore, independent of the government's fiscal stance, 1966 would likely have been the last year of the expansion and 1967Q1 and 1967Q2 (at least) would have been recession quarters.

But, that's not what happened and investment spending recovered in the second half of 1967, as did profits. Until 1968Q3, investment continued to contribute positively to GDP growth. Meanwhile, though still spending in deficit, the amount by which the government was doing so (as a percentage of GDP) steadily declined. This was by design as it was believed that "… restraint is essential to our economic health" (*Economic Report of the President* 1968: 10). The administration was thus not completely cured of the deficits-bad/surpluses-good conventional wisdom, but they had at least temporarily suppressed it.

4.3.2 Final Year of Expansion: 1969Q1 through 1969Q4

Though a recession was avoided in 1967, by late 1969 investment was shrinking once again, as were profits. At the same time, PMI was falling, but remaining over fifty. Meanwhile, inflation had accelerated, nominal interest rates were rising, and the budget deficit turned to surplus (for the first half of the year – it went back to deficit as unemployment started creeping back up). Because the marked increase in inflation was a major story at the time, it is worth taking a closer look.

Contemporary and modern accounts of this period point almost without exception to policy and, in particular, excessive money growth as the causes. However, as explained in Chapter 3, money growth cannot cause inflation because (a) it merely changes the form of wealth held by the private sector and does not increase it and (b) it is impossible to increase the supply of money beyond the demand since central bank money creation requires the conscious, voluntary cooperation of the counterparty.

Fiscal policy *can* increase incomes, however, and therefore cause demand to pull up prices (as it did in World War II). This, too, is a commonly invoked explanation of the inflation in this period (although often in concert with the monetary policy story). But what do the data suggest? The acceleration started in 1967, with the overall rate jumping from 1% in first quarter to 4.5% by fourth. According to the Bureau of Labor Statistics, "All major classes of goods and services contributed to the rise; consumer services accounted for almost one-half, nondurables other than food almost three-tenths, and durables about one-sixth" (BLS CPI Dec 1967: 2). Within consumer services, medical care alone rose by 7.9% – something unlikely to be bid up simply just because people had more money – and while mortgage rates had fallen, the cost of property taxes and insurance increased by almost 7%. Other consumer services witnessing a substantial increase in cost were "hotel and motel rooms, home repairs, housekeeping services (including laundry, fees for baby sitters, and domestic workers), barber and beauty shops, and recreational services (such as movie admissions and golf and bowling fees) (BLS CPI Dec 1967: 2)." It seems fair to say that these might well be the result of rising demand. On the other hand, other significant factors included poor agricultural harvests, rising state and local taxes, and apparel prices. Once more, part of this may be attributable to increased consumer spending, but clearly not all of it.

Inflation in 1968 was even higher, with prices rising over 4 percent. Again, consumer services were responsible for roughly half of this. Ironically, the rising interest rates – the result of policy intended to lower inflation – were contributing directly to significantly higher mortgage costs. Other costs related to home ownership followed suit. Rental prices rose in part due to high demand, but also because of "higher taxes and maintenance costs" (BLS CPI Dec 1968: 2). Food prices rose substantially, too, especially food away from home.

Price increases accelerated once again in 1969, with inflation around 5.5 percent. While it does appear that the traditional explanation, amended by

4.3 Vietnam Cycle

it not being driven by monetary policy, sheds some light on the situation – there were areas where rising demand seems the most likely culprit, for example, Food Away From Home (7.1% December 1968 to December 1969) and Apparel (5.2%) – other factors played a role, too:

- "The 12-month rise for automobile insurance rates quadrupled" (BLS CPI Dec 1969: 3);
- "Mortgage interest rose 12.5 percent, constituting one-tenth of the rise in the overall index" (BLS CPI Dec 1969: 3);
- "homeowners taxes and insurance increased 7.1 percent" (BLS CPI Dec 1969: 3);
- "Reduced supplies of fresh vegetables caused mainly by inclement weather brought increases of 6.6 percent in the fresh fruit and vegetables index" (BLS CPI Dec 1969: 4);
- "Declining milk cow herds contributed to an increase of 4.1 percent on dairy products during the year;" (BLS CPI Dec 1969: 4);
- "Tobacco products prices were raised 8.8 percent during the year, mainly because of widespread increases in State and local taxes on cigarettes" (BLS CPI Dec 1969: 4).

Though the prevalence of COLAs, or cost of living adjustments in contracts is often cited as a contributing factor, this appears to be more myth than fact (Rudd 2022: 2–3). In reality, only a small percentage of workers were covered and that coverage was often less-than-complete.

In terms of evolving policy responses, two considerations are relevant here. First, there is evidence that policymakers began to view higher rates of inflation as acceptable (Romer and Romer 2002). Second, the Federal Reserve determined that it was no longer required to pursue policies consistent with balance-of-payments/currency-market goals and could focus instead on the domestic macroeconomy (wherein they had already decided that higher inflation was acceptable; Bordo and Eichengreen 2008).

In any event, the bigger picture is that – as argued in Chapter 3 – inflation is complicated. It is likely that the late 1960s price increases were driven at least in part by rising demand, but (a) other factors clearly played a role, too, (b) rising interest rates contributed to rather than reduced inflation, and (c) there is no a priori reason to believe that those who presumably benefited from the rising prices, for example, those in the apparel and restaurant industry, should not have. If consumers wanted to dine out more often and this increased demand was causing higher prices, then this creates an incentive to build more restaurants. This is how the market system is supposed to work. If inflation is causing serious problems for certain segments of the population, for example, retirees on fixed incomes, then naturally this should be addressed. However, attempting to induce a recession by raising interest rates is neither the only nor the best solution.

4.3.3 Recession: 1970Q1 through 1970Q4

The recession was not particularly steep except for the fourth quarter, which was complicated by the General Motors strike that began on September 15.

As a result of the dispute, GM lost over $1 billion in profits, recording the biggest quarterly loss in its sixty-two-year history. Due to the industry's size – at the time, one in six American jobs were reportedly linked to automaking – the US economy lost over $1 billion in tax revenue and hundreds of millions of dollars in retail sales (Minchin 2023: 41–2).

Real GDP growth for 1970Q4 was –4.2 percent. Meanwhile, investment spending was slow and contracted over the course of the year as the "long upsurge of business investment in plant and equipment came to an end" (*Economic Report of the President* 1971: 23). Inflation remained high but decelerated as economic activity declined. Profits fell throughout the year, although slightly less than they had in the year before the recession. The budget deficit, of course, rose substantially as the automatic stabilizers kicked in. 1971Q1 saw very strong recovery, in large part due to inventory accumulation intended to catch up after a General Motors strike that had started in 1970Q3 and ended in 1970Q4.

4.3.4 Further Observations

The cycle was strongly affected by fiscal spending from the Vietnam War and Johnson's Great Society programs. While it is obviously difficult to say what would have happened without these, the data suggest that a recession might have occurred at least in 1966 had it not been for the fiscal stimulus. This is very instructive in terms of long-lasting lessons from the period. It drives home the fact that when one injection into the income stream falters – investment being the key one in this context – another – government spending – can take its place. Automatic stabilizers certainly help, but they only treat the symptom of lost income and not the disease of lost jobs. Chapter 5 will explain at length how this can be remedied.

One could imagine the Vietnam cycle being responsible for more broader trends, but the events of the next few years will trump that. Oil Shock I will be witness to the final collapse of Bretton Woods, the 1973 Arab–Israeli War and the subsequent oil crisis, the sole peacetime imposition of wage-and-price controls in US history, and the first-ever (and thus far only) resignation of an American president.

4.4 OIL SHOCK I CYCLE

Expansion: Dec 1970 ... Nov 1973 (36 months); 1971Q1 ... 1973Q4 (12 quarters)

Recession: Dec 1973 ... Mar 1975 (16 months); 1974Q1 ... 1975Q1 (5 quarters)

TABLE 4.6 *Key indicators Oil Shock I Cycle*

	Unemp	GDP	Inv	π	PMI	Gov't	Int	CPI
Early-to-mid expansion	5.78	5.67	15.50	4.92	58.25	−3.920	5.49	3.43
Last year of expansion	4.85	4.13	11.28	4.20	65.89	−2.296	8.02	8.40
Recession	6.16	−2.48	−17.96	−4.57	47.66	−3.347	10.43	11.38

Key: Unemp = unemployment rate; GDP = inflation-adjusted GDP growth; Inv = inflation-adjusted growth physical investment spending; π = inflation-adjusted growth of corporate after-tax profits; PMI = Purchasing Managers' Index; Gov't = federal government surplus as a percentage of GDP (negative indicates a deficit); Int = Prime interest rate; CPI = consumer price inflation.

Relevant Presidential Administrations
- Richard M. Nixon (R): January 20, 1969 to August 9, 1974
- Gerald Ford (R): August 9, 1974 to January 20, 1977

4.4.1 Early-to-Mid Expansion: 1971Q1 through 1972Q4

The year 1971 was a year full of momentous events:

Rarely has economic policy made so much news as in 1971. The freeze and Phase II, closing the gold window and prospective devaluation, domestic and international meetings at Camp David, the Azores, the Smithsonian Institution, and Bermuda, Key Biscayne, and San Clemente – all were continuing headline stories. These dramatic events were part of the process of dealing with problems in the forefront of public attention – inflation, unemployment, the international position of the U.S. economy (*Economic Report of the President* 1972: 19).

The period opened with a very strong 11.3 percent annualized rate of real GDP in 1971Q1, a result at least in part due to a liberalization of depreciation rules (*Economic Report of the President* 1972: 33) and the resolution of labor troubles at General Motors (*Survey of Current Business* Apr 1971: 1). The boom was driven primarily by investment spending, which rose by 55 percent and thereby offset the fall in demand created by the shift away from defense spending. The fact that most of the rise in investment was in inventory is consistent with the assumption that it was a result of the end of the strike. Meanwhile, unemployment declined slightly, hampered in part by the return of veterans to the workforce (*Economic Report of the President* 1972: 37–8).

However, economic activity slowed considerably over the rest of the year, dragged down by both a deceleration in investment and a continued drain from the adjustment in fiscal policy, plus the impact of what had become a chronic trade deficit. Although policy makers were keen to shift back to expansionary policies, they worried that this may reverse the downward trend in inflation. Instead, on August 15:

The United States suspended the convertibility of the dollar into gold or other reserve assets, for the first time since 1934. It imposed a temporary surcharge, generally at the rate of 10 percent, on dutiable imports. Prices, wages, and rents were frozen for 90 days, to be followed by a more flexible and durable – but still temporary – system of mandatory controls (*Economic Report of the President* 1972: 22).

The program was mandatory, as distinct from voluntary. A mandatory program means that it is backed by legal penalties. Most price violations were handled administratively rather than through legal action, such as through requiring firms to refund or reduce prices. However, about 300 legal actions were taken in the first year of Phase II (Frumkin 2010: 171).

In this manner, it was hoped that an expansionary fiscal policy could be pursued without negative repercussions in inflation or the balance of payments. This appeared to have the desired effect with respect to the former, as the rate of price increases decelerated from 5.9% in 1970Q4 to 3% in 1971Q4 and eventually 2.6% in 1972Q2; it was somewhat successful in terms of improving the trade balance.

The year 1972 saw a return to very strong GDP growth, supported by a substantial increase in investment spending. Attitudes in general became very positive as businesses and consumers believed that the policies enacted in the previous year were having the desired effect in terms of restoring growth and reducing inflation. By 1972Q4, the PMI was 69, real GDP growth was 6.9 percent, and unemployment was the lowest it had been in a little over two years. The only negative was the resurgence of inflationary pressures to 4.2 percent (the highest since 1970Q4).

4.4.2 Final Year of Expansion: 1973Q1 through 1973Q4

Events in late 1973 would change all that and play a role in the next three recessions. Until then, GDP growth and investment spending, with the exception of 1973Q3, stayed strong. In fact, the PMI was extremely high, hitting 70 in 1973Q1, 66 in 1973Q2, 61 in 1973Q3, and 66 in 1973Q4. But, on October 6, Egypt and Syria launched a surprise attack on Israel. The Egyptians were successful beyond their expectations; while the Syrians were not, it was nevertheless a close-run affair for some time. In response, the U.S. offered considerable support to Israel and by October 25 the war was over with the invaders pushed back to their starting lines. This did not go over well in the Arab world and the result was the Organization of the Petroleum Exporting Countries (OPEC) oil embargo.

4.4 Oil Shock I Cycle

Fuel oil and coal prices rose by 10% from October 1973 to November 1973, and 30% compared to the previous November. Overall inflation, already accelerating since 1972Q4, averaged 8.4 percent over the course of 1973 and would rise thereafter (some of this a function of the post-Bretton Woods collapse of the dollar). Investment and profits did not show the pattern suggested by the theory laid out in Chapter 2. There was a considerable decline in both in 1973Q3, but this had recovered by 1973Q4. It seems safe to say that the upcoming recession was the result of an exogenous event, that is, the oil embargo, and not an internal dynamic.

4.4.3 Recession: 1974Q1 through 1975Q1

Investment soon collapsed, falling an average of 16.9 percent each quarter from 1974Q1 through 1975Q2. Real GDP growth followed suit, as did unemployment which rose from 4.8% in the last quarter of the expansion to 8.3% in the last quarter of the recession. All this occurred despite a generally expansionary stance on the part of fiscal policy. As this was occurring, the Ford administration (Nixon had resigned in disgrace on August 9, 1974) was taking steps to help the economy to recovery:

To provide support for the economy, the President on January 13 proposed tax relief for individuals and business. For individuals the program calls for a tax rebate equivalent to 12 percent of total 1974 personal tax liabilities up to a limit of $1,000 per return. The rebate would total approximately $12 billion and would be paid in two instalments, the first in May and the second in September.

For business the President proposed a 1-year increase in the investment tax credit to 12 percent. Except for utilities, which now have a 4 percent credit, the present credit is equal to 7 percent of investment in equipment. For electric utility investment in generating capacity that does not use oil or gas, the higher tax credit would remain in force through 1977. The increase in the tax credit is expected to reduce tax liabilities of businesses by approximately $4 billion during 1975. The credit will apply to machinery and equipment put into service during 1975, as well as to orders placed during 1975 and put into service by the end of 1976 (*Economic Report of the President* 1975: 20).

Policies were also put into place aimed at reducing dependence on foreign energy (*Economic Report of the President* 1975: 21). These were necessary as a result of the continued extremely high rates of inflation, averaging 11.4 percent over the course of the recession. Energy prices played the central role:

In 1974, as in 1973, the largest increases among nonfood commodities were for petroleum products. Retail prices for gasoline rose 20.6 percent for the 12-months ending in December 1974, about the same as in the preceding 12-month period. Fuel oil prices rose 30.3 percent in 1974, following an increase of 46.8 percent in 1973. Prices for gasoline and fuel oil started to rise rapidly in early 1973 when shortages appeared in some areas and accelerated sharply during the Middle East crisis in late 1973 and early 1974 (BLS CPI Dec 1974: 6).

Unfortunately, oil prices tend to have significant spillover effects as their increase raises the costs of production in other sectors (Baba and Lee 2022).

4.4.4 Further Observations

While the central thesis of this volume is that expansions create the conditions that lead to recession, it is not denied that external factors can also play a decisive role. That is definitely the case with the Oil Shock I recession. It is not at all evident that the typical combination of optimistic expectations and disappointing profits was on the horizon. Instead, the terrible shock of massive price increases in energy created the downturn. They will continue to play a central role in the next two cycles (though systemic factors will reemerge in smaller roles).

4.5 OIL SHOCK II CYCLE

Expansion: Apr 1975 ... Jan 1980 (58 months); 1975Q2 ... 1980Q1 (20 quarters)

Recession: Feb 1980 ... Jul 1980 (6 months); 1980Q2 ... 1980Q3 (2 quarters)

TABLE 4.7 *Key indicators Oil Shock II Cycle*

	Unemp	GDP	Inv	π	PMI	Gov't	Int	CPI
Early-to-mid expansion	7.18	5.06	13.99	3.46	56.00	−4.015	7.82	7.13
Last year of expansion	5.98	1.43	−4.15	−2.04	49.63	−2.023	13.83	14.20
Recession	7.50	−4.25	−26.90	−6.83	37.95	−3.778	13.97	10.95

Key: Unemp = unemployment rate; GDP = inflation-adjusted GDP growth; Inv = inflation-adjusted growth physical investment spending; π = inflation-adjusted growth of corporate after-tax profits; PMI = Purchasing Managers' Index; Gov't = federal government surplus as a percentage of GDP (negative indicates a deficit); Int = Prime interest rate; CPI = consumer price inflation.

Relevant Presidential Administrations
- Gerald Ford (R): August 9, 1974 to January 20, 1977
- Jimmy Carter (D): January 20, 1977 to January 20, 1981

4.5.1 Early-to-Mid Expansion: 1975Q2 through 1979Q1

While the long recession finally ended in 1975Q2, employment was very slow to recover. Indeed, it continued to rise into the expansion and by third quarter thereof was still only at the level it had been in the last quarter of recession (8.3 percent). This was anticipated by the administration:

Because we began the present recovery with more slack than in any of the previous postwar cycles, a much longer period of above-average growth will be required for a return to full resource utilization. Even under the best of circumstances the return to full employment cannot realistically be accomplished this year or next. To ensure that we return to high levels of resource utilization – as is our objective – the recovery must therefore be a durable one (*Economic Report of the President* 1976: 19).

While investment spending was initially a drag on economic activity, it eventually became the engine of growth through the second half of 1975 and the first half of 1976. That said, consumption was also a significant contributor, with "over one-third of the $91-billion growth in personal income from 1974 ... due to the rise in government transfer payments" (*Economic Report of the President* 1976: 25). This was a result of the Tax Reduction Act of 1975.

The last three quarters of 1976 saw consistent but not particularly robust, growth. This was recognized and there was considerable concern that the foundation needed to be laid for a more accelerated growth path, especially if the unemployment problem were to be addressed. It was further believed that investment, in particular, needed to be stimulated, and so a variety of policies were into place in the hopes of accomplishing this (*Economic Report of the President* 1977: 31–5). Capital formation did, indeed, recover, with increases averaging 24 percent per quarter over the first three quarters of 1977. As predicted in Chapter 2, corporate profits responded in kind. There was some concern at the time that the increase in capital expenditures was not indicative of a trend (*Survey of Current Business* Oct 1977: 7). As feared, they, along with profits, declined in fourth quarter, although this was in part due to an especially severe winter and a coal mining strike. Unemployment continued to fall from 7.8% in 1976Q1 to 6.7% in 1977Q4 (*Economic Report of the President* 1979: 25).

Growth picked back up again in 1978 and was very strong in second quarter, but inflation once again accelerated. This time, energy prices were not the main culprit. Rather, increases were widespread across categories.

> The upward movement in these other prices was a response to a wide variety of forces – including the pass-through of higher import prices associated with depreciation of the dollar, the effects on home prices of incentives to invest in land and houses as an inflation hedge, and some supply bottlenecks in construction materials. A particularly troublesome phenomenon, however, was the slow growth in productivity. This added directly to costs of production and may indirectly have affected wage rates by increasing the demand for labor (*Economic Report of the President* 1979: 38–9).

This is consistent with reports from the *Federal Reserve Bulletin*:

> Developments in the farm and food sector exerted a major influence on measures of inflation in 1978. Retail food prices rose 12 percent over the year – the largest increase since 1974 ... Trends in energy prices were mixed in 1978 and the rise at retail amounted to about 8 percent, somewhat above the increase in 1977 ... Prices outside the food and energy areas rose faster in 1978. Service prices excluding energy accelerated to an annual rate of 9¼ percent from 8 percent last year. The homeownership component of the consumer price index was up 12½ percent, more than 3 percentage points above the previous year ... The decline in the dollar's exchange value also aggravated inflation (*Federal Reserve Bulletin* Jan 1979: 11).

Unfortunately, it was observed that "inflationary forces are likely to remain intense in 1979 – especially in view of the sharp increases in the price of oil and the continued rise in food prices" (*Federal Reserve Bulletin* Jan 1979: 12). Despite this, however, the PMI remained strong, actually rising above 60 in the second half of 1978 and still over 50 into 1979Q3.

4.5.2 Final Year of Expansion: 1979Q2 through 1980Q1

Consistent with the theory laid out in Chapter 2, investment rapidly decelerated in the last year of the expansion, showing negative growth for all four quarters. Profits of course shrank as well, save for 1979Q2, while the PMI averaged

4.5 Oil Shock II Cycle

barely under 50, at 49.6. In other words, while Purchasing Managers' expected economic activity to stay largely the same, it deteriorated. The economy was therefore ripe for a downturn as agents' expectations were disappointed.

On top of that was another oil shock occurring at the end of 1979 as a result of the Iranian Revolution. This was a substantial blow to an economy already showing signs of recession and it led to a rapid acceleration in inflation (rising to almost 17 percent in 1980Q1). Only the government's fiscal stance, boosted by the tax cuts inherent in the Revenue Act of 1978, kept real GDP growth positive. Eventually, even this proved insufficient as the economy shrank in 1980Q2 and 1980Q3.

Before proceeding to the review of the recession, another extremely important event with long-term consequences occurred during the last year of expansion:

> On October 6 the Federal Reserve announced a major shift in its technique for implementing monetary policy. Previously it had attempted to control the expansion of the monetary aggregates by adopting a target for the Federal funds rate. Under the new approach the object of open market operations would be to supply the volume of bank reserves consistent with desired rates of monetary growth (*Economic Report of the President* 1980: 54).

This was the Monetarist experiment, based on the assumption that it was money supply growth that caused inflation. It has already been argued in Chapter 3 that this is not actually the case and that the theory is based on several unwarranted premises. However, it is nevertheless what was believed at the Federal Reserve and by Federal Reserve Chair, Paul Volcker. This led the prime lending rate to rise from an average of 9.29% in 1979Q2 to 10.54% and 12.14% in the last two years of the expansion. This would not be their peak, though, as the discussion of the next cycle will show.

4.5.3 Recession: 1980Q2 through 1980Q3

While the recession was short, it was deep. Investment spending fell by an average of 27% over both quarters and real GDP growth was −8% in 1980Q2 and −0.5% in 1980Q3 (in contrast, the US trade balance turned positive, although this is not totally unexpected when domestic incomes decline). Unemployment jumped to nearly 8 percent. Recovery was rapid, however, and GDP growth – driven primarily by investment spending – was substantial as the upturn began.

4.5.4 Further Observations

In part, this downturn was driven by the same factor as the earlier one, that is, a spike in inflation. But there were also elements of a systemic downturn, with profits disappointing business expectations. Perhaps more important were two other events that had long-term consequences for economic policy making. One was the passage of the Humprhrey–Hawkins bill. It has been argued that this officially marked the shift from the primary target as full employment (officially endorsed in the Full Employment Act of 1946) to dual targets of inflation and employment (Goutsmedt 2022).

The integration of a numerical inflation target was seen as a victory for the Republican opposition to the bill. Consequently, the enactment of a largely amended version of the Humphrey-Hawkins bill remains regarded by historians as a failure of the Democratic Party, a sign of the moving political balance of power and the transformations of the economic intellectual landscape in the 1970s ... With the introduction of the inflation goal, the "doctrine of monetarism was riding to victory on the legislative carcass of the fading orthodoxy of Keynes" (Goutsmedt 2022: 620; quote is from Greider 1989: 97).

In the end and as will be seen in subsequent descriptions in this chapter, the full-employment half of the bill was largely forgotten (Goutsmedt 2022: 647–8). Indeed, as often as not, low unemployment will hereafter be interpreted as a negative, something liable to drive up wages and, therefore, prices.

However, this is not the same as saying that a full-fledged Monetarist frame had been adopted. First, there is evidence that the transformation manifested in the Humphrey–Hawkins bill was actually a function of arguments employing the Neoclassical Keynesian Phillip's Curve (Goutsmedt 2022: 648). Second, even when it was openly stated that the Federal Reserve was conducting a Monetarist experiment, it "was not really monetarist! Rather, the new techniques were conditionally adopted for pragmatic reasons" (Lindsey, Orphanides, and Rasche 2005: 77). Furthermore, a major target of the high-interest policies was not inflation at all, but support of the dollar. For example, "Chairman Volcker arrived in Washington on Tuesday, October 2, with his ears still resonating with strongly stated European recommendations for stern action to stem severe dollar weakness on exchange markets (Lindsey, Orphanides, and Rasche 2005: 19; further references to attempts to shore up the dollar appear throughout the paper)."

In any event, we emerge from Oil Shock II with a shift away from treating unemployment as the key problem in the macroeconomy and toward inflation, and addressing the latter by means of high interest rates. This remains true as of the time of this writing.

4.6 Volcker Cycle

Expansion: Aug 1980 ... Jul 1981 (12 months); 1980Q4 ... 1981Q3 (4 quarters)

Recession: Aug 1981 ... Nov 1982 (16 months); 1981Q4 ... 1982Q4 (5 quarters)

TABLE 4.8 *Key indicators Volcker Cycle*

	Unemp	GDP	Inv	π	PMI	Gov't	Int	CPI
Early-to-mid expansion	NA	NA	NA	NA	NA	NA	NA	NA
Last year of expansion	7.40	4.45	23.55	-1.94	50.63	-2.871	18.80	10.85
Recession	9.40	-1.98	-15.52	4.42	38.38	-5.325	15.29	4.90

Key: Unemp = unemployment rate; GDP = inflation-adjusted GDP growth; Inv = inflation-adjusted growth physical investment spending; π = inflation-adjusted growth of corporate after-tax profits; PMI = Purchasing Managers' Index; Gov't = federal government surplus as a percentage of GDP (negative indicates a deficit); Int = Prime interest rate; CPI = consumer price inflation.

Relevant Presidential Administrations
- Jimmy Carter (D): January 20, 1977 to January 20, 1981
- Ronald Reagan (R): January 20, 1981 to January 20, 1989

4.6.1 Early-to-Mid Expansion: NA

This was the shortest expansion of the period under study, lasting only one year. There is not, therefore, an early-to-mid expansion distinct from the last year thereof. This does not mean that there is nothing to say in this section, but the theory laid out in Chapter 2 really cannot be used here since it hinged on changes that took place up to versus during the last year of expansion.

4.6.2 Final Year of Expansion: 1980Q4 through 1981Q3

Ronald Reagan took office on January 20, 1981, and ushered in a new set of policy priorities:
The key elements of the proposed program were:

- cutting the rate of growth in Federal spending;
- reducing personal income tax rates and creating jobs by accelerating depreciation for business investment in plant and equipment;
- instituting a far-reaching program of regulatory relief; and
- in cooperation with the Federal Reserve, making a new commitment to a monetary policy that will restore a stable currency and healthy financial markets (*Economic Report of the President* 1982: 23).

The last point suggests that the administration agreed with the pseudo-Monetarist path taken by the Federal Reserve, which is indeed true. Eventually, the prime rate peaked at 20 percent in April 1981.

Despite this, however, there was a substantial increase in investment spending over the first half of the expansion, with inflation-adjusted growth rates of 43 percent during each quarter.[5] Both were marked by a large rebuilding of inventories, and the first quarter also by a significant rise in fixed investment. At the same time, the PMI held no clear trend and fluctuated between optimism and pessimism, while inflation-adjusted profits fell over the entire expansion (with the exception of a weak increase in 1980Q4). In short, there was a great deal of confusion and angst interspersed with hope over the first year of the new presidency.

4.6.3 Recession: 1981Q4 through 1982Q4

Eventually, however, the extremely tight monetary policies had their desired effect and the US entered into a sixteen-month recession. Not only was this the longest since the Depression, but, until the COVID recession, it "boasted" the highest peak rate of unemployment. However, as suggested, this was all according to plan. The core assumption driving this was that the real culprit in the roughly two decades of inflation was government policy, particularly monetary:

Inflation is essentially a monetary phenomenon. This is not to deny the importance of other factors, such as changes in the price of petroleum, in causing increases in the general price level. What the statement does deny, however, is that persistent inflation can be explained by nonmonetary factors (*Economic Report of the President* 1982: 54).

The popular axiom that attributes inflation to "too much money chasing too few goods" reflects a basic truth: it is difficult to imagine a sustained inflation that is not supported by excessive money growth (*Economic Report of the President* 1983: 20).

In addition to excessive money growth, they blamed the continued price increases on forecasts of future inflation on the part of firms and households (Kliesen and Wheelock 2021). Hence, what they believed they needed to achieve was not just a downturn, but one of sufficient depth and duration to change these expectations. And so it was that both the White House and the Federal Reserve endorsed the policies that caused a severe recession.

4.6.4 Further Observations

Inflation did fall, spectacularly. In the last quarter before the recession (1981Q3), it had been 11.6 percent. In the first quarter after the recession (1983Q1), it was 0.3 percent. It rebounded, but never again reached post-OPEC embargo

---

[5] Note that this occurred during a period of extremely high interest rates, raising some questions about the Neoclassical position that interest rates are the key determinant of investment.

4.6 Volcker Cycle

levels until the early 1990s and Desert Storm. Even then, it fell quickly and did not witness a sustained increase until the post-COVID years.

Should we then celebrate this as a victory of economic policy? Those at the Federal Reserve certainly believed we should, and still do:

> Ultimately, this persistence paid off. By October 1982, inflation had fallen to 5 percent and long-run interest rates began to decline. The Fed allowed the federal funds rate to fall back to 9 percent, and unemployment declined quickly from the peak of nearly 11 percent at the end to 1982 to 8 percent one year later. The threat of inflation was not completely gone, as the Fed would face a number of "inflation scares" throughout the 1980s. However, the commitment of Volcker and his successors to aggressively targeting price stability helped ensure that the double-digit inflation of the 1970s would not return (Sablik 2013).

I, however, am less convinced. My reasons are based on the inflation theory laid out in Chapter 3. There, it was argued that the line of causation posited by the Monetarists and many Neoclassical Keynesians is impossible, that is, that the central bank can force unwanted money onto the private sector, which the private sector then spends and drives up prices. But the Federal Reserve has no policy tools that allow it to raise anyone's income and can only change the form of one's wealth. In addition, their explanation for inflation hinges on it being demand-pull, which further requires that we be at or near full employment. While Volcker, et al., amended this to argue that expectations can lead firms and workers to raise prices and wages in anticipation of inflation, thereby creating a self-fulfilling prophecy, this represents an ad hoc addition that does not fit with the rest of their theory and is entirely unnecessary to explain what really occurred.

Rather, a reexamination of the events of those years suggests a more convincing explanation. To give credit where credit is due, there may well be some truth to the inflationary-expectations theory. It was the case that throughout much of this period, some workers had Cost of Living Adjustments built into their wages, particularly those who were unionized. This was not a major factor, but it did play a role. Even those who did not were liable to point to union wage settlements as a standard against which theirs should be measured. This meant that every episode of inflation was guaranteed to have second-round effects as labor costs, too, rose in many industries. However, as is well-known, Reagan was not friendly toward unions and their strength declined throughout his and subsequent administrations (Jacobs and Myers 2014). While this certainly contributed to the reduction in inflation, it had nothing to do with monetary policy nor did it require that the economy suffer the worst recession since the Great Depression.

Reagan-era deregulation, regardless of the later consequences, also allowed prices to at least decelerate. On the other hand, higher interest rates certainly raised costs. All that said, the most important developments were no doubt those related to the major cause of the increase in prices in the first place: oil. Three major adjustments had occurred. One, the high price of energy had made new exploration cost-effective. Fresh supplies had been discovered (Tussing 1983: 17). In addition, production processes had been modified so that they were less dependent on petroleum and related products (Tussing 1983: 16). Finally and most important, the OPEC oil cartel had collapsed. Though several factors played a role, the key one was the Iran–Iraq War (1980–8). While initially causing a spike, eventually the fact that both countries – desperate for income – were cheating on the quotas led others to do the same. This had significant consequences (Tahmassebi 1986). From 1973 to 1980, the price of a barrel of West Texas Intermediate Crude Oil had risen from $3.873 to $37.375 (annual averages, data from FRED). By 1986, this had fallen to $15.04. This was a massive relief to the oil-importing world and it played a significant and likely the major role in the deceleration of inflation. Furthermore, natural gas deregulation may have contributed to the deceleration (Schmidt 1983); though, that said, not everyone agrees (Trebing 2008).

The most significant legacy of the Volcker Cycle is the lasting impact on monetary policy. While the general approach began during Oil Shock II, the decline in the rate of price increases that occurred alongside the extremely high rates of interest and unemployment served to convince policy makers that their new approach was, indeed, the correct one. Contractionary policy has become standard operating procedure in the face of accelerating prices, regardless of the causes of the latter. At the time of this writing, US and Eurozone central banks have undertaken significant interest rate hikes in response to inflation that is clearly being caused by Russia's invasion of Ukraine and lingering issues related to COVID. There is absolutely no logical reason for their policy. We have the coincidental decline in inflation after the Volcker recession to blame for this.

4.7 DESERT STORM CYCLE

Expansion: Dec 1982 ... Jul 1990 (92 months); 1983Q1 ... 1990Q3 (31 quarters)

Recession: Aug 1990 ... Mar 1991 (8 months); 1990Q4 ... 1991Q1 (2 quarters)

TABLE 4.9 *Key indicators Desert Storm Cycle*

	Unemp	GDP	Inv	π	PMI	Gov't	Int	CPI
Early-to-mid expansion	6.94	4.66	8.60	0.71	54.25	−4.413	9.91	3.65
Last year of expansion	5.43	1.75	−1.58	1.45	47.76	−3.849	10.14	5.58
Recession	6.35	−2.75	−16.65	1.38	40.77	−4.128	9.60	5.00

Key: Unemp = unemployment rate; GDP = inflation-adjusted GDP growth; Inv = inflation-adjusted growth physical investment spending; π = inflation-adjusted growth of corporate after-tax profits; PMI = Purchasing Managers' Index; Gov't = federal government surplus as a percentage of GDP (negative indicates a deficit); Int = Prime interest rate; CPI = consumer price inflation.

Relevant Presidential Administrations
- Ronald Reagan (R): January 20, 1981 to January 20, 1989
- George H. W. Bush (R): January 20, 1989 to January 20, 1993

4.7.1 Early-to-Mid Expansion: 1983Q1 through 1989Q3

This period opened with unemployment over 10 percent, but inflation a fraction of what it had been over the previous decade. Regardless of what caused the latter, the PMI recovered from an average of thirty-eight over the recession to sixty-seven a year into the expansion. Investment spending, which had declined every single year of the downturn and sometimes significantly so, was ripe for recovery. As commented at the time, "In comparison to previous recoveries, the current recovery in plant and equipment expenditures looks strong" (*Survey of Current Business* Dec 1983: 20). In addition to the need to restock and retool after such a long decline, there were changes in the depreciation rules that made investment more profitable (*Economic Report of the President* 1984: 34). The fact that this was occurring despite extremely high interest rates was recognized at the time and explained as a result of the change in tax and other laws (*Economic Report of the President* 1984: 35). It is worthy of note that policy makers were concerned that the rising budget deficit might eventually crowd out private investment and thereby reduce growth (*Economic Report of the President* 1984: 35–41). Yet despite this lip service to "fiscal responsibility," the Reagan administration was about to preside over a massive increase in the debt and deficit – indeed, had they not, the expansion would have come to a screeching halt after just two years.

In mid 1984, the Leading Economic Index indicated that a recession was on the horizon. It was a false alarm, however (Woodham 1984). Given the composition of the index, it is quite possible that it was triggered by the fact that investment spending had rapidly decelerated and then declined in 1984Q3 and 1984Q4. In addition, inflation-adjusted corporate profits fell over the last three quarters of 1984. With the PMI still above 50, this is precisely the scenario argued in Chapter 2 that can lead to recession. The reason it did not occur is similar to that in 1966 when the index gave a false alarm: the federal government's budget deficit kept economic activity from further decline. This pattern continued even after the brief scare. From 1984Q4 through 1986Q3, investment spending continued to decline every single quarter but two (1985Q2 and 1985Q4), an even worse performance than in the previous recession. However, at the same time and from the administration that had promised the opposite, government budget deficits hit record levels.

To get a sense of the impact of these fiscal stimuli, consider the relative contributions of investment and government spending to GDP growth. Over the period in question (1984Q4 through 1986Q3), real GDP grew by an average rate of 3.69 percent. According to Federal Reserve data, the contribution of real investment spending to that 3.69 was −0.34 – that is, investment spending was a net drag. At the same time, real government spending contributed 1.38 to those 3.69 percentage points, more than offsetting the negative impact of investment.

Investment largely recovered thereafter, from 1986Q4 through 1989Q3 (the last quarter before the last quarter of the recession) contributing an average of 0.67 percentage points to GDP growth (which averaged 3.8 percent) as compared to 0.44 for government spending. The dollar's fall from its spectacular rise through 1985 also helped as net exports added 0.60 to the 3.8. The remaining 2 percentage points came from consumption spending; however it is difficult to separate that completely from investment spending, government spending, and net exports given that those three inject income into the macroeconomy, which is then subject to a multiplier effect that manifests itself through consumption.

Unemployment was slow to recover but it did start to fall and by the end of early-to-mid expansion (1989Q3) it stood at 5.2 percent, precisely one half of where it had started. Inflation, too, had returned to more reasonable levels which, though it fluctuated somewhat, averaged 3.65% (over the Volcker Cycle it had been 7.54%). Interest rates, however, at first dipped and then rose once again as the period came to a close. Given that inflation rates had declined, this implied even higher real interest rates (interest minus inflation) than earlier.

Despite all these positives, however, the stock market crashed in October 1987:

The stock market had soared more than 40 percent in value from the start of the year through its August peak, but, by the close of business on October 16, nearly half of

4.7 Desert Storm Cycle

that gain had been erased. And the following Monday, October 19, after stock markets elsewhere in the world had posted sharp declines, the Dow Jones Industrial Average lost 22.6 percent in a single day. Trading volume was enormous, the markets were chaotic, many stocks opened very late, and the word "panic" aptly described the atmosphere. It was a worldwide phenomenon with potentially worldwide consequences (*Economic Report of the President* 1988: 40).

The Federal Reserve acted quickly to provide liquidity and order was restored, but the question remained as to why the bust had occurred. All of the erstwhile fundamental factors appeared to be positive, with corporate profits rising every quarter since 1986Q3 and unemployment falling a full percentage point since then. Real GDP growth had averaged 3.3% over the same period and was about to hit 7% in 1987Q4.

Reviews of the event offered a variety of possible explanations, the most compelling being (a) the magnitude of the increase up to October was unjustified in terms of actual economic performances, especially as interest rates began to ratchet up and press coverage of the "twin deficits" increased, and (b) the relatively new phenomenon of computerized trading created automated herd behavior. The latter meant that after the decline started: "trading systems created a domino effect, continually accelerating the pace of selling as the market dropped, thus causing it to drop even further. The avalanche of selling that was triggered by the initial losses resulted in stock prices dropping even further, which in turn triggered more rounds of computer-driven selling (CFI Team 2022)."

The policy response to the impact of computer trading included circuit breakers, which closed trading whenever price declines reached a particular threshold.

For example, as of 2019, if the S&P 500 Index falls by more than 7% from the previous day's closing price, it trips the first circuit breaker, which halts all stock trading for 15 minutes. The second circuit breaker is triggered if there is a 13% drop in the index from the previous close, and if the third circuit breaker level is triggered – by a 20% decline – then trading is halted for the remainder of the day (CFI Team 2022).

The market recovered thereafter, though at a more restrained pace. It did not reach precrash levels again until mid 1989.

The expansion continued, largely uninterrupted, throughout the rest of the early-to-mid expansion period (i.e., through1989Q3). Unemployment fell from around 5.8% during the quarter of the crash to 5.2% and GDP growth continued to be robust, dipping below 3% only twice. Inflation accelerated briefly in 1989Q2, due largely to a severe drought (*Economic Report of the President* 1990: 49). All that said, 1989Q2 was the first of three consecutive quarters of negative growth in real investment spending. While this would normally signal the onset of recession, in each case this drag was entirely (1989Q2 and 1989Q3) or almost entirely (1989Q4) offset by the stimulative effect of government spending. This takes us into the last year of the expansion.

4.7.2 Final Year of Expansion: 1989Q4 through 1990Q3

The last year witnessed an average rate of growth of real investment spending of − 1.58 percent. Inflation-adjusted corporate profits still rose 1.45 percent/quarter. Meanwhile, the mean PMI was forty-eight and so slightly pessimistic. Of course, as already stated above, there would almost certainly have been a recession already back when investment turned negative in 1984 or 1989, but these were offset by government spending. Hence, while the last year of the expansion showed tepid GDP growth, rates didn't turn negative until the occurrence of an what was, indeed, an external event at work: Iraq's August 1990 invasion of Kuwait. This added uncertainty and the economy then slipped into recession as investment fell for four consecutive quarters. The weakness in the economy was reported to be widespread (*Survey of Current Business* Apr 1991: 2).

4.7.3 Recession: 1990Q4 through 1991Q1

The recession was brief, with two quarters of average real GDP growth of −2.75%. Unemployment rose significantly, however, going from 5.3% in 1990Q2 to 6.6% in the last quarter of the recession to an eventual peak of 7.6% during the subsequent expansion. This very weak response of employment to the upturn lead analysts to dub the latter a "jobless recovery." This will be addressed in the next cycle.

4.7.4 Further Observations

One of the items of note emerging from the Desert Storm Cycle is the evidence of the degree to which mainstream Neoclassical/Monetarist economic theory had taken clear control of the policymaking reins. It was already mentioned above that the pseudo-Monetarist experiment at the Federal Reserve had started in October 1979, and the 1990 *Economic Report of the President* echoed the orthodox macroeconomics belief that full-employment is the default state of the economy and only shocks can temporarily knock it off that path: "Historical and international evidence shows that economic expansions do not die of old age. Expansions end because of particular external shocks to the economy, policy errors, or widespread imbalances, such as an overaccumulation of inventories, developing throughout the economy (*Economic Report of the President* 1990: 33)."

This adds yet another nail to the coffin of the philosophy underlying the Employment Act of 1946 for, if the economy automatically creates a job for every willing worker then there is no need for the government to prod it into doing so. Obviously, there may need to be action in response to "particular external shocks to the economy, policy errors, or widespread imbalances," but in general it can be left on automatic pilot.

4.7 Desert Storm Cycle

This was perfectly consistent with the Reagan administration's (and his vice president's) overall approach. "Reaganomics" had many facets and sources, not all of which were mutually consistent (Samuelson 1987). In general, however (and going into only as much detail as is relevant for present purposes), the president had been faithful to three themes: "taxes should be cut, government spending and involvement in private affairs should be reduced, and national defense spending should be increased to ensure that the United States was strong enough to meet any challenge (Campagna 1994: 32)."

With respect to details, he, personally, did not go much further than this. "He knew what he wanted to achieve and delegated much of everything else to his aides. His was not an analytical mind, and he did not think in the abstract (Campagna 1994: 32)." But details did follow, of course, as his staff developed policy (largely) consistent with his philosophy.

What was achieved with more or less success were tax cuts (Bischoff, Kokkelenberg, Terregrossa 1991: 23–4 and Burtless 1991: 43); deregulation (Boettke 1991: 120–2 and Davis and Lehn 1991: 129–30); and the shift in macroeconomic policy already discussed. There is considerably controversy regarding their role in creating superior economic outcomes. Some contend, for example, "that the reduction in marginal tax rates succeeded in encouraging investment, savings, and work effort" (Sahu and Tracy 1991: 11). Others are less generous:

... the long-term consequences of his policies were far-reaching because they set into motion policies that locked the society into an inferior set of institutions, ideology, income distribution, and educational system that had powerful deleterious impact in the decades to come (Arthur 1989). The accumulated effect of his tax cuts, deficits, and the income inequality that increased enormously ultimately led to a business-friendly legal framework, more deficits, and more inequality .... The inequality eventually led to the accumulation of so much despair among the have-nots, the less educated, the evicted, and the downwardly mobile, that they eventually reached for the pitchforks to overthrow the establishment and put a strongman into the White House come what may. Trump, therefore, is Reagan's ultimate legacy (Komlos 2018: 2–3).

I would not go as far as Komlos, but would generally point to the Reagan era as one that sent us down a unfortunate path. It is a path that George H. W. Bush, Bill Clinton, and George W. Bush also followed, however, so it seems unfair to lay everything at Reagan's feet. One way or another, New Deal-style protections to incomes, health and safety, and financial health were being systematically dismantled.

A pillar of Reaganomics that was never achieved, incidentally, was a reduction in government spending. Indeed and ironically, had this been done then the long recovery under Reagan would likely not have occurred (as argued at numerous places above). The willingness to spend in deficit should actually be viewed as one of the positive legacies of his administration.

4.8 SEPTEMBER 11 CYCLE

Expansion: Apr 1991 ... Mar 2001 (120 months); 1991Q2 ... 2001Q1 (40 quarters)

Recession: Apr 2001 ... Nov 2001 (8 months); 2001Q2 ... 2001Q4 (3 quarters)

TABLE 4.10 *Key indicators September 11 Cycle*

	Unemp	GDP	Inv	π	PMI	Gov't	Int	CPI
Early-to-mid expansion	5.71	3.77	8.49	0.96	52.60	−3.160	7.74	2.62
Last year of expansion	4.00	2.25	1.47	−0.68	48.33	0.909	9.22	3.43
Recession	4.90	0.67	−8.73	−2.71	43.71	−1.457	6.36	1.20

Key: Unemp = unemployment rate; GDP = inflation-adjusted GDP growth; Inv = inflation-adjusted growth physical investment spending; π = inflation-adjusted growth of corporate after-tax profits; PMI = Purchasing Managers' Index; Gov't = federal government surplus as a percentage of GDP (negative indicates a deficit); Int = Prime interest rate; CPI = consumer price inflation.

Relevant Presidential Administrations
- George H. W. Bush (R): January 20, 1989 to January 20, 1993
- Bill Clinton (D): January 20, 1993 to January 20, 2001
- George W. Bush (R): January 20, 2001 to January 20, 2009

4.8.1 Early-to-Mid Expansion: 1991Q2 through 2000Q1

The expansion opening 1991Q2 would ultimately last 120 months and be one of the longest and strongest in US history. It did not start out that way, however: "Initially, recovery from the 1990–91 recession was hampered by several special factors including large household and business debt burdens, high vacancy rates in commercial real estate, tight credit practices by many lenders, stagnant growth in much of the rest of the world, and declining Federal purchases, especially of military goods and services (*Economic Report of the President* 1995: 49)."

Its character changed around 1993, but this was too late for George Bush, who lost the 1992 presidential election to Bill Clinton largely on the basis of the economy. While Clinton's administration argued that issues like income distribution and declining productivity were now paramount, he nevertheless fell in line with the previous two Republican ones in terms of worry over the debt and deficit (*Economic Report of the President* 1993: 26–9). This would have consequences and it is one of the reasons that the government's deficit shrank throughout the expansion (the other of course being the automatic stabilizers moving into reverse).

Real GDP growth in 1993 was mixed but ended on a high note at 5.6 percent for 1993Q4. 1994 as a whole proved to be the strongest year thus far in the expansion, with real GDP growth around 4.1% and inflation remaining moderate at 2.6%. The former was attributable to a very large increase in

4.8 September 11 Cycle

investment, in which fixed played a considerably larger role than inventory. This was in part attributable to firms adopting computer technology:

> The extraordinary growth in PDE (producers' durable equipment) reflects the strong growth posted by spending on both computers and noncomputer equipment. Since the current expansion began, real investment in computers and peripheral equipment has increased at an average annual rate of 33.9 percent, while real spending on equipment other than computers has increased at an annual rate of about 8 percent. As a share of real GDP, noncomputer investment during 1994 was higher than at any time since separate records were first kept for computer and noncomputer investment spending (*Economic Report of the President* 1995: 52).

This was a key characteristic of the expansion in general. GDP growth slowed somewhat in early 1995, while remaining positive, and unemployment continued to fall. Part of the former was attributed to the December 1994 Mexican financial crisis, which led to a reduction in Mexican imports from the US (*Economic Report of the President* 1996: 46), plus weak contributions from consumption (concentrated in durables) and investment (*Survey of Current Business* Apr 1995a). But these recovered in the second half and there was strong growth thereafter through 1999 (an average of 4.5 percent per year).

This period was witness to several major trends. The key one, as already mentioned, was the investment in computer technology. Over the course of the decade, "IT investment grew from 3% of GDP at the beginning of 1991 to 4.9% – more than one-third of total investment – at the end of 2000" (Weller 2002). Not only did this by itself stimulate growth, but there was an increase in the depreciation rate and, therefore, in replacement investment. This was "due to a shift in the composition of capital towards computers, which depreciate more rapidly than other types of equipment" (Tevlin and Whelan 2003: 1–2). This sudden shift in investment priorities had its origins in a marked increase in productivity in the IT industry which:

> resulted in higher rates of decline in IT prices, stimulating decisions by firms, households, and governments to invest in IT equipment and software. As a result, rising IT investment contributed 0.72 points to the jump in output growth. Jorgenson (2001) has traced the accelerated price decline to a substantially shorter product cycle in the production of the key electronic components of IT equipment (Jorgenson et al. 2007: 230).

This raised both GDP growth and overall productivity, but "The IT boom of the last half of the 1990s faded considerably after the dot-com crash of 2000" (Jorgenson et al. 2007: 230). This brings us to the second major theme, the overvalued stock market.

Not only did tech drive physical investment, it was a darling of financial investment, too. To some extent, this makes perfect sense: why not fund enterprises whose products were increasingly popular and apparently profitable? This is, indeed, what occurred.

In the late 90s, low interest rates made speculative equity investments more attractive than bonds, and at the same time, innovative internet companies grew in popularity among retail investors, professional traders, venture capitalists, and alike. When the Taxpayer Relief Act of 1997 passed, the top capital gains tax rate was lowered, providing yet another incentive for equity speculators to pour money into the fledgling internet industry (Salvucci 2023).

In addition, "Investment banks earned massively by facilitating IPOs for one tech company after another" (Salvucci 2023). From 1995 to its peak in early 2000, the Nasdaq increased over fivefold (in nominal terms).

The overvaluation arose for reasons related to the character of financial markets as discussed in Chapter 2. There, it stated that the financial sector must:

1. be capable of providing sufficient funding to support investment (and other forms of spending); and
2. practice portfolio management policies that encourage financial sector stability, especially in terms of making reasonably accurate evaluations of the credit worthiness of borrowers.

The chapter further argued that while the market can do #1 with ease, #2 is problematic. Deciding who was the most worthy of investment cash is necessarily problematic. Consistent with this, an account from around the time of the crash stated, "the capital markets did a great job of channeling money into the new business sector that the dot-coms represented. But they did a lousy job of selecting which start-ups to support" (Mills 2001). In an environment of *uncertainty*, panic and – particularly important in this case – euphoria become possible in a manner they do not under *risk*. And, as Keynes argued in the *General Theory*, in a booming financial market "there is an inducement to spend on a new project what may seem an extravagant sum, if it can be floated off on the Stock Exchange at an immediate profit" (Keynes 1936: 151). This happened time after time.

It eventually stopped happening, however, around March 2000. Many possible triggers for the bust have been suggested, including rising interest rates, a recession in Japan, and reports that asset issuers were underperforming (Salvucci 2023 and Geier 2015). I have argued elsewhere, however, that these are coincidental and that "although their outward manifestations may vary, all such events have at their heart the same cause: the development of increasingly optimistic forecasts alongside economic forces that cannot justify those expectations (Harvey 2010: 62)."

In other words, the bust occurs because there was a boom, or a significant separation of expected financial market gains versus those actually earned by asset issuers. What bursts the bubble is historical accident. Note, incidentally, that it is not necessary for the savvy players in the market to be ignorant of the overvaluation. As Keynes observed, "The actual, private object of the most skilled investment to-day is 'to beat the gun', as the Americans so well express it, to outwit the crowd, and to pass the bad, or depreciating, half-crown to the other fellow (Keynes 1936: 155)." So long as you find a "muppet" to whom to sell the asset once the collapse begins, there is money to be made.

4.8 September 11 Cycle

The consequences of the boom went beyond the financial chaos caused by the bust. For one, it may have damaged the manufacturing sector:

The stock market run-up and manufacturing's decline may have been related. The rapid rise in the stock market may have given lenders an incentive to invest primarily in companies that saw large increases in their stock prices, thereby possibly raising financial constraints for firms located in sectors where stock prices did not rise as fast. This seemed to have been especially true for most of the manufacturing sector (Weller and Helppie 2005: 359).

In addition, "large stock market gains may have made investments in fixed assets less attractive," which had the additional effect of inducing corporations to use resources to boost asset prices through dividend payouts and share repurchases rather than reinvestment in productive capacity (Weller and Helppie 2005: 359). Even worse is the fact that the preference for boosting paper profits over real ones did not appear to end with the collapse of the dot-com boom. Rather, it may have become institutionalized and linked to CEO remuneration (Boyer 2005). This may be part of the reason for the general slowdown in physical investment spending in the 2000s (Maas 2017).[6]

The last important trend to mark here was the increase in consumer indebtedness. The related developments are nicely summarized in a report by Demos:

The mid and late 1990s will always be remembered as an era of unprecedented prosperity. But for most American families, the roaring '90s had a dark underbelly – it was also the Decade of Debt.

Between 1989 and 2001, credit card debt in America almost tripled, from $238 billion to $692 billion. The savings rate steadily declined, and the number of people filing for bankruptcy jumped 125 percent.

How did the average family fare? During the 1990s, the average American family experienced a 53 percent increase in credit card debt, from $2,697 to $4,126 (all figures measured in 2001 dollars). Low-income families saw the largest increase – a 184 percent rise in their debt – but even very high-income families had 28 percent more credit card debt in 2001 than they did in 1989.

Credit card debt is often dismissed as the consequence of frivolous consumption. But an examination of broad structural and economic trends during the 1990s – including stagnant or declining real wages, job displacement, and rising health care and housing costs – suggests that many Americans are using credit cards as a way to fill a growing gap between household earnings and the costs of essential goods and services. Usurious practices in the credit card industry, in the form of high rates and fees, have taken advantage of the increased need for credit. As a result, a growing number of American families find themselves perpetually indebted to the credit card industry, which – despite claims of losses and chargeoffs – remains one of the most profitable sectors of the banking industry (Druat and Silva 2003: 9).

Their reference to "stagnant or declining real wages, job displacement, and rising health care and housing costs" is key here. Deindustrialization had already

---

[6] Recall the discussion of money-manager capitalism under secular stagnation in chapter 3.

been taking place for well over a decade (High 2021), union strength was waning in the aftermath of the Reagan Revolution (Rosenfeld 2019), social support mechanisms had been cut away by every president since 1981 (including Clinton; Rasmus 2020), and the health care industry was becoming increasingly concentrated (Fulton 2017). Without sufficient income, households turn to debt, and "from 1970 to 2018, the share of aggregate income going to middle-class households fell from 62% to 43%" (Horowitz, Igielnik, and Kochhar 2020).

4.8.2 Final Year of Expansion: 2000Q2 through 2001Q1

The strength and duration of the expansion led pundits, policy makers, politicians, and analysts to claim the emergence of a "New Economy," one marked by "sustained high investment rates, continued strong productivity growth, and low unemployment with stable core inflation" (*Economic Report of the President* 2001: 56). This was not to last, however. The first indicator of weakness was the stock market crash in 2000Q1. Although this preceded the last year of the expansion and was over a year before the recession, this had the effect of changing the atmosphere in which business took place. To begin, the PMI dropped from 56 to 53 to 51 by 2000Q3. Of course, this still indicates an expectation of improvement, which the economy did not deliver. Instead, the rate of growth of inflation-adjusted corporate profits was negative from 2000Q1 through 2000Q4, setting the stage for disappointment. That a downturn did not occur earlier than it did is related to the continued strong, if diminishing, increases in consumption spending (*Economic Report of the President* 2001: 60-2). These were related to the increases in consumer debt referenced above and could not therefore continue indefinitely. But, by 2001Q1, this too had declined to the point that it was no longer sufficient. The bottom line is that firms had reached capacity:

In particular, the productivity gains offered by the more intensive use of computers, fiber optic technologies, and the Internet drove an investment boom in which the Nation's businesses retooled and upgraded their workplaces for the 21st century. Not surprisingly, the rapid pace of investment then slowed as the need to adopt the new technologies began to be satisfied and a more mature investment phase began (*Economic Report of the President* 2002: 36).

4.8.3 Recession: 2001Q2 through 2001Q4

Real GDP actually contracted in the quarter before the official start of the recession in 2001Q2, although if you look only at the NBER's monthly dating of the downturn it was in March 2001 (i.e., the last month of 2001Q1). Investment spending shrank every quarter but one from 2001Q1 through 2001Q4, the exception being a growth rate of 0.6 percent in 2001Q2. Both fixed and inventory investment were responsible. The new George Bush administration claimed that, until the September 11 attacks, it appeared as if the economy might recover:

4.8 September 11 Cycle

The terrorist attacks of September 11 changed the direction of the macroeconomy. Before the attacks, the economy had been showing tentative signs of stabilizing after its long deceleration, and many forecasters expected real GDP growth to accelerate in the third and fourth quarters of 2001. Immediately after the attacks, however, the economy turned down because of the direct effect of the assault on the Nation's economic and financial infrastructure and because of the indirect, but more significant, effect on consumer and business confidence. The drop was sufficient to turn the sluggish period of economic activity into a recession (*Economic Report of the President* 2002: 30).

There is no question that the September 11 attacks had a significant impact on the economy, but it is not entirely evident that recovery was around the corner. Indeed, the economy continued to sputter for the next year. However, it is difficult to separate from subsequent events that which was caused by the shock of the attacks and those things that would have happened anyway.

4.8.4 Further Observations

The expansion that ended in the last year of the twentieth century was at that point the longest in history at 120 months. Investment was steady if not spectacular throughout the period. The only time that declines in investment were grouped together took place in 1995Q2 and 1995Q3. Contemporary commentary suggested that consumption behavior was very unusual in this period in that even with a rise in unemployment and a fall in personal income, spending rose (*Survey of Current Business* Aug 1995b: 3). This implies debt. Indeed, rising private-sector debt, especially as the public sector moved to surplus, is a hallmark of this expansion (Papadimitriou and Wray 1998). That stock prices were skyrocketing also no doubt affected households' willingness to spend from current income.

In general, however, it was a typical Keynes-style upswing with investment in the driver's seat. The latter was focused particularly on computer equipment. Similar to the long expansion of the 1920s being driven by the gearing up of automobile and related industries, so there was a unique technological innovation behind this one (Tevlin and Whelan 2003). Note, too, that the existence of very little price inflation meant that the central bank did not feel compelled to raise interest rates (even if this is a secondary factor). But, eventually entrepreneurs reach the point at which they are satisfied with capacity, thus setting the stage for a fall in demand and disappointment of entrepreneurial expectations.

Real investment spending started falling around 2000Q3, while the PMI moderated but remained above fifty. In contrast, realized profits were declining. The recession followed shortly thereafter (officially dated as 2001Q1 to 2001Q4, although real GDP growth was an anemic 0.33 percent in 2000Q3) and the economy was already in decline before the terrorist attacks. The long-term effects of the latter are difficult to quantify, but, while there was clearly a shock in the 2001 recession, it occurred after the downturn was underway. Consistent with Keynes' view, the expansion had continued until investment and then the realized profits fell, creating disappointment and collapse.

4.9 SUBPRIME CRISIS CYCLE

Expansion: Dec 2001 ... Dec 2007 (73 months); 2002Q1 ... 2007Q4 (24 quarters)

Recession: Jan 2008 ... Jun 2009 (18 months); 2008Q1 ... 2009Q2 (6 quarters)

TABLE 4.11 *Key indicators Subprime Crisis Cycle*

	Unemp	GDP	Inv	π	PMI	Gov't	Int	CPI
Early-to-mid expansion	5.39	3.06	5.33	4.85	53.86	−3.777	5.46	2.67
Last year of expansion	4.63	2.18	−1.75	−1.43	51.23	−2.682	8.05	4.05
Recession	6.80	−2.53	−19.70	0.64	43.31	−7.367	4.48	1.08

Key: Unemp = unemployment rate; GDP = inflation-adjusted GDP growth; Inv = inflation-adjusted growth physical investment spending; π = inflation-adjusted growth of corporate after-tax profits; PMI = Purchasing Managers' Index; Gov't = federal government surplus as a percentage of GDP (negative indicates a deficit); Int = Prime interest rate; CPI = consumer price inflation.

Relevant Presidential Administrations
- George W. Bush (R): January 20, 2001 to January 20, 2009
- Barack Obama (D): January 20, 2009 to January 20, 2017

4.9.1 Early-to-Mid Expansion: 2002Q1 through 2006Q4

The first year of the expansion saw rather tepid GDP growth with rates at 3.4%, 2.5%, 1.6%, and 0.5%. This matches the pattern of changes in real investment spending at the same time. Consumption, on the other hand, rose over the course of the year, possibly boosted by the reduction in marginal tax rates enacted in June (*Economic Report of the President* 2003: 16): "Robust consumption, in turn, was a crucial locus of strength in the overall economy, contributing an average of 2.1 percentage points to real GDP growth during the first three quarters of the year (*Economic Report of the President* 2003: 28)." It was 2.2 percentage points in 2002Q4, but those data were not available when the above was written.

Contributing to the consumption spending and of interesting note given what will happen at the end of this expansion is the following:

Along with healthy growth of disposable income, another positive determinant of consumption growth in 2002 was the strength of the housing market ... Housing wealth is more widely distributed among American families than stock market wealth, and housing equity continued to rise in 2002. A common way for this equity to support consumption is through borrowing against home equity: the outstanding value of revolving home equity loans at commercial banks rose from $155.5 billion in December 2001 to $212.3 billion in December 2002. Another way that homeowners can tap the equity in their homes, for higher consumption or for spending

4.9 Subprime Crisis Cycle

on home improvements, is by refinancing their outstanding mortgages when interest rates have fallen. Of course, simply refinancing a mortgage at a lower interest rate can reduce monthly mortgage payments and free up extra cash. Many refinancers, however, choose to remove equity from their homes by taking out a new mortgage with a larger principal than the amount outstanding on the original mortgage. These "cash-out" refinancings boomed in 2002 as a result of the continued appreciation in housing prices and declining long-term interest rates. According to the Federal Home Loan Mortgage Corporation (Freddie Mac), holders of conventional, conforming mortgages liquefied about $59 billion in equity in the first three quarters of 2002 (*Economic Report of the President* 2003: 33).

Although not exactly the phenomenon that will play such a critical role in the Financial Crisis of 2007–2008, the subprime lending crisis could not have occurred in the absence of a booming housing market. Residential housing played a role, but not the only one: "Much of the growth of private demand during 2003 was attributable to the effects of expansionary fiscal and monetary policy designed to counteract the lingering effects of the stock market decline, the capital overhang, worries about geopolitical developments, and concern about accounting scandals (*Economic Report of the President* 2004: 84)."

While the direct contribution of government spending to GDP growth was small (adding roughly 0.36 percentage points to the 4.30 of overall GDP growth in 2003), this does not account for the impact on consumption of the tax cuts. But it was investment that was most significant, with nonresidential and residential leading the way (*Survey of Current Business* Mar 2004: 2). Purchases of high-tech equipment and software increased substantially (*Economic Report of the President* 2004: 90).

All this began, incidentally, against a backdrop of worries and uncertainty over excess capacity, corporate scandals, and uncertainty about economic and geopolitical events:

> Over the past several years, this Nation has faced major economic challenges resulting from the decline of the stock market beginning in early 2000, a recession that began shortly after, revelations about corporate governance scandals, slow growth among many of our major trading partners, terrorist attacks, and the war against terror, including in Afghanistan and Iraq (*Economic Report of the President* 2004: 3).

The strong growth in 2003 was therefore especially welcome.

The year 2004 was not as robust but still represented a solid performance. In addition, unemployment continued to decline, if not dramatically. "Growth was supported by gains in consumer spending, business fixed investment, and, to a lesser extent, housing investment, inventory accumulation, and government spending" *Economic Report of the President* 2005: 31). Again as a foreshadowing of later woes there was reference to housing prices:

> The strength in housing demand has been reflected in home prices. An index of prices for houses involved in repeat transactions (that is, sales prices of the same house over

time) increased by 13 percent during the four quarters ended in the third quarter of 2004 – the biggest four-quarter increase since the late 1970s. The rapid increase in demand and prices has further helped support gains in home construction. Housing starts totaled 1.95 million units during 2004, making it the strongest year for housing starts since 1978 (*Economic Report of the President* 2005: 34).

The economy continued at a similar pace in 2005 and for largely the same reasons, although there was a dip in investment in 2005Q2 due to inventory run downs. Inflation accelerated in 2005Q3 as a result of "rising energy prices and a devastating hurricane season," but slowed by 2006Q4 when the CPI actually fell (*Economic Report of the President* 2006: 25; CBC Staff 2006). Developments in housing continued to be of interest:

During the past five years, home prices have risen at an annual rate of 9.2 percent. This increase was largely supported by two factors: first, an increase in housing demand, driven by a rise in nominal per capita disposable income of 3.4 percent per year; second, a decline in the cost of financing house purchases, due to a drop in the monthly payment on 30-year fixed-rate mortgages of 4.3 percent per year. Housing demand was also boosted by increased household formation and a strengthening job market. Supply constraints, due to limits on the supply of buildable land in some areas, also contributed to rising prices over the past five years (*Economic Report of the President* 2006: 30).

This continued at a slower pace in 2006. Up to that point, "the cumulative increase in inflation-adjusted housing prices during the 6 years from 1999 to 2005 is one of the largest on record, exceeded only by the period immediately following the Second World War" (*Economic Report of the President* 2007: 27). By contrast, residential investment was a significant net drag on GDP growth in 2006. It would not, however, be until the next year that the term "subprime" would make an appearance in the *Economic Report of the President*.

The rate of real GDP growth had already been slowing since 2003, when it was 4.3 percent. It subsequently fell to 3.4% in 2004, 3% in 2005, 2.6% in 2006, and 2.2% in 2007, which was the last year of the expansion. The primary reason for this was the slowdown in investment. Its contribution to GDP had been consistently positive from 2003 through 2004 and was only negative once in 2005 (2005Q2). But 2006 through 2007 showed only two quarters when investment contributed positively to overall growth. Some of this was a consequence inventory adjustment, while most was due to a decline in residential investment (which became a consistent drag from 2005Q4 through the end of the expansion in 2007Q4). Were it not for continued significant contributions from consumption, the recession would have almost certainly started earlier (at least by 2007Q1 instead of 2008Q1).

But consumption did rise. The "rapid increase in consumer spending in 2006 was supported by rising employment, gains in real income, increases in household wealth, and favorable financial conditions" (Federal Reserve Board

2006). Indeed, unemployment had finally fallen below 5 percent in 2006 and inflation remained moderate, particularly by earlier standards. Unfortunately, however, debt also clearly played a role as household debt service as a percentage of disposable personal income hit a new high by the end of the year and it would continue to climb to what remains an all-time high in 2007Q4 – the last quarter of the expansion.

While there was little to no mention of this in the Bush administration or among orthodox economists, at least some scholars noted these developments with concern. A report from the *Levy Economics Institute*, for example, reported: "U.S. household deficit spending has achieved an alarming trajectory. So, too, has the ratio of household debt to income" (Parenteau 2006: 24). It continued:

Even under optimistic assumptions, the trajectory of U.S. household spending growth is likely to slow further. With the end of the housing boom, various major lines of household credit have already slowed dramatically, which suggests that the pace of household deficit spending is likely to reverse course. If, as is typically the fashion, banks become concerned with creditworthiness, as the slowdown unfolds, a credit crunch could sharply curtail household credit growth and force a dramatic reversal of household deficit spending (Parenteau 2006: 25).

It would not be the last time that the Levy Institute sounded the alarm. In addition, in December 2005, economist Steve Keen also began warning the world of an impending crisis though his blog, debtdeflation.com. His analysis, based on a model he had published in 1995, suggested that the rising levels of private-sector debt were leading to a collapse of potentially catastrophic proportions. These warnings, coming primarily from Post Keynesian economists, would increase in frequency throughout the last year of the expansion. They would, however, ultimately be ignored.

4.9.2 Final Year of Expansion: 2007Q1 through 2007Q4

The last year began on the tail of two consecutive quarters of decline in real investment spending (again, due largely to residential construction). This would continue for all except one quarter of 2007 (that one quarter showing 0.8 percent growth), while the PMI never fell below 50. The rate of growth of inflation-adjusted, after-tax corporate profits fell by an average of 1.43 percent in the last year of the expansion. All this sets up the scenario described in Chapter 2 wherein agents' expectations (as represented by the PMI) are disappointed (in the form of a decline, rather than the expected rise, in profits) and, in an environment of *uncertainty*, this leads them to replace their error of optimism with an error of pessimism.

At the same time, of course, subprime mortgages and their effect on financial markets were adding further instability to the economy. Their role was finally being acknowledged more widely. Even with that, however, the 2008

Economic Report of the President (which covers the previous year's events) identified it as the sixth of seven "key points of this chapter" (*Economic Report of the President* 2007: 25–6). The administration's economic forecast of GDP growth for 2008 was 2.7% and 2009 was 3.0%. In reality, those numbers were −2.5% and 0.13%. Granted some politics may enter into such calculations, but they were not out of line with those found at other institutions dominated by economic orthodoxy. The Federal Reserve Bank of Chicago, for example, offered forecasts of 2.5 percent for both 2008 and 2009 (Strauss and Engel 2008: 1). The International Monetary Fund was somewhat more cautious, but still expected a positive 1.9 percent in 2008 (Callen 2007). Only economists like Steve Keen[7] and those at the Levy Institute were less optimistic (see, for example, Papadimitriou, Hannsgen, and Zezza 2007 and Whalen 2007).

4.9.3 Recession: 2008Q1 through 2009Q2

Real GDP growth turned negative in 2008Q1, as consumption no longer held up the economy and actually shrank. The PMI dipped below 50 and did not rise above it again until 2009Q3 (the first quarter of the subsequent expansion). The rate of growth of inflation-adjusted, after-tax corporate profits was negative for 2008, at −13.5%, while unemployment rose from 4.8% in the last quarter of the expansion to 9.3% in the last quarter of the recession (it would eventually climb to 10% in October 2009, eclipsed only by the peak after the Volcker recession and the massive spike after COVID).

4.9.4 Further Observations

The expansion that started in 2002 was not very strong, with the lowest average real GDP and investment growth of any since 1950 (Aron-Dine, Stone, and Kogan 2008). In fact, the recession could have started in 2006Q2 rather than 2007Q4, when there was the first of four consecutive declines in real investment spending and GDP grew at 1.45% (to be followed by 0.11% in 2006Q3). Though in general this whole period was consistent with Keynes' explanation of the business cycle, several longer-term issues came into play and should be explained.

The financialization of the US economy, or a shift in orientation toward managing financial wealth as opposed to production of commodities (referenced under secular stagnation in Chapter 3), had been taking place since the 1980s. Encouraged by both the economics discipline and neoliberal governments, it was based on the former's premise that markets were rational and efficient and led to the latter's deregulation of the financial industry and

---

[7] See the summaries of his DebtWatch blogs at www.debtdeflation.com/blogs/pre-blog-debtwatch-reports/.

increasingly hands-off approach to economic policy. It both contributed to and was in turn encouraged by the massive run up of the stock market in the 1990s and it led to an excessively short-term orientation for financial and non-financial business and an increased role for agents' expectations and levels of confidence. Firms, households, and governments became convinced that real returns well in excess of historical rates of real GDP growth could be consistently realized in financial markets (Wray 1998).

A second emerging factor was the shift toward greater income inequality that had been taking place since the late 1960s and accelerated in the 1980s (Weinberg 1996). One study argues that the period 1994–2000, was witness to an especially rapid deterioration (Galbraith and Hale 2004). This not only has a tendency to lower the marginal propensity to consume and thus the overall level of economic activity, but it was exacerbated by financialization (Palley 2007) – and, in combination with it, created the third problem.

Last, while household income distribution was becoming more skewed, financial institutions were encouraging those with declining income shares to borrow more and more in order to maintain spending. Headlines focused on how this played out in the subprime mortgage market, though it was certainly system-wide and had started in the previous cycle (as referenced above). Financial investment in search of quick and substantial capital gain must take on risk, and so risk was created by loaning to those who were less likely to be able to repay.

Hence, by the time investment was wavering in 2006Q2, the macroeconomy had already been weakened by (1) a shift in income toward those who spend the least, (2) the superimposition of short-term, psychology-dominated expectations from finance to the economy at large, and (3) the existence of very high debt-to-income ratios. None of these is inconsistent with the Post Keynesian view, of course, but they were more long-term than cyclical issues. That real GDP growth managed to stay positive for another six quarters was a function of consumer spending and consumer debt. When these accelerated, economic growth remained robust despite investment; when it did not, the economy experienced low but positive growth.

In the last year of the expansion, the rate of growth of real investment spending had slowed and realized profits were falling, but, as hypothesized, the PMI still averaged above 50. While this by itself would be sufficient to create disappointment, as the extent of the situation in the financial industry became clear the balance between unfounded optimism and real returns was upset. The PMI fell to its lowest level since the oil crises and the two-year collapse in investment starting in 2007Q3 was the largest in the post–World War II era. All of this, of course, fits quite well into the Post Keynesian scheme.

4.10 COVID CYCLE

Expansion: Jul 2009 ... Feb 2020 (128 months); 2009Q3 ... 2019Q4 (42 quarters)

Recession: Mar 2020 ... Apr 2020 (2 months); 2020Q1 ... 2020Q2 (2 quarters)

TABLE 4.12 *Key indicators COVID Cycle*

	Unemp	GDP	Inv	π	PMI	Gov't	Int	CPI
Early-to-mid expansion	6.67	2.25	7.12	1.13	54.71	−6.737	3.54	1.80
Last year of expansion	3.70	2.58	0.90	−0.99	51.20	−5.825	5.28	2.03
Recession	8.45	−18.2	−27.05	−10.11	47.88	−15.59	3.84	−1.05

Key: Unemp = unemployment rate; GDP = inflation-adjusted GDP growth; Inv = inflation-adjusted growth physical investment spending; π = inflation-adjusted growth of corporate after-tax profits; PMI = Purchasing Managers' Index; Gov't = federal government surplus as a percentage of GDP (negative indicates a deficit); Int = Prime interest rate; CPI = consumer price inflation.

Relevant Presidential Administrations
- Barack Obama (D): January 20, 2009 to January 20, 2017
- Donald Trump (R): January 20, 2017 to January 20, 2021

4.10.1 Early-to-Mid Expansion: 2009Q3 through 2018Q4

GDP growth, which had been negative for the previous five of six quarters, finally turned positive again in 2009Q3. It remained so for the remainder of that year and the next, due in no small part to the $831 billion American Recovery and Reinvestment Act of 2009 (Feyrer and Sacerdote 2011). However, the Obama administration almost immediately began expressing concerns about the federal budget balance (*Economic Report of the President* 2010: 137–57). Indeed and in stark contrast to the needs of the economy, *government spending was a net drag on economic activity every single quarter from the second half of 2010 through to the first quarter of 2014*. This led to the expansion being among the weakest – perhaps the weakest – since World War II. This did not go unnoticed by contemporary observers (see, for example, Long and Luhby 2016, Morath 2016, Papadimitriou, Nikiforos, Zezza, and Hannsgen 2014).

Looking at the data from the first quarter of recovery through the last quarter of Barack Obama's presidency (i.e., 2009Q3 through 2016Q4), the average rate of real GDP growth was 2.17 percent. This is below that of every other expansion covered in this volume (note the consecutive declines in the 1990s and 2000s, evidence of secular stagnation to be addressed later):

4.10 COVID Cycle

4.1%	Ike I expansion (1954Q3 ... 1957Q3)
5.6%	Ike II expansion (1958Q3 ... 1960Q2)
4.9%	Vietnam expansion (1961Q2 ... 1969Q4)
5.2%	Oil Shock I expansion (1971Q1 ... 1973Q4)
4.3%	Oil Shock II expansion (1975Q2 ... 1980Q1)
4.5%	Volcker expansion (1980Q4 ... 1981Q3)
4.3%	Desert Storm expansion (1983Q1 ... 1990Q3)
3.6%	Sept 11 expansion (1991Q2 ... 2001Q1)
2.9%	Subprime Crisis expansion (2002Q1 ... 2007Q4)

The average was somewhat higher from Donald Trump's first quarter through the last quarter before COVID (2017Q1 through 2019Q4), but still fell below all of the above at 2.54 percent. Overall, the COVID-Crisis expansion averaged 2.3 percent.

The primary reason for the acceleration in the Trump administration was the shift in fiscal policy. Under Obama and even including the immediate postrecession years when the American Recovery and Reinvestment Act of 2009 was in play, government spending on average *lowered* real GDP growth by 0.13 percentage points. The equivalent figure under Trump (up to the last quarter before COVID, i.e., 2017Q1 through 2019Q4) was +0.28 percentage points. The net difference is 0.41 percentage points, almost exactly the same size as the difference in real GDP growth rates under each administration (0.37 percentage points). This misapplication of fiscal policy is a recurring theme and will be addressed at length in the Chapter 5.

Even taking this into account, however, growth was very slow after the subprime crisis. Table 4.13 shows the percentage point contribution of the various components of GDP to real GDP growth after each recession. In the Ike II-Cycle expansion, for example, real GDP growth was 5.63 percent.

TABLE 4.13 *Contributions to GDP growth by category*

	Growth	Percentage point contribution			
Period	GDP (%)	C	I	G	NetX
Ike I exp (1954Q3 ... 1957Q3)	4.08	2.58	1.20	0.19	0.12
Ike II exp (1958Q3 ... 1960Q2)	5.63	3.08	2.06	0.24	0.26
Vietnam exp (1961Q2 ... 1969Q4)	4.94	2.87	1.21	0.94	−0.08
Oil Shock I exp (1971Q1 ... 1973Q4)	5.12	2.88	2.19	0.20	0.28
Oil Shock II exp (1975Q2 ... 1980Q1)	4.33	2.34	1.66	0.40	−0.06
Volcker exp (1980Q4 ... 1981Q3)	4.42	1.37	3.63	0.25	−0.83
Desert Storm exp (1983Q1 ... 1990Q3)	4.29	2.53	1.14	0.76	−0.15
Sept 11 exp (1991Q2 ... 2001Q1)	3.63	2.55	1.26	0.23	−0.41
Subprime exp (2002Q1 ... 2007Q4)	2.91	1.96	0.73	0.37	−0.15
Average	4.37	2.46	1.68	0.40	−0.11
COVID exp (2009Q3 ... 2019Q4)	2.29%	1.53	0.94	−0.01	−0.17

Consumption spending was responsible for 3.08 of those percentage points, investment for 2.06, government spending 0.24, and net exports 0.26. Up through the Subprime Crisis-Cycle expansion and even including that anemic recovery, the average rate of growth of real GDP was 4.41 percent with contributions from consumption, investment, government spending, and net exports at 2.45, 1.74, 0.42, and −0.14. As indicated above, our COVID-Cycle expansion can be explained in part by the drastic change in the contribution of the public sector. For the first time over the entire period studied, government spending was a net drag. This may have been small, but it nevertheless stands in stark contrast to the earlier average of 0.42. Changing that cell alone would have raised real GDP growth to 2.72 (which does not account for the fact that consumption would also have increased given the net injection of income).

But that's clearly not the only story here. Indeed, the table suggests that another fundamental shift took place and one that actually outweighs the impact of that affecting fiscal policy: investment spending. After contributing an average of 1.68 percentage points to real GDP growth up through the Financial Crisis of 2007–2008, it drops to 0.94 (which is actually a slight improvement over the previous expansion). This is a decline of 0.74 percentage points, again without considering the effect this would have on consumption. Changing government and investment spending to their earlier averages raises real GDP growth in the COVID expansion to a much more robust (though still below pre-subprime cycle) 3.44 percent.

Why have these shifts occurred? The reduction in government spending resulted from a policy choice. In spite of the American Recovery and Reinvestment Act of 2009 which, while undersized, helped the US recover from the crisis far more quickly than Europe, austerity was the buzz word of the day. It was in this period that the famous Rogoff and Reinhart controversy occurred, wherein their paper – purportedly showing that high levels of government spending reduced GDP growth – was shown (by a graduate student in a nonmainstream economics department) to have serious data errors (Alexander 2013). Once these were corrected, the analysis supported just the opposite. But that didn't matter to the Republicans, who were intent on criticizing the Democratic administration. Even the Democrats, for that matter, were at least partly on the austerity bandwagon so that they could claim Clinton-like fiscal "responsibility."

And now that our economic recovery is gaining strength, Democrats and Republicans must come together and restore the fiscal responsibility that served us so well in the 1990s. We have to live within our means. We have to reduce our deficit, and we have to get back on a path that will allow us to pay down our debt. And we have to do it in a way that protects the recovery, protects the investments we need to grow, create jobs, and helps us win the future (President Barack Obama's speech at George Washington University, April 13, 2011).

It is worth noting that the 1990s Obama references were witness to a dramatic increase in private-sector debt.

4.10 COVID Cycle

Reversing that trend requires a political decision. However, as difficult as that seems in the current divisive and polarized environment, the issue with declining investment may be more deeply seated and intractable. As can be seen on Table 4.13, this was not new to the COVID expansion. While the post-Volcker and post-Desert Storm expansions showed some slowdown, the dramatic change comes in the 2000s. A number of authors have studied this troubling phenomenon, with one general conclusion being that the issue is not that firms believed that investment would not be profitable (see, for example, Fu, Huang, and Wang 2022, Furman 2015, Gutiérrez and Philippon 2016, Stewart and Atkinson 2013). Rather, firms are simply reacting differently. Empirical evidence suggests that this is because levels of competition have declined and there is tighter governance on the part of shareholders (Gutiérrez and Philippon 2016: 48). The first means that firms have less reason to innovate and expand, while the second leads to pressure for dividends and stock buy backs rather than capital expansion. Both, argue the authors, lead to short-termism.[8] These are structural and institutional problems that have evolved over decades and cannot be reversed easily.

All this said, while growth under Obama was tepid, unemployment did fall from 10% to just under 5%. However, labor force participation also fell, from 65.7% in January 2009 to 62.8% in January 2017. This continued and accelerated a trend that had started around January 2000, when the rate had been 67.3 percent. This might not seem terribly significant, but had the participation rate still been at its January 2009 level in January 2017, the unemployment rate would have been 8.9% instead of 4.7%. In fact, at January 2000 participation rates, January 2017 unemployment would have been a post-Depression (but pre-COVID) high of 11.1 percent. Labor force participation rebounded slightly under Trump before collapsing after the COVID recession.

About a third of the decline is simply due to demographics: baby boomers are retiring (Hornstein, Kudlyak, Meisenbacher, and Ramachandran 2023). But nearly as important have been those claiming disability, some of whom are those same baby boomers who have developed health problems as they aged (Dotsey, Fujita, and Rudanko 2017). That is not everyone, however, though it is difficult to differentiate. Some have argued that disability has become a place for those without competitive job skills (Joffe-Walt undated). With the reduction in social programs undertaken by Reagan and Clinton, they perhaps see this as their only choice. "Somewhere around 30 years ago, the economy started changing in some fundamental ways. There are now millions of Americans who do not have the skills or education to make it in this country (Joffe-Walt undated)."

---

[8] They also investigated the claim that investment data simply don't reflect firms' focus on intangibles like research and development. However, while they found this to be statistically significant, it was quantitatively small (Gutiérrez and Philippon 2016: 4). Furthermore, it shows a similar pattern of decline over this period.

There are concerns that one of the effects of COVID may be to even further increase the percentage of Americans on disability (Roberts, Ives-Rublee, and Khattar 2022).

The last factor most commonly cited in explaining the declining labor force participation rate is an increase in working-age individuals going to school (Bauer et al. 2019). With roughly the same magnitude of impact as those on disability (and 75 percent of that of retirees), some of this is a reflection of fewer teenagers working during the school year, but "the decline in teen labor force participation during the summer is even more dramatic" (Bauer et al. 2019).

the reasons for declining teen labor force participation seem to reflect increasing time spent in school during the summer as well as a decline in labor force participation while in school during the academic year. In both cases, the increased attention to academics may in fact be a better outcome for society than increased youth employment (Bauer et al. 2019).

4.10.2 Final Year of Expansion: 2019Q1 through 2019Q4

As explained above, real GDP growth was marginally higher under Trump as government spending became a consistent positive contributor. Unemployment fell to 3.6% by 2019Q4 (albeit at a participation rate of 63.3%), inflation was moderate by historical standards, and the expansion had become the longest in history. The PMI had slipped below 50, however, and investment spending had declined for the first time since 2017Q1, but in general there seemed to be no reason to expect a downturn.

4.10.3 Recession: 2020Q1 through 2020Q2

The reasons for this recession are clear enough. A global pandemic drove US unemployment to 14.8% in April 2020 and led to a contraction in real inflation-adjusted GDP of 31.2% (annualized). Investment collapsed, along with consumption. Only government spending and net exports contributed positively to GDP.

4.10.4 Further Observations

Once again, one of the lessons of the cycle regards the strength and utility of fiscal policy. The Obama administration's timid response – even with an $800-billion recovery package – contributed to the recovery being the weakest since WWII. That continued under President Trump, but to a lesser extent given his willingness to run deficits. This will be a key consideration in the Chapter 5. Also important in this cycle was the tremendous decline in the labor force participation rate. It has recovered somewhat since a deep dip after COVID, but has yet to return to even immediate pre-COVID levels, let alone

4.11 Conclusions

those experienced before the Financial Crisis of 2007–2008. While some of this may simply be a result of demographics, at least a portion – that related to disability – is actually a function of a broken system. This, too, is something that will be addressed in the Chapter 5.

4.11 CONCLUSIONS

The above offers statistical and anecdotal evidence in support of the Keynes' view of the business cycle. This is not to say that shocks and policy have no effect, but their impact is supplementary. *There is simply no way to explain the US economy since 1954 without reference to endogenous fluctuations in investment, particularly as related to systematic changes in the relationship between expected and realized profits.* This is important for policy because it argues that the economy does not tend toward full employment, something suggested by even left-leaning Mainstream economists. Recessions occur without the existence of government intervention or other exogenous forces. Chapter 5 will outline a policy designed to not only create a cushion against downturns (and one that is much more effective than current automatic stabilizers), but to also offer solutions for emerging crises like elder care and the climate and to give the disillusioned in the labor force a reason for hope.

5

Policy and Conclusions

Chapter 4 recounted the events associated with the ten business cycles that occurred in the United States from 1954 to 2020. Over that period, millions became unemployed for reasons that had nothing to do with their personal choices, values, or qualifications, but because (a) downturns are built into our system, (b) we have experienced a secular decline in economic growth, and (c) current orthodox economic scholarship falls well short of understanding, let alone addressing, this. In contrast, Institutionalist and Post Keynesian inspired work gets to the root of the problem, identifies the manner in which our economy generates cyclical and longer-term job losses, and offers a solution. Their position is that the unemployment that results from a recession serves no useful purpose and is not a side effect of some otherwise welcome process. We should be acting decisively to prevent it.

This is precisely what a Job Guarantee – a program whereby the government stands ready to employ anyone willing to work but unable to find a job – would do. It is simple, reasonable, and well within our means – indeed, it is shockingly affordable. It offers protection from both cyclical and longer-term and chronic joblessness. In addition, the program could focus on addressing many of the social problems we face today. A Job Guarantee, while not promising a utopian paradise, would unquestionably create a world far more civilized, prosperous, and pleasant than the one in which we live today.

Before going into the details of the manner in which a Job Guarantee would operate, consider for a moment the illogic of our current system. Why does increasing our ability to produce goods and services lead to both cyclical and long-term reductions in the public's ability to actually acquire those goods

I owe a great debt to Pavlina Tcherneva and L. Randall Wray, who kindly reviewed this chapter for me (particularly with reference to the Job Guarantee and Modern Monetary Theory). Any remaining errors are, of course, my responsibility.

5 Policy and Conclusions

and services? This is what was argued in Chapter 2, albeit more formally. Physical investment spending adds to productive capacity. However, as firms reach targets for the latter, they reduce investment. This raises unemployment, making some of that new capacity redundant. We enhance our ability to produce goods and services and then – ironically – reduce households' ability to purchase a share of it. That's the cyclical half of the problem.

Over the longer term, every laborsaving innovation makes the maintenance of high levels of employment more difficult (Murray 2013). While some technological advances may actually enhance job creation by creating new demands and markets, that is not true of self-checkout lanes at grocery stores and ordering screens at fast food restaurants. And yet we should be celebrating laborsaving technology as, in an ideal world, these would give us more leisure time. This has certainly been the effect within the economy of the household where dishwashers, washing machines and dryers, vacuums, lawnmowers, leaf blowers, etc. have given families much more room to pursue individual interests or to socialize. But in the household, places at the dinner table are not restricted to those who performed some given quantity of labor services. Hence, a reduction in the total volume necessary for the maintenance of the household does not create the dilemma that it does in the market system. That's the long-term half of the problem: increases in labor productivity – despite their theoretical ability to raise our standards of living – increase job insecurity (recall the Vatter and Walker argument under secular stagnation in Chapter 3).

Now imagine that those who are laid off for any reason – a cyclical downturn, a new invention, or mandated social isolation from a pandemic – could, after some period of searching for new employment in the private sector, go to a local government office and be placed in a job. Unemployment rates would fall to zero save for those still in the search process. Later, I will show in detail how incredibly inexpensive such a program would be; first, however, consider the cost of the American Recovery and Reinvestment Act of 2009. The final price tag was in the range of $831 billion (for further discussion, see Tcherneva 2009). The goal was to bring down unemployment, which was 8.3 percent in the month the bill became law (February 2009). Unemployment would actually continue to rise through October 2009, when it hit 10 percent, and it did not return to its prerecession level of 4.7 percent until November 2016 – seven years and nine months since the beginning of the program.

What if a Job Guarantee had already been in place? In February 2009, that 8.3 percent represented 12.898 million people. If each had been paid $25/hour not just for that month, but for an entire year – something that would almost surely not have been necessary given the strong stimulative effect the program would have had on the private sector – the total cost would have been[1]:

---

[1] Other obvious and necessary costs will be added later, but the total bill will remain small.

$25/\text{hr} \times 40 \text{ hours} \times 52 \text{ weeks} \times 12.898 \text{ million unemployed}$
$= \$670.696 \text{ billion}$

Not only is this less than the $831 billion for the American Reinvestment and Recovery Act, but the expenditure is not made in the hope that we might get unemployment back to the prerecession level of 4.7 percent in another seven years and nine months, *but to drop it to near zero almost immediately*. A Job Guarantee is a much more efficient means of lowering unemployment, and there are many other benefits as well.

5.1 STRUCTURE OF A JOB GUARANTEE PROGRAM

A national Job Guarantee would be designed as follows[2]:

- *All voluntary applicants accepted*: While the private sector selects only those whose qualifications meet firms' profit-oriented requirements, a Job Guarantee strives instead to create employment that matches workers' existing skills.
- *Job training*: In the event that those skills are particularly ill-suited to any available work (under either the Job Guarantee or in the private sector), training will be available and could even be provided by other Job Guarantee employees.
- *Living wage*: Wages would not be set by the market, but based on living wage calculations like those maintained at the MIT Living Wage site (https://livingwage.mit.edu/). These could vary by locale. For example, at the time of this writing (February 2023), the living wage for Cook County, Illinois, is $20/hour; it is just under $16/hour in Knox County, Tennessee; and just over $15/hour in Gilmer County, West Virginia. These are, incidentally, hardly generous, as will be shown below.
- *Child care*: The above wages would have to be significantly higher for those requiring child care. So as to avoid the necessity of a multitier wage structure designed to take this into account, free child care would be available to all Job Guarantee workers. This, like job training, could be provided by other Job Guarantee employees.
- *Health care*: Just as with child care, omission of this from the benefits could create serious disparities in terms of how well the wage actually supported the individual worker. The health care provided would not represent actual medical services, but federal government insurance along the lines of Medicare or the programs already available to retired military (i.e., Tricare). Given the massive inefficiency of our current system, this would actually represent a tremendous savings (see below).

---

[2] For a more comprehensive outline, see especially Tcherneva 2018.

- *Local control and administration*: While some programs would necessarily be designed and implemented at the national level, it is assumed that for the most part local communities know best their wants and needs. Those wants and needs could be jointly determined by government, nonprofit, and even private-sector entities.
- *Federally funded*: For reasons that will become clear later in this chapter, such a program would need to be federally funded. For one, state and local revenues are going to vary cyclically, while Job Guarantee-related spending would need to vary counter-cyclically. In addition, although this mismatch is also nominally true at the federal level, the fact that the federal government does not face a budget constraint makes this a moot point. State and local dollars come from taxes and fees; federal dollars come from a keyboard. Again, this is explained in detail later in the chapter.

5.2 BENEFITS OF A JOB GUARANTEE PROGRAM

Such a program would boast many benefits, both economic and social. Consider for example:

- *Very low unemployment rates*: This may seem rather obvious, but it's significant. As suggested in the above example of how the Job Guarantee would have operated after the Financial Crisis, the economy will operate with rates closer to 1 percent, it will reach those levels very quickly, and it will actually require less government spending than is true under current policies.
- *More efficient use of government spending*: Again as already demonstrated in the Job Guarantee vs American Recovery and Reinvestment Act example above, a Job Guarantee is much more efficient. At present, our primary method of stimulating the economy is to try to increase demand (via tax cuts, government spending, interest rate cuts, and the like) sufficiently to induce the private sector to rehire unemployed workers. Labor, however, is a cost to the private sector, so it is something to be minimized. Given that, what size increase in demand would realistically be necessary to induce a grocery store to rehire those made redundant by new self-checkout lanes? What is far more likely is that any consequent government stimulus money would generate very few jobs and simply end up in firms' profits (Tcherneva 2014). There's nothing wrong with firms earning profits, of course, but if the goal of the policy is to increase employment then it is missing its target. If the government hopes to see the unemployed employed, then why not simply employ them? It is neither fair nor realistic to expect the private sector to absorb the extra workers – that's the government's job.
- *Experienced employees*: The numbers involved in the Job Guarantee would fluctuate counter-cyclically, with more joining during downturns and then going back to the private sector once an expansion is underway. One of the

problems returning workers currently face is the fact that their job skills will have deteriorated during their period of unemployment and they become less employable (Tcherneva 2020). This would no longer be true as those reentrants will have been continuously working under the Job Guarantee.

- *Skilled employees*: Furthermore, as workers reenter the private sector, those whose skills had been less useful will now have been retrained and therefore more productive and competitive.
- *Private-sector stimulus*: Job Guarantee wages will stimulate private-sector employment and profits, particularly because those participating are likely to spend a high percentage of their income. Generally speaking, the wealthiest 20% of households in the US spend roughly 60% of their income (BLS 2023). The other 80% spend nearly 100%. Unemployment tends to be concentrated among those in that lower end. This not only means that their high rates of spending will be a boon for business, but not every unemployed person need take Job Guarantee employment since the private sector will need them to meet the increased demand.
- *Automatic*: As a result of the Financial Crisis of 2007–2008, unemployment soared from roughly seven million in 2007 to eleven million by the end of 2008 and fifteen million by close of 2009. While, as discussed in Chapter 3, there are some automatic stabilizers built into the system, these obviously fell far short of what was needed. This meant that legislation was required. Because this necessitates researching the magnitude of the problem (which, in the event, seriously underestimated the size of the downturn), writing the bill, debating the bill, voting on the bill, putting – if passed – the bill's programs into action, etc., there can be a significant lag between the emergence of the crisis and any real efforts to address it. A Job Guarantee, on the other hand, stays permanently in place and automatically starts hiring those affected by the downturn in question. Nor does the magnitude of the crisis need to be estimated. The unemployed self-identify and we immediately know without error how much is needed (assuming, of course, sufficient outreach to make those eligible aware of the relevant programs).
- *Less prone to abuse*: The fact that it is automatic also makes it less prone to abuse. With the American Recovery and Reinvestment Act of 2009, there was a huge incentive for governors and other state officials to game the system in order to get as large a share as possible from the federal stimulus. While no system is completely immune to such shenanigans, the formulaic nature of the Job Guarantee (the funds you receive equal your number of unemployed times the wage they are to be paid) makes this more difficult. Money will actually go to where it is needed rather than where political pressures redirect it.
- *Less political partisanship*: No Republican voted for the American Recovery and Reinvestment Act of 2009, despite the fact that it was plain that the country was experiencing the most serious economic challenge since the Depression (Calmes 2009). While the stated reasons were related to the size

of the package and the Republicans preference for tax cuts over spending, there can be little question that a great deal of the resistance was due to the fact that President Obama was a Democrat. Although initial creation of a Job Guarantee is likely to be marked by partisan bickering, once in place it is automatic and no longer subject to hostage taking by the party out of the White House.

- *Local tax revenue*: State and local coffers would benefit directly not only from the spending by Job Guarantee employees, but also those in the private sector whose jobs resulted from the former's spending. This would be an especially welcome boost when they might otherwise be facing shortfalls.[3]
- *Improved mental and physical health*: There is a great deal of evidence that job loss leads to deteriorations in mental and physical health.[4] This was among the concerns of health care professionals in the face of the economic slowdowns created by COVID:

> The mental health impacts of today's job losses are likely to be significant, given a large body of research showing that unemployment is linked to anxiety, depression and loss of life satisfaction, among other negative outcomes. Similarly, underemployment and job instability – two additional results of the coronavirus pandemic – create distress for those who aren't counted in the unemployment numbers (Pappas 2020).

Pappas goes on to explain, "Research on unemployment shows that losing one's job is detrimental to mental health – and often physical health – even without serious financial strain." A Job Guarantee would seriously reduce the mental and physical cost to those whose unemployment results from the structure of our current system.

- *Inoculation against the spread of job loss*: Tcherneva (2017) makes a powerful case for understanding job loss as a disease. She writes (even before COVID put this in the forefront of our minds!):

> Fourth, and perhaps most striking, is the discernable geographic pattern of the evolution in unemployment over time. A region affected by mass layoffs quickly sees its unemployment problem spread to an ever-increasing area. The radius of the affected area grows in recessions. Like the ripple effect of a pebble tossed in a lake, mass layoffs in a distressed community produce higher unemployment rates in the surrounding areas.
>
> ....
> This pattern suggests that unemployment behaves much more like a virus or an infectious disease than a random shock event. Not only does it propagate in a specific geographic pattern, but it also inflicts severe consequences on individuals and communities. (Tcherneva 2017: 5–6).

---

[3] Recall from above that the funding for the Job Guarantee would come from the federal government.
[4] See, for example, Farré, Fasani, and Mueller 2018; Milner, Page, and LaMontagne 2014; and Strandh, Winefield, Nilsson, and Hammarström 2014, among very many. Tcherneva 2017 also includes a useful summary.

The implication here is that stopping the initial outbreak is key to preventing the spread. Conventional economic policy – other than automatic stabilizers, which are clearly insufficient to prevent large fluctuations in employment – suffer from a number of lags. By the time policy is put into effect, the disease has spread. A Job Guarantee, on the other hand, acts as an immediate inoculation in precisely the areas where the problems are emerging.

- *Addressing social inequities*: A Job Guarantee can help to address inequities that exist elsewhere in the economy. For one, no one is turned away because of their race, ethnicity, gender, sexual orientation, etc. If an individual is denied opportunity in the private sector, they can get it in the public sector. Furthermore, the experience and training they receive may allow them to break down erstwhile barriers in business. At the very least, it would provide them with a path out of poverty – and it is no secret that poverty is concentrated among particular social groups for historical and cultural reasons.
- *No minimum wage law*: With the Job Guarantee jobs available, private-sector firms no longer need to be forced to pay a minimum wage. They may pay whatever they like, along with any benefits package, and if workers would prefer their employment, then so be it.

5.3 JOBS CREATED UNDER A JOB GUARANTEE PROGRAM

First and foremost, they should not be profitable. That's the private-sector's domain. If supplying some good or service costs less than the revenue from selling it, then this is an incentive to do so. No government agency or charitable foundation needs to set up a business selling sporting goods or pet supplies, as the private sector already does a satisfactory job of pursuing these profitable undertakings. The role of the government should be to supply those things that are (a) socially beneficial but (b) unprofitable or of insufficient profit to cause them to be supplied in a socially desirable quantity. While we immediately face a problem in that people may disagree regarding what they view as socially beneficial, there are candidates that seem fairly neutral. National defense, for example, is not profitable. The army does not fund itself by going door-to-door to convince private citizens to sign up for one of their protection services. Instead, they are funded by the government. Education is already provided by the private sector, but in quantities that most would say are insufficient if we are to be a healthy democracy with a thriving economy. We all benefit from the fact that those otherwise unable to afford a basic education are nevertheless provided one. Of course, each of those is already provided by the government and would therefore not be one of the activities pursued by those employed by the Job Guarantee (though some connections could be imagined, like Job Guarantee employees running after-school programs). However, the basic concept is the same: if something is unprofitable but nevertheless deemed to be socially beneficial (or the private sector generates an insufficient supply), then it is fair game for a Job Guarantee.

5.3 Jobs Created under a Job Guarantee Program

There are many activities that would fall under these categories. Consider the following candidates:

- *Environmental support*[5]: Generally speaking, environmental support is not profitable. It is therefore either not undertaken by the private sector or is not addressed sufficiently. Among the Job Guarantee jobs that might be created to address these problems are:

    … soil erosion, flood control, environmental surveys, species monitoring, park maintenance and renewal, removal of invasive species, sustainable agriculture practices to address the "food desert" problems in the United States, support for local fisheries, community supported agriculture (CSA) farms, community and rooftop gardens, tree planting, fire and other disaster prevention measures, weatherization of homes, and composting (Tchnerva 2018: 18).

    Many of these do not require highly specialized skills and could therefore be undertaken quite quickly. For those that do, training would be available.

- *Community support*: Anyone who has driven through poverty-stricken areas of cities, towns, and countryside has observed the bleak and sometimes downright dangerous conditions that exist. Those seeking employment but not finding it in the private sector could become involved with:

    … cleanup of vacant properties, reclamation of materials, restoration of public spaces, and other small infrastructure investments; establishment of school gardens, urban farms, coworking spaces, solar arrays, tool lending libraries, classes and programs, and community theaters; construction of playgrounds; restoration of historical sites; organization of carpooling programs, as well as recycling, reuse, and water-collection initiatives, food waste programs, and oral histories projects. (Tchnerva 2018: 18–9)

    Again, few of these would generate any monetary profit, and so without public sector involvement they would not get done; but, under a Job Guarantee, local labor that might otherwise be idle will instead be helping to revitalize their own communities. The benefits would be tangible and many, including to the private sector.

- *Social support*: Homo sapiens are social animals. Generally speaking, however, social support is not profitable. It is therefore either not undertaken by the private sector or is not addressed in sufficient quantity. Among the Job Guarantee jobs that might be created to address these problems are:

    … organizing afterschool activities or adult skill classes in schools or local libraries; facilitating extended-day programs for school children; shadowing teachers, coaches, hospice workers and librarians to learn new skills and assist them in their duties; organizing nutrition surveys in schools; and coordinating health awareness programs for young mothers.

---

[5] The following three categories are, while renamed, adopted directly from Tcherneva 2018 (17–19).

Other examples include organizing urban campuses, co-ops, classes and training, and apprenticeships in sustainable agriculture, and all of the above-mentioned community care jobs, which could produce a new generation of urban teachers, artists and artisans, makers, and inventors. (Tcherneva 2018: 19)

Again, many of these do not require highly specialized skills and could therefore be undertaken quite quickly.

- *Elder care*: The U.S. is facing an eldercare crisis. Not only are we already seriously understaffed, but the "percentage of people over the age of 85 – the group that most needs care – is predicted to double to 14 million by 2040" (Moe 2022). Worse still, the U.S. was already near the bottom of many categories of care even before the mass exodus of eldercare workers that occurred after COVID (Seegert 2017). The social benefit of providing care to our elderly seems clear, but couldn't the private sector provide this? In point of fact, about 70 percent of all nursing homes are, indeed, for-profit (Nguyen 2021). And yet, this must not be a particularly profitable undertaking, for most of the funding actually comes from the government: "It's very hard for a facility to survive completely on private-pay revenues," Konetzka said. "The vast majority of them depend on Medicaid and Medicare revenues. Medicare revenues come through the post-acute short-stay residents, and Medicaid revenues from the majority of long-stay residents" (Nguyen 2021).

  In other words, nursing homes could not stay in business if they were dependent on private-sector spending. Worse still, "'Medicaid doesn't kick in until basically you've impoverished yourself,' Konetzka said" (Nguyen 2021). The provision of elder care would be an excellent use of the labor not employed by the private sector.

- *Climate change*: There is no more pressing issue facing the planet than the one about which there is near unanimity among scientists: climate change (NASA 2020). Among the many consequences will be hotter temperatures, more severe storms, increased drought, warming and rising oceans, loss of species, insufficient food supplies, increased health risks, and poverty and displacement (UN undated). The next century will almost certainly be marked by the causes and effects of warming global temperatures. Fortunately, we are not short of potential solutions (Harvey 2020a: 158). Unfortunately, next to none of them are profitable and so there is no reason to expect the private sector to undertake them. This is an ideal, indeed critical, place for the Job Guarantee to play a role. Job Guarantee jobs, because they are concerned with social benefit and not the corporate bottom line, can focus on tasks that will (a) help the environment absorb more carbon and (b) accelerate the shift from carbon-based fuels. Nor is it necessary to continue the debate regarding whether or not a Green New Deal would lower employment (Brown and Ahmadi 2019). Such arguments are moot when we are no longer depending on the private sector to hire those made redundant by either cyclical or structural issues.

- *Degrowth*: Closely related to the previous section is the general principle of creating jobs that do not contribute even more to greenhouse gas emissions. This means moving away from our current economic paradigm where growth is encouraged for growth's sake. Under capitalism, goods and services must be produced and reproduced and reproduced and reproduced for profits to be generated and employment maintained. Were everyone to suddenly become content with their cell phone, for example, this would be a terrible blow to that industry. At the same time, however, it would be a boon for the environment and possibly even children's welfare (Byrne and Hudson-Edwards 2018 and Kara 2018). Degrowth is an economic paradigm by which we would attempt to decouple economic prosperity from economic growth and is as much a philosophical shift as a physical one. Moving to degrowth "requires rethinking our understanding of prosperity. Essentially, it requires a move away from high-resource-consuming and high-greenhouse-gas-emitting lifestyles, to decarbonized, low-materials lifestyles (Millstone 2018)."

A Job Guarantee can contribute to this by prioritizing employments that encourage a movement toward such an economy (Hickel 2019).

What would happen if we ran out of unprofitable social problems to address? Then perhaps we can revert to the sort of lifestyle enjoyed by humans throughout most of our history, wherein we spent the vast majority of our time "on other purposeful activities such as making music, exploring, decorating their bodies, and socializing" (Stillman 2020). Of course, we may need to replace these with more modern activities such as reading, fishing, playing games, and wine tasting, but in any event, this would hardly be a disaster!

5.4 POTENTIAL CRITICISMS OF A JOB GUARANTEE PROGRAM

Some may argue that Job Guarantee jobs pay too well. After all, the living wage is well above current minimum wages, and it promises benefits such as health and child care. How is the private sector to compete with this? The quick answer is that, if they cannot, then perhaps they should not be in business in the first place. A living wage is not particularly generous and expecting someone to survive on less – especially in an economy with the technology and resources to provide a standard of living above anything heretofore possible – is inhumane, unjust, illogical, and unnecessary.

As evidence of this, consider the wage suggested by the MIT Living Wage Calculator for my current home, Fort Worth, Texas. Fort Worth is in Tarrant County, the 2023 living wage for which is listed at $31,488/year (after taxes, for a single adult with no children). This includes $3,926 for food. That translates to $10.76 per day, or $3.59 a meal. Meanwhile, livingcost.com lists the price of a fast-food meal as $8.49 and the expected annual cost of food for a single individual as $7,056.[6] The living wage allowance is only 56 percent of this.

The living wage allocation for housing in Tarrant County is $11,568 per year, or $964/month. According to Rent.com, "The average rent for apartments in Fort Worth, TX, is between $1,247 and $1,552 in 2023. For a studio apartment in Fort Worth, TX, the average rent is $1,306. When it comes to 1-bedroom apartments, the average rent in Fort Worth, TX, is $1,247. For a 2-bedroom apartment, the average rent is $1,552."

That leaves our living wage recipient with a monthly housing deficit of $1,247 − $964 = $283. They may well be able to find a cheaper place, but that then entails other costs like higher utilities due to inferior insulation and perhaps an undesirable neighborhood. The amount set aside for transportation is $5,477, or $456/month. As Fort Worth lacks effective public transportation, this almost certainly means buying a vehicle, maintaining it, purchasing fuel, and being insured. The average price of a used car in Texas is $35,061 (Blackley 2023). As current (February 2023) forty-eight-month used car interest rates are 6.88 percent (Betterton 2023), this yields a monthly payment of around $840 – already well in excess of the allowance. Annual car insurance is going to be around $1,400,[7] while annual fuel and maintenance costs should come in around $1,600 and $1,400 (AAA Staff 2021). Those same numbers translate to $116, $133, and $116 on a monthly basis, which sums to $365. Even if our representative individual isn't still paying for the used vehicle and even if their repair costs don't exceed the average (which they almost certainly will give that the maintenance numbers were for new, not used, cars), that leaves a $91/month cushion. Perhaps that can be put toward the $283 monthly housing deficit!

Long story short, a living wage is hardly a luxury wage. And, to repeat the point from above, if paying someone a living wage means that a private sector firm can no longer compete for that worker, one has to wonder whether or not such a firm should have existed in the first place. So, yes, some firms may suddenly find themselves unable to hire workers at the old wage. Net, however, society is better off.

Another potential criticism is that it may cause inflation. First and foremost, one must have a proper understanding of inflation. This is discussed at length in Chapter 3, but by way of summary, (1) it must always be viewed sectorally, and (2) rising prices can actually play a positive role. Whether or not a policy response is necessary must be determined on a case-by-case basis. Given that, will a Job Guarantee cause inflation? There is no question that it would lead to a once-and-for-all increase in prices as wages for the poorest workers rise. That will make goods and services more expensive in industries where they were concentrated, which may in turn initiate shifts in consumption patterns away

---

[6] Prices undated but checked on February 24, 2023.
[7] www.thezebra.com/auto-insurance/texas-car-insurance/fort-worth-tx-car-insurance.

5.4 Potential Criticisms of a Job Guarantee Program

from such sectors and raise costs in others. Because "Food preparation and serving related occupations" employ just over half of all those working at or below the minimum wage, it is likely that restaurants will be one of the sectors most affected (BLS 2021). People might not be able to afford to eat out as often.

Whether or not this is a strike against the Job Guarantee, however, is a very different question. A minimum-wage employee in Texas earns $7.25/hour (as of February 2023). That yields an annual gross (at forty hours per week for fifty-two weeks) of $15,080 – *less than half of the living wage*. It has already been demonstrated that a living wage is hardly generous. Refusing to support policies that would raise the standard of living of restaurant and other low-wage workers to even the meager level provided by a living wage is not an economic problem, it is a moral one. No one should be put in the position of struggling to survive just so the rest of us can go out for fajitas more often.

What about thereafter? Recall first that inflation must always be understood as sectoral. It is never just a single number, and until the specific source and cause are identified, it is impossible to offer any policy recommendations. Chapter 3 described six distinct varieties:

- Demand-pull inflation: Prices are bid up because demand is outstripping producers' ability to supply;
- Demand-pull inflation/labor market: Special case of the demand-pull inflation phenomenon is when the bottlenecks make themselves felt in the labor market;
- Cost-push inflation/market power: Rising costs (especially as profits) due to firms' exercise of market power;
- Cost-push inflation/supply shock: Rising costs due to a noneconomic phenomenon (e.g., war, weather event, pandemic, natural disaster);
- Speculation: Rising prices due to a good or service being the direct target of speculative demand or because the value of an asset derivative of that good or service is being bid up;
- Currency depreciation: The increase in the price of imports due to a loss in the value of domestic currency.

Of these, it is the first two to which detractors point when they say that a Job Guarantee is inflationary. But this ignores a critical fact: the fiscal impact of the Job Guarantee automatically shrinks as we approach full employment. It does not operate such that demand continually rises regardless of our position on the production possibilities frontier. Hence, while there may be adjustments between markets as, say, the demand for carpenters rises versus that for plumbers, there is no systemic tendency to drive aggregate demand beyond the capacity to supply. Furthermore, in the event of cost-push/supply shock inflation, Job Guarantee workers can be employed in sectors directly addressing the bottlenecks (in the manufacture of medical alcohol during COVID, for example). With respect to the last three sources, none would be in any way directly affected by a Job Guarantee (nor have even opponents suggested this).

Another criticism leveled at the Job Guarantee is that it is coercive in that it forces recipients to work. First off, and as suggested earlier, there is no reason why it should not be voluntary. This would not be problematic because, in point of fact, people want to contribute. We are social animals, and it is in our nature to desire to be perceived as an upstanding member of the tribe (Deranty 2019). What is not in our nature is that such contributions be limited to those earning profit for the owners of capital. Because a Job Guarantee offers applicants the opportunity to use (and/or develop) their talents as they see fit, it would not be necessary to make it compulsory.

Others have argued that a universal basic income policy would be a superior alternative. But a number of objections can be raised:

- A universal basic income does not magically free society from undertaking labor. Those choosing to draw their income solely from such a source would be enjoying the goods and services produced by others.[8]
- While a universal basic income addresses some of the same problems as the Job Guarantee, it leaves totally untouched the ability to use the program to address key social problems. It has been suggested that perhaps people can volunteer to help with various projects. This seems as realistic as President Bush's Thousand Points of Light, wherein it was expected that private charity would spontaneously reach out to help all those in need. Such an approach leaves us *hoping* that enough people volunteer to care for the elderly, to work to address climate change, to help with after-school programs, and so on. The social problems we face are serious and many and realistic and effective solutions will require organization at the national, state, and local level. It cannot be left to chance.

5.5 COST OF A JOB GUARANTEE PROGRAM

Going into more detail on the cost of a Job Guarantee, let us assume a system based on the living wage for 2022, which was $17.46 (Vaghul, Fenelon, and Glasmeier 2022). Given what has already been said regarding the less-than-generous nature of these calculations, let us set the Job Guarantee wage at $20/hour.[9] This yields an annual income of $41,600. That covers just wages, but the program outlined above also included health care and child care. With respect to the former, Galvani and Fitzpatrick estimate that a single-payer health care system in the U.S. in 2020 would have cost $3 trillion (Galvani and Fitzpatrick 2020). With a population of 329.5 million that same

---

[8] One possible exception is parents with children, particularly preschoolers. No one should be forced to work outside the home in order to pay for child (or elder) care, when they could be doing it themselves. In many respects, this is merely a redefinition of "work," one that is more equitable and inclusive.

[9] For simplicity, this example will assume a single wage for the entire country. Regional adjustments may be necessary.

5.5 Cost of a Job Guarantee Program

year, that averages to $9,105/person. To be conservative, let us set the cost of health care for Job Guarantee participants at $10,000. Note that this is likely a substantial overestimate, as the average per capita cost in OECD countries similar to the US – nations with superior life expectancy and infant mortality numbers – is $6,651 (2022; Wager et al. 2024). Furthermore, even at $10,000/person, this represents a net savings over the current number ($12,555 in 2022; Wager et al. 2024). Despite this, for purposes of argument, it will continue to be counted as a "cost."

Regarding child care, Child Care Aware of America suggested that the 2020 cost was around $10,174/child (Child Care Aware of America 2021). To determine the number that would need to be covered, consider first the fact that Isaacs and Lovell estimate that there were 4.8 million children with an unemployed parent in December 2007 (Isaacs and Lovell 2010). Unemployment that same month was 7.645 million, suggesting 0.63 children per unemployed individual. This would add 0.63 × $10,174 = $6,409.62 to the cost of employing someone under the Job Guarantee, which I will round to $6,500.

All those add to the following in terms of the costs of a Job Guarantee (plus another 10 percent to each for administrative costs):

wage = $41,600
health care = $10,000
child care = $6,500
admin costs = $5,810
TOTAL = $63,910

These are likely overestimates not only for the reasons suggested above, but also because (a) the private sector would respond to the Job Guarantee employees' spending and reabsorb some of those laid off and (b) none of the savings from the reduced use of unemployment and income support programs is factored in.

Even at these totals, however, the cost is remarkably low – especially as this is to reduce unemployment to near zero and offer all the benefits reviewed above. Take the 2000s through 2020 as an example. This period includes two of the worst downturns since World War II and expansions that were only moderately strong, something that should stack the deck against the Job Guarantee. But, structured as explained above, a Job Guarantee in place from 2000 to 2020 would have cost on average the equivalent of 3.2% of the actual government spending for that period, ranging from 4.89% in 2009Q4 to 1.81% in 2019Q3 and 2019Q4.[10] To offer a comparison to other budget items, defense spending is around 10% of the annual budget, while Social Security is about 20%. In short, for (at worst) 1/3 the cost of defense or 1/6 the cost of Social Security, we could have an economy that would be the envy of the world. Unemployment would drop to near zero, health and child care

---

[10] This estimation set the 2020Q4 wages as shown above and then adjusted them for inflation going back to 2000Q1.

would become more widely available, workers would be more experienced and better trained, the private sector would receive a large boost in sales, state and local tax coffers would benefit, people would enjoy improved mental and physical health, social inequities could be addressed, and we might actually be able to begin seriously tackling climate change – all through a process that is more effectively insulated from political partisanship and abuse than our current system.[11]

5.6 HOW THE FEDERAL GOVERNMENT FUNDS A JOB GUARANTEE

Still, adding another 3.2 percent (at worst) to government spending might be of concern to some. It should not be, but unfortunately the manner in which the federal government's budget really operates is widely misunderstood (including among economists and policymakers). Explaining how a Job Guarantee would be financed requires clearing up many misconceptions.[12]

5.6.1 Myth #1: The U.S. Government Can Be Forced to Default on Its Debt

It is widely believed that after the U.S. reaches a certain level of total national debt, it will find itself unable to meet its obligations to borrowers. But because our debt is in a currency that we also issue, forced default is impossible (Wray 1998 and 2023). This is not a theoretical issue, it is a legal one and it has been addressed many times by policymakers, scholars, and market analysts:

- "In the case of governments boasting monetary sovereignty and debt denominated in its own currency, like the United States (but also Japan and the UK), it is technically impossible to fall into debt default." Erwan Mahe, European asset allocation and options strategies adviser (Mahe 2011).
- "As the sole manufacturer of dollars, whose debt is denominated in dollars, the U.S. government can never become insolvent, that is, unable to pay its bills. In this sense, the government is not dependent on credit markets to remain operational." Federal Reserve Bank of St. Louis (Fawley and Juvenal 2011).
- "The United States can pay any debt it has because we can always print money to do that. So there is zero probability of default." Alan Greenspan 1987–2006 (Allen 2011).

---

[11] See Wray et al. 2018 for an extensive discussion of the Job Guarantee.
[12] For the excellent explanations of how government budgeting truly works, see Kelton (2020) and Wray (2023).

- "Central banks can issue currency, a non-interest-bearing claim on the government, effectively without limit." Alan Greenspan, Chair of the Federal Reserve 1987–2006 (Greenspan 1997).
- "A sovereign government can always make payments as they come due by crediting bank accounts – something recognized by Chairman Ben Bernanke when he said the Fed spends by marking up the size of the reserve accounts of banks." L. Randall Wray, Professor of Economics at the University of Missouri-Kansas City and a Senior Scholar at the Levy Economics Institute (Wray 2011).
- "In the case of United States, default is absolutely impossible. All U.S. government debt is denominated in U.S. dollar assets." Peter Zeihan, Vice President of Analysis for STRATFOR (STRATFOR 2011).
- "Reagan proved that deficits don't matter." Dick Cheney, Vice President of the United States 2001–2009 (Nichols 2013).
- "The necessity for a government to tax in order to maintain both its independence and its solvency is true for state and local governments, but it is not true for a national government." Beardsley Ruml, Chair Federal Reserve Bank of New York 1937–1947 (Ruml 1946: 35).

This is not to say that there are no consequences to federal government deficit spending and accumulated debt; it is to say, however, that default risk is absolutely, positively not one of them.

5.6.2 Myth #2: Federal Government Budget Surpluses Help the Private Sector

For each deficit, there must be a corresponding surplus. This is an inescapable accounting identity. Every nation on earth cannot have a trade deficit, for example, as you have to have a deficit with respect to some other nation. Hence, the sum total of all deficits and surpluses on the planet must be zero. And yet, as easy as that is to understand, the corollary with respect to government budgeting is almost completely missed: The federal government's budget deficit must, by definition, be the nongovernment sector's budget surplus. Whenever the government spends more than it taxes, the nongovernment sector experiences an influx of income; and when the government taxes more than it spends, the nongovernment sector's income is reduced by the size of the government's surplus. Many politicians over time have promised to reduce the government's deficit. Imagine how well this would go over with voters if it were framed in terms of its accounting equivalent: a reduction of the nongovernment sector's income.

It is worth considering this in a bit more detail. We could, for example, divide the world into three sectors: the domestic private, the domestic public, and the foreign (i.e., non-U.S.). Each one spends and earns income as shown in Table 5.1. The US private sector earns income and spends; the US public sector's budget is credited via tax revenues and debited when the government spends; and the foreign sector earns income from US imports and spends by the amount of US exports. It is not necessary that the total value of each income source be equal to that row's spending type (e.g., US imports need not be equal to US exports); but – as these are the only three sectors that exist in our example – the balances on each must add to zero.

Some real-world scenarios may be useful. Examine the values for the Sample 1980s line on Table 5.2 (all data from Federal Reserve Bank of St. Louis). That year, the US had a trade deficit of $154 billion, and hence the foreign sector had a surplus of that same amount. This already puts the private sector in a hole in that they have spent more on imports than they earned on exports. However, during that same quarter, the government spent in deficit by $209 billion, injecting that much more into the private sector than it drained through taxation. This meant that, net, the private sector actually ended up with a surplus of $209 − $154 = $55. The same basic math holds for all of other rows (each selected with the goal of illustrating different combinations of surpluses and deficits and specific historical events). At the start of the 1990s expansion, for example, the US had a trade surplus. The foreign sector therefore had a deficit, which, along with the government deficit, contributed to the private sector's surplus of $328 billion. At the end of the Clinton Administration (January 2001), the government and foreign sectors both had a surplus, leading to a huge deficit for the private sector. The row showing one of the quarters before the Financial Crisis of 2007–2008 (which started in 2008Q1) indicates that the government had a deficit, which helped the private sector, but it was too small

TABLE 5.1 *The economy in three sectors*

Sector	Income source	Spending type
Domestic private sector	US private sector income	US private sector spending
Domestic public sector	Taxes	Government spending
Foreign sector	US imports	US exports

TABLE 5.2 *Sectoral balances in selected periods*

| Scenario | Date | Balances in billions | | | |
		Foreign	Govt	Pvt	Sum
Sample 1980s	1987Q2	$154	−$209	$55	$0
Start 90s expansion	1992Q1	−$42	−$286	$328	$0
Clinton surplus	2001Q1	$376	$111	−$487	$0
Pre-financial crisis	2006Q1	$792	−$436	−$356	$0
Fiscal stimulus	2009Q1	$393	−$1,708	$1,315	$0

5.6 How the Federal Government Funds a Job Guarantee

to offset the foreign sector's surplus. The private sector thus once again experienced a deficit. And last, note how the very large public sector deficit arising from the American Recovery and Reinvestment Act far offset the foreign sector's surplus, giving the private sector a sizeable surplus.

The bottom line here is that if a Job Guarantee is to be a net injection of income to its employees, the private sector must end up with a surplus. That income must come from either a foreign or public sector deficit. Some nations such as, Germany specifically target the former so that the foreign sector's consequent deficit can – even with a government budget that is balanced or close to it – represent a surplus for the private sector. But this is obviously not an available option for every country on the planet since for every trade surplus there must be a trade deficit. In addition, it is not the foreign sector's responsibility to see to it that every willing worker has a job – it is the government's. And so, a government deficit is necessary for a Job Guarantee to work, particularly if the US continues to import more than it exports.

5.6.3 Myth #3: To Spend in Deficit, The Government Must Borrow from the Private Sector

Even if one agrees to this point that the U.S. cannot default and that public sector deficit spending is necessary to finance a Job Guarantee, another potential worry remains: what if the private sector will not lend the money to the Treasury? This concern is easily dismissed, however, for (a) the Treasury does not need to borrow in the first place, it can spend money into existence, and (b) while there currently exists a legal requirement for the Treasury to sell securities and do so to entities other than the Federal Reserve, this can be and is easily bypassed (Tymoigne 2014: 652–7). It is worth emphasizing the first point: there is no economic reason that the Treasury should be required to sell securities at all; constraining them in this manner is a political choice. Indeed, as a moment's reflection makes clear, the government cannot "borrow" or recollect as taxes dollars that have not already been issued by them (Bell 1998: 18–22). And if the government must create the money first, this means they are not reliant on the private sector for funding (via either taxation or borrowing).

One can find examples of policymakers openly acknowledging this necessary sequence. The Massachusetts Bay Colony, for instance, issued currency to be used for government purchases "in anticipation of taxes" (Davis 1901: 10; quoted in Tymoigne 2014: 3). The taxes were clearly not necessary for funding since the government's purchases had already been made: The only reason for the subsequent taxation was to get the public to willingly accept the currency in the first place. Furthermore, when taxes were paid, the notes were destroyed (just as one might destroy an IOU after its conditions had been fulfilled). Interestingly, they eventually discovered that they faced a dilemma:

> The retirement of a large proportion of the circulating medium through annual taxation, regularly produced a stringency from which the legislature sought relief through

postponement of the retirements. If the bills were not called in according to the terms of the acts of issue, public faith in them would lessen, if called in there would be a disturbance of the currency (Davis 1901: 21; quoted in Tymoigne 2014: 4).

In other words, while it was the very fact that the bills were necessary to pay taxes that made them valuable, the government also discovered that the public wished to hold some bills for personal and commercial use. To satisfy both, a public sector deficit was necessary. It is certainly a more complex situation today, particularly with banks and other depository institutions having the power to create money, but the essential issue remains: Not only does the Treasury not need to borrow its own money from the private sector, it must logically have spent it first in order to recollect it.

All that said, the Treasury *is* legally required to sell securities. To reiterate, it is not an economic necessity, but it is a political reality. Does that therefore mean that the US federal government's budget is dependent on private sector loans? It does not, for, as Tymoigne explains, there are at least four means by which the Treasury can and has bypassed the legal requirement:

The first one is the issuance of monetary instruments by the Treasury. The second way is to allow banks to buy treasuries by crediting TT&Ls [Treasury Tax and Loan] instead of paying with Federal Reserve currency. The third way is to allow the Federal Reserve to provide an emergency or regular credit line to the Treasury (part 2). The fourth way is for the Federal Reserve to provide funds indirectly to the Treasury through financial institutions (part 1) (Tymoigne 2014).

I direct the reader to the original article for an explanation of the first three. The fourth, however, is both the easiest to follow and the most important in terms of real-life usage. It is very easy for the Treasury to sell securities to the private sector, particularly a primary dealer, who then sells them to the Federal Reserve. Hence, for all intents and purposes, the Treasury is funded by the central bank, but via an intermediary.

This requires the voluntary cooperation of both the primary dealer and the Federal Reserve. However, there is every reason to believe it would be forthcoming. Beginning with primary dealers, the system works as follows:

Selection criteria for primary dealers typically include financial strength as indicated by adequate capitalization; an active role in government securities markets and financial expertise, such as skilled management and staff, together with access to appropriate technology. Obligations generally include one or more of the following: (I) participating in the primary market in a substantial and consistent manner; (ii) serving as a market maker in the secondary market by providing two-way quotes, either indicative or firm, for specified groups of securities; and (iii) providing market-related information to the public debt manager, whose main objective is to ensure that the government's financing needs and its obligations are met at the lowest possible cost, consistent with a prudent degree of risk. Privileges, or supporting arrangements, which vary widely among countries, generally involve the granting of some aspect of exclusivity – for example, the exclusive right to participate in the auction for treasury bills, and/or the right to serve as a counterparty to the central bank when it conducts

5.6 How the Federal Government Funds a Job Guarantee

open market operations, and/or access to a line of credit or permission to borrow particular issues from the central bank (Arnone and Iden 2003: 4).

In short, primary dealers are stable financial institutions who, in exchange for their willingness to buy Treasury securities in whatever volume they are offered, gain certain privileges. This system is widely used throughout the world and guarantees that the Treasury is able to sell the volume of securities it wishes.

This does not explain, however, the role of the central bank. The reason is as follows. Let us say the Treasury sells $5,000-worth of Treasury securities to a primary dealer. This means that $5,000 in reserves has been drained from the financial sector. If the Federal Reserve does nothing, interest rates will almost certainly rise as banks and other institutions compete for the now-fewer reserves (which they demand even in the absence of an official requirement). Unless the Federal Reserve has changed their interest-rate target to match the new actual rate, they are obliged to intervene by injecting into the system the $5,000 of lost reserves. How do they do this? They purchase $5,000-worth of Treasury securities from the private sector. The Treasury did not sell the securities straight to the central bank, but they may as well have done so. This is, incidentally, why the Federal Reserve will want to be informed of any upcoming Treasury transactions. They want to be standing ready to offset any possible impact on the interest rate.

Now imagine another scenario: that the Treasury spends instantly simply by having the Federal Reserve credit the private-sector accounts of those receiving the income from the government (say, for example, a Marine or a scientist at NASA). In this instance, the Federal Reserve faces the opposite problem, that is, that reserves have risen by the amount of spending by the Treasury. As this will tend to drive interest rates lower, it will be the Federal Reserve that has to sell Treasury securities (which they do not issue but already have in great supply) to absorb the excess!

Long story short, and regardless of the political constraints placed on the Treasury and Federal Reserve, the federal government is not logically dependent on the private sector for funding. There is no risk that the private sector will not finance government spending.

5.6.4 Myth #4: Money Is Wealth

In everyday conversation we may think of wealth and money as being the same thing. What I mean by wealth in the current discussion, however, consists of the goods and services we consume, the leisure time we enjoy, our health and mental well-being, etc. More broadly, it is our standard of living. Money is only the ability to access those other things, it is not those other things. Hence, just because the federal government does not face a budget constraint does not mean that we can all be wealthy. *The resources have to be there!* We cannot suddenly make Somalia as wealthy as Denmark just by creating more money. If Somalia lacks the infrastructure, institutions (political, social, and economic), assets, resources, and productive capacity of Denmark, then it cannot be Denmark – not yet, at any rate. This essential point is regularly overlooked by critics of the approach forwarded in this chapter, which is often called Modern Monetary Theory, or MMT. They say that MMT claims that we can have anything we want because we can "print" as much money as we like. And yet not a single, solitary MMT scholar has ever said that. It is a straw man. Rather, what they *all* say is that the government's lack of a budget constraint means that it can activate idle resources at will. If the private sector is not using a thousand willing workers in Fort Worth, Texas, then the government can. It is never unable to do so because it lacks the funds.

But those thousand people cannot be employed to produce something for which we don't have the resources. They cannot, for example, become engaged in the production of maple syrup, because the climactic conditions in Fort Worth are not favorable to the transformations that are necessary to make it profitable to tap the tree for syrup (it's too hot!). On the other hand, they can produce those things for which we do have resources, with the above list of potential Job Guarantee jobs showing many examples. In addition, doing so gives them the income to be able to share in the country's wealth. For example, we clearly have more than enough empty housing to shelter the homeless (Sylvester 2019). This does not literally mean that those individuals could move into those particular properties, as some are in serious need of repair, some are actually inhabited for part of the year, and some are simply in transition between owners. But the actual ratio of empty houses to homeless, somewhere in the range of 30-to-1, suggests that this is a solvable problem. The resources exist, it just remains to create incomes for potential inhabitants.

5.6.5 Myth #5: Interest Payments on Rising Debt Would Cause Inflation

The basic idea here is that because the interest payments could, if not returned to agents' savings portfolios in a different form, be spent, this could cause inflation. This would be particularly true at high levels of debt and high interest rates. While this is theoretically possible, avoiding it is simple. First off, most of that income would actually go to financial institutions and foreigners who would be unlikely to use it to add to the demand for goods and services and thereby contribution to inflation. But even barring that, Scott Fullwiler demonstrates that so long as the rate of interest is held below nominal GDP growth, this would never occur (Fullwiler 2016: 87–92). And, since the rate of interest is a policy variable, there is absolutely no reason that it cannot be set at a level that prevents the interest on the debt from becoming a source of inflation. Indeed, this should be a policy goal regardless: there is no logical reason for high interest rates (Galbraith 2023).

5.7 CONCLUSIONS

Ecological economist Richard Norgaard writes of something he calls *economism*, or the tendency to reduce all social relations to market logic (Norgaard

5.7 Conclusions

2015). It is, he argues, a modern religion and one that blinds us to the true nature of the problems that face us.

This modern "religion" is essential for the maintenance of the global market economy, for justifying personal decisions, and for explaining and rationalizing the cosmos we have created. This uncritical economic creed has colonized other disciplines, including ecology, as ecologists increasingly rely on economistic logic to rationalize the protection of ecosystems. More broadly, economism often works syncretically with the world's religions even though it violates so many of their basic tenets. A Great Transition is needed to replace economism with an equally powerful and pervasive belief system that embraces the values of solidarity, sustainability, and well-being for all (Norgaard 2015).

More than anything else, he argues, this is what is preventing the implementation of the policies necessary to address climate change. The idea that the market system is natural and that any solution must be devised within it is so deeply embedded in our collective psyche that it never crosses our minds that alternatives exist.

We face an analogous situation when it comes to addressing unemployment and poverty. People – lay persons, economists, and policymakers – have a very difficult time seeing beyond our current economic system. It is not that they outright reject what has been outlined above, they just cannot imagine it. The framework into which they place any policy is that of the market system. This is true even of the political party that is supposedly on the side of Main Street rather than Wall Street: The Democrats. Under Building a Stronger, Fairer Economy is the section, "Investing in Engines of Job Creation." There, it states: "Democrats know that small businesses are among the best job creators in our country" (Democratic Party 2020: 18). While there is mention of some government programs like infrastructure repair, it is clear that this is intended to be temporary and expected to, once complete, hand the baton off to the private sector to continue the job of boosting employment. In some respects, the overall sentiment is not inconsistent with what has been argued here, but it suffers from Norgaard's economism in that it takes the very system that is causing the problem as a given.

One can find similar perspectives in the State of the Union addresses of Barack Obama and Joe Biden. In his January 13, 2016 speech, for example, President Obama discusses the role of laborsaving technology in reducing job security. That is certainly reasonable. However, he then goes on to argue that one of the key parts of a solution is education: "We agree that real opportunity requires every American to get the education and training they need to land a good-paying job" (Obama 2016). But this assumes that a job exists for each individual. If not, we simply get better educated people in the unemployment line. *The problem is not with the individual, it is with the system.* Of course, more education is better than less, but not because it will guarantee everyone a job. As further evidence of his economism, President Obama states: "I believe a thriving private sector is the lifeblood of our economy." Meanwhile, in President Joe Biden's 2023 State of the Union Address, he laments the size of the national debt and claims with pride, "In the last two years, my administration cut the deficit by more than $1.7 trillion – the largest deficit reduction in American history." He thereby betrays his economism by confusing the public sector's budget with the private sector's (Biden 2023). Hillary Clinton, too, promised not to add to the national debt if elected (Clinton 2023).

That's the depressing part. On the plus side and in spite of economism, there actually appears to be a great deal of support for a Job Guarantee among the public. Tcherneva reports:

When the job guarantee reentered the political discourse in the US in 2018, a number of surveys tried to gauge its popularity. A HillHarrisX poll from October 2019 found that a whopping 78 percent of voters supported the job guarantee, including 71 percent of Republicans, 87 percent of Democrats, 81 percent of Independents, 78 percent of leaning Conservative, and 52 percent of strongly Conservative voters (Tcherneva 2020: 114).

And it would appear that younger people are more open to policies like a Green New Deal (and much less enamored of the system that got us to this point).

In any event, the only problems we face today are philosophical. We have the tools necessary, just not the collective understanding or will to use them. Let us hope that the data Tcherneva cites is more indicative of the common mood with respect to a Job Guarantee and that one of the political parties finally picks up on this. Otherwise, history may not look kindly on the decisions we are making today.

Appendix: Critical Survey of Business Cycle Theories

The business cycle theory presented in this volume is based on the work of Wesley Clair Mitchell (1874-1948), John Maynard Keynes (1883-1946), Michal Kalecki (1899-1970), Hyman Minsky (1919-1996), and Paul Davidson (1930-2024). While the degree to which each directly influenced the current analysis varies, they are nevertheless key in setting the stage and themes that run throughout the volume. In order to give the reader a clear understanding of those foundational elements, a critical survey of the original work follows. The appendix closes with a brief discussion of Neoclassical business cycle theories.

A.1 INSTITUTIONALIST/POST KEYNESIAN INFLUENCES

A.1.1 Wesley Clair Mitchell (1874-1948)

Wesley Clair Mitchell was a pioneer in the development of business cycle theory. His work was meticulously researched, empirically grounded, and intended to be practical as well as scholarly. Because the *National Bureau of Economic Research* and *Index of Leading Economic Indicators* are part of his vast legacy, he is one of the few Institutionalists whose name might be familiar to Neoclassicals. He even served as the President of the American Economic Association in 1924. And yet, despite all this, his efforts are often discounted: "Another institutional economist who left a lasting mark on the economics profession through his leadership of the National Bureau of Economic Research was Wesley C. Mitchell, *who eschewed theory in favor of meticulous empirical investigation* (emphasis added; Williamson 1996: 391)." That is impossible. Without theory, there is no guide to what variables should be studied in the first place. Obviously, Mitchell had one. Rather, what Williamson is really trying to say is that Mitchell did not include enough math. In Neoclassicism, any theory, no matter how complex or relevant, is not respectable if it does not include equations and proofs.

This is why, sadly, Mitchell's outstanding work is largely forgotten. Not here, however. A useful starting point is his definition of "business cycle." Arthur Burns' characterizes his then recently deceased colleague's view thusly:

> Business cycles are not merely fluctuations in aggregate economic activity. The critical feature that distinguishes them from the commercial convulsions of earlier centuries or from the seasonal and other short-term variations of our own age is that the fluctuations are widely diffused over the economy – its industry, its commercial dealings, and its tangles of finance. The economy of the western world is a system of closely interrelated parts. He who would understand business cycles must master the workings of an economic system organized largely in a network of free enterprises searching for profit. The problem of how business cycles come about is therefore inseparable from the problem of how a capitalist economy functions (Burns 1951: 3).

Two things stand out. First, for Mitchell a distinguishing feature of business cycles is that they are widespread, crossing not only over many industries and enterprises, but including finance as well as commerce. It represents a general downturn and not simply a crisis in one sector or another. Second, the common bond among all those affected is monetary: "the industrial process of making and the commercial process of distributing goods are thoroughly subordinated to the business process of making money" (Mitchell 1913: 570). Ultimately, every business, regardless of specialization, must worry about the bottom line (Minsky's work also emphasizes this essential fact).

Given these premises, it is not surprising that Mitchell's focal points were profits, prices, and finance – but especially profits. Particularly important to him was how these were affected by the pressures created by expansion and recession. Take, for example, what happens in the opening phases of an upturn. Businesses start to buy again and while at first this may be confined, the need for "materials, wares, and current supplies from other enterprises" means it soon spreads (Mitchell 1913: 571). Banks are loaning money again, too, and "all this while, the revival of activity is instilling a feeling of optimism among business men, and this feeling both justifies itself and heightens the forces which engendered it by making everyone readier to buy with freedom" (Mitchell 1913: 571).

Along with the rise in output and employment comes a rise in prices. But, they do not do so equally or at the same time or speed, and therein lies the key:

> In the great majority of enterprises, larger profits result from these divergent price fluctuations coupled with the greater physical volume of sales. For, while the prices of raw materials and of wares bought for resale usually, and the prices of bank loans often, rise faster than selling prices, the prices of labor lag far behind, and the prices which make up supplementary costs are mainly steroryped for a time by old agreements regarding salaries, leases, and bonds (Mitchell 1913: 572).

Appendix: Critical Survey of Business Cycle Theories

In other words, though nonlabor costs for firms may rise at a rate faster than their selling prices and volume, labor and other overheads lag behind. Profits are thus high as is optimism and all the various positive effects reinforce one another. Orders of capital equipment also increase.

However, a number of forces – all a function of the expansion – come to weigh heavily. First, once contracts and other agreements expire, labor and supplemental costs *do* begin to rise under the pressure of increased demand. Second is the

> stress is the accumulating tension of the investment and money markets. The supply of funds available at the old rates of interest for the purchase of bonds, for lending on mortgages, and the like, fails to keep pace with the rapidly swelling demand. It becomes difficult to negotiate new issues of securities except on onerous terms, and men of affairs complain of the "scarcity of capital." Nor does the supply of bank loans grow fast enough to keep up with the demand. For the supply is limited by the reserves which bankers hold against their expanding demand liabilities. Full employment and active retail trade cause such a large amount of money to remain suspended in active circulation that the cash left in the banks increases rather slowly, even when the gold output is rising most rapidly (Mitchell 1913: 573–4).

Note that when this was written, the US was still on a gold standard and would remain so until 1933.

Third, Mitchell believed that the industries dependent on the demand for industrial equipment would add disproportionately to the rising costs. Because of the expenses involved, their capacity is generally geared only toward "repairs and renewals." However,

> ... when to this regular work of maintaining the efficiency of the existing equipment and to these odd contracts for new construction there is added the rush of orders from the many enterprises which see their own trade outrunning their facilities and from the numerous new projects launched on the rising tide of prosperity, then the construction trades have a season of activity which few of the industries for which they are working can match (Mitchell 1913: 484).

This, too, contributes to the squeezing of profits that occurs as the expansion matures.

In summary then, in early expansion profits are rising because sales and output are going up while all other costs save raw materials are stable. This is true of labor and overhead because they are contracted; in finance and industrial equipment, the mounting pressure has simply not yet had an impact. But, as contracts expire, reserves dwindle, and capacities are strained, so profits begin to be squeezed. It is not necessary for this to be universal or even widespread. Indeed, it will likely only be a minority of firms who find themselves in trouble. But, just as the upturn is marked by feedback and multipliers, so is the slow down. Interestingly and in stark contrast to mainstream approaches, Mitchell points to the financial market in explaining the path by which the contagion occurs:

Now such a decline of profits threatens worse consequences than the failure to realise expected dividends. For it arouses doubt concerning the security of outstanding credits. Business credit is based primarily upon the capitalized value of present and prospective profits, and the volume of credits outstanding at the zenith of prosperity is adjusted to the great expectations which prevail when the volume of trade is enormous, when prices are high, and when men of affairs are optimistic. The rise of interest rates has already narrowed the margins of security behind credits by reducing the capitalized value of given profits. When profits themselves begin to waver the case becomes worse. Cautious creditors fear lest the shrinkage in the market rating of the business enterprises which owe them money will leave no adequate security for repayment. Hence they begin to refuse renewals of old loans to the enterprises which cannot stave off a decline of profits, and to press for a settlement of outstanding accounts.

Thus prosperity ultimately brings on conditions which start a liquidation of the huge credits which it has piled up. And in the course of this liquidation prosperity merges into crisis (Mitchell 1913: 575–6).

This causes a significant shift in priorities as "the problem of making profits on current transactions, is subordinated to the more vital problem of maintaining solvency" (Mitchell 1913: 576).

The dismal state of affairs can be expected to continue, but not indefinitely. First, the same differential rate of change of prices now works in favor of economic recovery. Raw materials prices can be expected to fall more rapidly than those of final sales, mitigating if not reversing the decline in profits. Second and more significantly, demand eventually recovers. Stocks accumulated during the expansion are run down and so new orders are placed; consumers and businesses find it increasingly necessary to replace durable items; new tastes emerge; and the demand for capital equipment is resurgent as credit is easy, untapped technological advances exist, "and contracts can be let on most favorable conditions as to cost and prompt execution" (Mitchell 1913: 579). The cycle begins again.

This, in a nutshell, is Mitchell's view of business cycles. Profits are squeezed in the upturn and inflated during the slump. During each stage, momentum gathers quickly as prosperity or depression multiplies. Both the expansion and the recession are marked by changes in the level of economic activity that occur across sectors and industries and ultimately center on pecuniary, not "real," forces. This is so because, as quoted above, "the industrial process of making and the commercial process of distributing goods are thoroughly subordinated to the business process of making money" (Mitchell 1913: 570). One can find parallels to Keynes, Kalecki, Minsky, and Marx in his discussion.

A.1.2 John Maynard Keynes (1883–1946)

No one's influence on the preceding chapters was greater than Keynes'. The concept of *uncertainty*, the central role of investment spending, and the basics of the forces turning expansion into recession all come from him. Regarding the business cycle, he writes in the opening of chapter 22 of the *General Theory*:

Appendix: Critical Survey of Business Cycle Theories

Since we claim to have shown in the preceding chapters what determines the volume of employment at any time, it follows, if we are right, that our theory must be capable of explaining the phenomena of the Trade Cycle.

If we examine the details of any actual instance of the trade cycle, we shall find that it is highly complex and that every element in our analysis will be required for its complete explanation. In particular we shall find that fluctuations in the propensity to consume, in the state of liquidity-preference, and in the marginal efficiency of capital have all played a part. But I suggest that the essential character of the trade cycle and, especially, the regularity of time-sequence and of duration which justifies us in calling it a cycle, is mainly due to the way in which the marginal efficiency of capital fluctuates (Keynes 1936: 313).

While Keynes cites Mitchell on a few occasions in the *Treatise on Money* and was therefore obviously familiar with his work, there is otherwise little evidence to suggest that Mitchell was a direct influence on him. That said, their theories are nevertheless compatible, if not identical. For both, for example, rising interest rates may play a role; in Keynes, however, this factor is not only unlikely to be the precipitating cause, but it is expected to be more significant *after* the crisis than before. They agree that an increase in the price of capital goods can add pressure over the course of the upturn, although under Keynes this is typically offset by the fact that "the later stages of the boom are characterised by optimistic expectations as to the future yield of capital-goods sufficiently strong to offset … their rising costs of production" (Keynes 1936: 315). And neither sees overinvestment as the culprit, with Keynes suggesting that the condition we reach is generally "not one in which capital is so abundant that the community as a whole has no reasonable use for any more" (Keynes 1936: 321).

Keynes' believes the business cycle to be endogenous and marked by "the phenomenon of the *crisis*" (Keynes 1936: 314). Downturns may occur suddenly and catastrophically, while upturns emerge more slowly. As has already been explained at length, key to this behavior is the manner in which expectations are formed and the contrast that may exist between forecasts and realized results in each stage of the cycle. Recall first that Keynes argues that economic agents necessarily operate in an environment of fundamental *uncertainty*. Under these conditions, we know neither all the possibilities nor their likelihoods: "By 'uncertain' knowledge, let me explain … about these matters there is no scientific basis on which to form any calculable probability whatever. We simply do not know (Keynes 1937a: 213–14)."

Yet even though we cannot create expected values,

… the necessity for action and for decision compels us as practical men to do our best to overlook this awkward fact and to behave exactly as we should if we had behind us a good Benthamite calculation of a series of prospective advantages and disadvantages, each multiplied by its appropriate probability, waiting to be summed (Keynes 1937a: 214).

It is the existence of animal spirits, or spontaneous optimism, that allows us to make the necessary leap of faith. Particularly relevant to the current discussion is the fact that agents "... assume that the present is a much more serviceable guide to the future than a candid examination of past experience would who it to have been hitherto. In other words we largely ignore the prospect of future changes about the actual character of which we know nothing (Keynes 1937a: 214)." Profits today are predictive of profits tomorrow.

Such a world is volatile, particularly in the face of disappointment. When our expectations lack a firm foundation, panic (and euphoria) becomes a distinct possibility. Recessions are not, however, simply the result of a self-fulfilling prophecy. Indeed, the problem is not that entrepreneurs become pessimistic, but that they remain too optimistic. Consider the early stages of an expansion. Expectations are likely to still be somewhat pessimistic in light of the recent recession (because, again, they expect those conditions to continue). Eventually, however, firms find it necessary to replace durable goods and equipment and inventories. Investments coming on line in this period will therefore earn higher-than-expected profits since they were conceived during the depths of the recession. In an *uncertain* world, this serves to boost optimism, which leads to an upward revision of forecasts and an acceleration in investment. For a time, the optimistic expectations are justified (and reinforced) by results. The boom is well underway.

Unfortunately, this cannot continue because investment spending will necessarily decline. This is so in part because the cost of capital equipment may rise, interest rates increase, and the propensity to consume fall. All of these are secondary, however, when compared to the real culprit: the saturation of the market for capital (Harvey 2014a: 392–3). As investors reach target levels of capacity, so they reduce their spending. While this makes perfect sense at the individual level, it has an unintended macro consequence: as investments come on line in late expansion, total spending has decelerated.

By itself, this might cause the economy to slowly settle into a steady state wherein investment exactly offsets depreciation. Recall, however, the buoyed expectations of profit from investment. These will not be realized. At first, shortfalls may be perceived as temporary aberrations. Eventually, however, it will become clear that the actual profits earned by completed investment projects are consistently falling short of the forecasts that motivated entrepreneurs to undertake them in the first place. Even though these realized levels might have been acceptable under other circumstances, they are a disappointment. If that disappointment is sufficiently large, panic and even catastrophic collapse may result (Harvey 2014a: 394).

When the disillusion comes, this expectation is replaced by a contrary 'error of pessimism'" (Keynes 1936: 321–2). The boom is over and the slump has begun.

One might conclude from this that Keynes believes the solution to be a dampening of the optimistic expectations that led to the upturn or an increase in the rate of interest sufficient to offset them. This would, however, "misinterpret my analysis" and "involve serious error" (Keynes 1936: 320). This is so because he

Appendix: Critical Survey of Business Cycle Theories 135

does not believe, like the Austrians for example, that over-investment is characteristic of the expansion. It is not that all socially useful investment opportunities have been exhausted, but that entrepreneurs overestimated the profitability of those that they did undertake. Some projects may be misdirected, but "a state of full investment in the strict sense has never yet occurred, not even momentarily" (Keynes 1936: 324). Keynes sees theories that advocate raising interest rates to stifle booms as resulting from "confusion of mind" (Keynes 1936: 328). He adds: "I can make no sense at all of these schools of thought; except, perhaps, by supplying a tacit assumption that aggregate output is incapable of change. But a theory which assumes constant output is obviously not very serviceable for explaining the trade cycle (Keynes 1936: 329)."

Thus, in Keynes the business cycle results from fluctuations in investment, a key contributor to which is the fundamental *uncertainty* of the world in which entrepreneurs must operate. It is only because of their animal spirits that any capital formation takes place at all. Even then, there is a systemic tendency for investment to fall short of the level that would satiate all socially useful opportunities. Perhaps the most important of his conclusions in this area of inquiry is that "the duty of ordering the current volume of investment cannot be safely be left in private hands" (Keynes 1936: 320).

A.1.3 Michal Kalecki (1899–1970)

Michal Kalecki published a number of important works on business cycles between 1931 and 1968. While his approach evolved over this period and included both endogenous and exogenous elements, I will focus on the former since it is most relevant to this volume. To begin, it's important to see the categories into which he divided economic activity. Keynes focused on types of spending: consumption, investment, government spending, and net exports. Kalecki did not ignore that, but he also wanted to include income distribution as a focal point. He therefore decided to break the economy into two classes: workers (or consumers) and capitalists (or entrepreneurs or investors). Workers earn wages (W, which is equal to the wage per worker) and capitalists earn profits (π, which is equal to total profits for the entire class). Total income for capitalists is π and total income for workers is the number employed (N) times the wage: NW. Assuming a closed economy with no government sector, this leaves two sectors: consumption goods and services (indicated by subscript C) and investment goods and services (indicated by subscript I). Using P for price level and Q for quantity, the total dollar value of all goods and services produced and sold is therefore:

$$PQ = P_C Q_C + P_I Q_I. \tag{A.1}$$

And total employment is:

$$N = N_C + N_I. \tag{A.2}$$

Kalecki assumes that workers spend all of their income and capitalists none of theirs such that:

$$P_C Q_C = W_C N_C + W_I N_I, \tag{A.3}$$

where the left-hand side is the total dollar value of sales in the consumption goods industry and the right hand side represents the total income of all workers. Hence, workers spend their entire income on consumption goods and capitalists save all of theirs (which explains the absence of π in the equation). With respect to workers' consumption, that is fairly accurate. In 2017, the bottom 80% of American households spent on average nearly 100% of their income. If we can assume that those are all workers, then Kalecki's statement that "workers spend what they get" is not terribly far off. However, the top 20% of Americans (assuming they are representative of capitalists) actually do spend at least some of their income, in fact around 60%. So while this is a simplification, it can be easily shown that relaxing it leaves us with the same conclusions, albeit with a number of extra steps. For present purposes, it is not worth the extra complication.

Profits in the consumption goods sector are shown in Eq. (A.4):

$$\pi_C = P_C Q_C - W_C N_C. \tag{A.4}$$

They are equal to the dollar value of their total sales ($P_C Q_C$) minus their total costs ($W_C N_C$). Note the implicit recognition that at the macro level, the only costs are labor costs. At the micro level we have rent, interest, labor, raw materials, and more, but not so at the highest degree of aggregation.

Comparing Eq. (A.3) to Eq. (A.4) reveals an important fact. If we know from the latter that $\pi_C = P_C Q_C - W_C N_C$ and from the former that $P_C Q_C = W_C N_C + W_I N_I$, then:

$$\pi_C = P_C Q_C - W_C N_C = W_I N_I. \tag{A.4'}$$

This says that $\pi_C = W_I N_I$, or that the consumption goods industry's profits come entirely from the spending of investment-goods workers. This makes perfect sense because the consumption-goods sector cannot make a profit if all it does is sell back to its own workers. *They must sell to someone that got their paycheck somewhere else.*

Eq. (A.5) shows the investment goods industry.

$$P_I Q_I = W_I N_I + \pi_I, \tag{A.5}$$

where $P_I Q_I$ is total sales and, therefore, total income, all of which takes the form of either wages or profits. Profits are in the investment-goods industry are shown in Eq. (A.6):

$$\pi_I = P_I Q_I - W_I N_I. \tag{A.6}$$

Just as in the consumption-goods industry, total profits in the investment-goods industry (π_I) are equal to total sales in the investment-goods industry ($P_I Q_I$) minus total costs in the investment-goods industry ($W_I N_I$).

Appendix: Critical Survey of Business Cycle Theories

Eq. (A.7) shows total profits:

$$\pi = \pi_C + \pi_I. \tag{A.7}$$

Substituting in Eqs. (A.4′) and (A.6) yields:

$$\pi = W_I N_I + P_I Q_I - W_I N_I = P_I Q_I. \tag{A.8}$$

In other words, total profits (π) are equal to investment spending ($P_I Q_I$). This shows directly a relationship that was vital to the analyses in Chapters 2 and 4. In the real world, the relationship is not one-to-one like this because other types of spending also contribute to profits (government spending, for example; Tcherneva 2012). But, the correspondence is extremely close. This is why Kalecki argues that "investors get what they spend" and it will be important to his business cycle theory.

Another key consideration was an explicit modeling of a gestation period for the creation of physical capital. In "A Theory of the Business Cycle" (after establishing that workers spend what they get while capitalists get what they spend) Kalecki writes:

> We wish now to state that the present investment, i.e. the value of present investment output, is a result not of *present* but *former* investment decisions, for, as we shall see immediately, a certain relatively long time is needed to complete the investment projects. This fact is of fundamental importance for the dynamics of an economic system (Kalecki 1937: 80–1).

This creates two important lags: that between the initial decision and the expenditure for a given portion of the project and that between the latter and the new unit of capital coming on line and being available for use by the entrepreneur. This creates a situation like that shown below (also in Chapter 2):

Here, the starting point is the decision to invest (1), which is based on factors available to the entrepreneur at that moment in time. Next, some fraction of the project is paid for and completed (2, 2′, and 2″). Assuming each of the above segments to be equal, this example has one-third being finished per period. Finally, on the far right, the investment process ends and the life of the newly produced capital stock begins (3).

At this point in the discussion, Kalecki has already argued the central importance of investment in the economy. Consistent with Keynes, he contends that it determines income, output, wages, consumption, employment, and (most

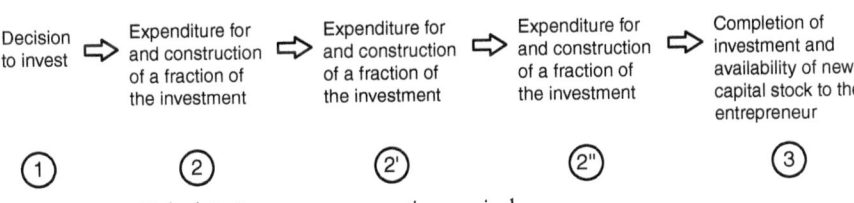

FIGURE A.1 Kalecki's investment-gestation period

important for the current discussion) profits. What happens on the far left of the above sequence therefore takes on critical importance and begs the question, why do firms invest in the first place? Kalecki says firms do so up to the point that the gross rate of profit (profits divided by the value of the capital stock) is equal to the rate of interest. This fact, in combination with the events shown in Figure A.1, introduces a dynamic element into the analysis. Because investment spending creates profits, this means that stages 2, 2′ and 2″ raise the gross rate of profit (since profits rise but the stock of capital does not until stage 3). Assuming along with Keynes that "the facts of the existing situation enter, in a sense disproportionately, into the formation of our long-term expectations" (Kalecki 1937: 84, quoting Keynes 1936: 148), this encourages more investment (López and Assous 2010: 93–4). However, at the same time firms throughout the economy may be reaching stage 3, thereby increasing the capital stock and lowering the gross rate of profit. This would depress expectations (Kalecki 1937: 89). We therefore have two opposing forces at work in Figure A.1, the relative weights of which determine where we stand in the business cycle. When stages 2, 2′ and 2″ dominate, we expand because investment spending creates profits that raise the gross rate of profit; eventually however, the rise in the stock of capital resulting from firms reaching stage 3 – which both increases the denominator in the gross rate of profit and signals the end of investment spending for a given project – will take over. Various forces create momentum in each stage. Note the endogeneity of expectations here. As suggested above, a rising rate of profit is likely to cause an optimistic revision of forecasts, and vice versa. In addition, Kalecki thought this phenomenon might be s-shaped in the sense that there may be little positive reaction at the beginning of an upturn, after which expectations become relatively elastic relative to realized results before once again becoming dulled as the upturn matures (Kalecki 1939).

Figure A.2 offers a graphical representation of his theory (Kalecki 1937). The line labeled D is the investment-decision curve, which shows how entrepreneurs' react to the profit created by given levels of investment. For example, if investment in period t is I_t, then, according to the above analysis, profits are also equal to I_t. According to the D curve, this leads firms to make decision D_t. They act on decision D_t in period $t+1$ by investing I_{t+1} (as both axes are scaled the same, the 45-degree line is used to translate decision D_t into action I_{t+1}). Profits in period $t+1$ will equal I_{t+1}, spurring agents to make decision D_{t+1}; that leads to investment level I_{t+2}, and so on. The investment-decision curve is less than 45° because even though rising investment raises profits and therefore encourages even more investment, as this process continues so the cost of purchasing and financing investment goods will rise. Ceteris paribus, investment will reach an equilibrium where the investment-decision curve intersects the 45° line.

This is not a cycle, however. Kalecki argues that one results once we take into account the fact that the investment-decision curve will shift in response

Appendix: Critical Survey of Business Cycle Theories

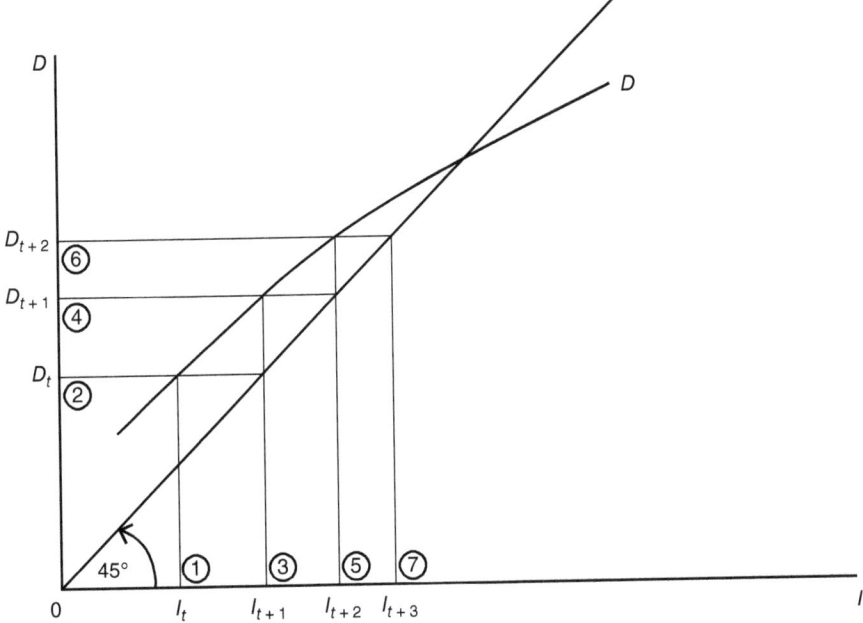

FIGURE A.2 Kalecki's investment-decision curve

to changes in the size of the stock of capital. The higher the stock of capital, the lower the rate of profit/factory since there are more factories. This which will have a depressing effect on expectations and shift the investment-decision curve down. If the stock of capital declines, the curve will shift up. Adding this to the above figure requires including a vertical line showing the level of investment necessary to exactly offset depreciation. This is $I = d$ on Figure A.3. Any investment level to the left of that results in negative net investment and thus a decrease in the capital stock; any one to the right shows positive net investment and an increase in the capital stock.

The vertical and 45-degree lines divide the diagram into four parts (labeled 1 to 4 on the figure). Given the assumptions above, the economy can be expected to cycle through the four quadrants as the D curve – not pictured since it will move around the diagram – shifts and levels of investment rise and fall (Table A.1 summarizes the events about to be described). If we begin at a point on a D curve that lies above the 45-degree line and to the left of $I = d$ (i.e., quadrant 1), next period's investment will be higher due to the former and next period's capital stock (K) will be lower due to the latter. D will shift up and there will be a rightward movement along it. This will continue until the rising D curve moves the economy into quadrant 2 (the equivalent of mid expansion). There, investment is still rising (moving along the D curve to the right) because the relevant points on the D curve lie above the 45-degree line; but now $I > d$ so the rising capital stock causes D to begin shifting down. Eventually, D

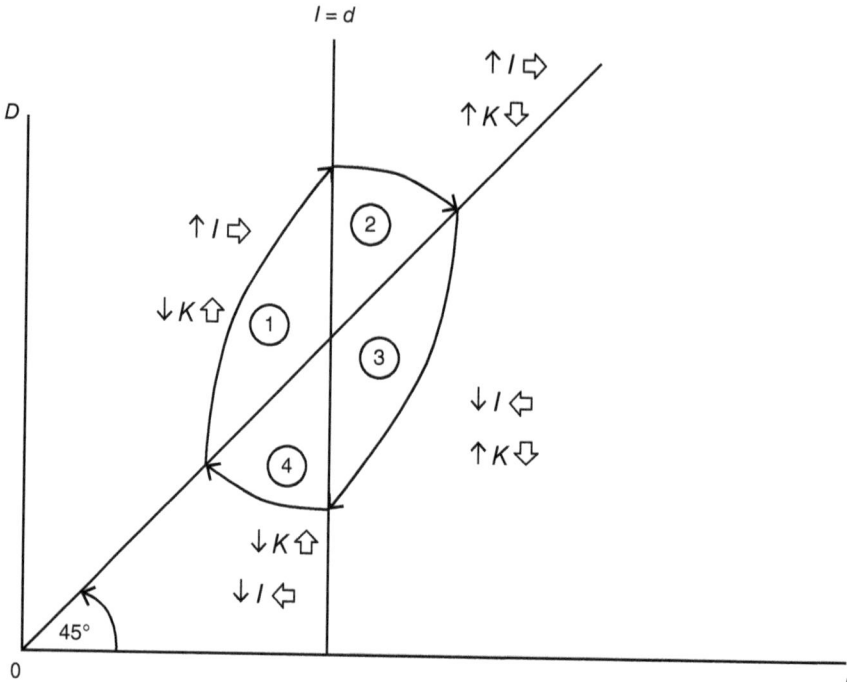

FIGURE A.3 Shifts in the investment-decision curve creating a cycle

TABLE A.1 *Stages in Kalecki's cycle*

Quadrant	Cycle stage	Point vs 45° ⇒ ΔI		I vs d ⇒ ΔK		D Shift
1	Early expansion	Above	Rise	$I < d$	Fall	Up
2	Mid expansion	Above	Rise	$I > d$	Rise	Down
3	Late expansion	Below	Fall	$I > d$	Rise	Down
4	Recession	Below	Fall	$I < d$	Fall	Up

will have shifted below the 45-degree line, putting the economy in quadrant 3 (late expansion). Here, investment is still net positive (shifting D further down) but declining (because the relevant point on D is below the 45-degree line). Finally, the falling investment drops below d and leads to recession in quadrant 4. There, investment continues to fall, but, as this is to the left of $I = d$, D is shifting upward. Eventually, D rises enough to return the economy to quadrant 1 and expansion. Note that only if the economy happened to start off at the intersection of the 45° line and $I = d$ would we be a stable equilibrium.

To this core Kalecki added a number of innovative concepts. One of the most discussed is the principle of increasing risk. It emerged from the consideration of the following question: if rising investment tends to raise expectations even further, are there no limits to the volume of capital a firm might add during a period of optimism? Kalecki argued that the relevant constraint was related to the fact that:

The rate of risk of every investment is greater the larger is this investment. If the entrepreneur builds up a factory he incurs a certain risk of unprofitable business, and these losses, if any, will be more significant for him the greater proportion the investment considered bears to his wealth. But besides this, in "sacrificing" his reserves (consisting of deposits or securities) or taking credits, he exhausts his "sources of capital," and if he should need this "capital" in the future he may be obliged to borrow at a high rate of interest because he has overdrawn the amount of credit considered by his creditors as "normal." Thus both these aspects of risk incurred by investment shot that the rate of risk must grow with the amount invested (Kalecki 1937: 84–5).

Thus, an additional check on entrepreneurs' investment is the increasing risk they face. The greater the investment relative to the stock of capital, the greater that risk and thus the faster the entrepreneur reaches her limit.

Kalecki also considered the role of profits in financing further investment and he attempted to build a model that accounted for both the cycle and trend in a capitalist economy. Though convinced that our economic system was inherently unstable, he experimented with models that included stochastic elements (like changes in technology) and various levels of internal stability. It is also significant that he believed that we rarely reach the level of full capacity, which distinguishes his from some other approaches (though not Institutionalist and Post Keynesian ones). Perhaps most significant of all is

the fact that he was the first economist to provide a rigorous analytical framework, an alternative to the general equilibrium theory, to study the general properties, and more specifically the stability properties, of a capitalist (or decentralized, to use the parlance of the general equilibrium theory) economy. Within this analytical framework, the issue of unemployment in capitalism can be given a dynamic explanation (López and Assous 2010: 118).

A.1.4 Hyman Minsky (1919–1996)

Hyman Minsky is, of course, best known for his financial instability hypothesis (see, for example, Minsky 1982). It argues, in short, that during upturns economic agents become increasingly optimistic and consequently reduce margins of safety between debt repayment schedules and expected income. The financial system thereby becomes increasingly fragile meaning that the magnitude of the shock necessary to cause a collapse becomes smaller and smaller. Stability creates instability.

His interest in and work on business cycles, per se, go back many decades. The Minsky Archive at the *Levy Institute* even includes his lecture notes from Oscar Lange's University of Chicago undergraduate business cycle course from spring 1942 (Minsky 1942). While Minsky's early research follows fairly standard lines, focusing on the accelerator, multiplier, and stochastic shocks and variations (see for example Minsky 1954a, 1954b, 1954c), starting in at least 1959 one sees an increasing emphasis on the integral role of the financial sector (Minsky 1959). Interestingly, the focus in the following is much more positive than that reflected in his later financial-fragility work. It is nevertheless suggestive of the direction he would take:

> In addition if, as suggested earlier, the exploitation of an innovation in a favorable financial environment leads to capital gains for the innovator, then the payoff from the success scenarios will depend upon the nature of the financial system. A financial system that facilitates the exploitation of investment opportunities opened by innovation, and that protects the position of the innovator will make returns from the success scenarios larger, sooner and more secure. They will be larger because of the leverage in "other people's money" that is involved, they will be sooner because they will take the form of immediate capital gains – rather than savings out of income –, and they will be more secure, because they will enable the innovator to hedge on future possibly unfavorable second and subsequent acts by selling out a part of the position: he can realize part of his capital gains and diversify his portfolio immediately after some initial success (Minsky 1959: 25).[1]

In the following 1960 publication, however, the financial instability hypothesis is clearly visible:

> In this study the validity and implications of a number of hypotheses relating to the interaction between the financial and real sectors of the economy will be explored. The broadest hypothesis is that the behavior of an economic system with respect to the real variables is not independent of the financial structure of the economy. A hypothesis more closely related to the terms of reference of this paper is that the likelihood of a financial crisis occurring is not independent of the financial structure of an economy and the financial structure reflects the "past" of the economy. The third hypothesis is the most precise and is really a way of phrasing the fundamental problem of this paper. It is that the financial changes that take place during a sustained boom generated by private demand are such that the domain within which the financial structure is stable is decreased as the boom continues, so that the likelihood that a disturbance of the financial system will lead to a financial crisis is increased as the boom lengthens (Minsky, Friend, and Andrews 1960: 3).

Indeed, almost every element appears, including the concept of a margin of safety (Minsky, Friend, and Andrews 1960: 35), the reduction thereof over the boom (Minsky, Friend, and Andrews 1960: 39), and the key role of the government as lender-of-last-resort (Minsky, Friend, and Andrews 1960: 49).

In terms of his business cycle work, "For Minsky, the modern business cycle *is* a financial cycle" (Wray 2015: 31). While this is clearly the case, there

---

[1] For materials drawn from the Minsky Archive, page numbers correspond to the scans rather than those of the original documents.

Appendix: Critical Survey of Business Cycle Theories

exists some controversy regarding other aspects of it. For example, though his approach definitely does not fit into the mainstream tradition wherein economies automatically seek full-employment equilibrium, "it would yet be misleading to draw from it the conclusion that Minsky's contribution to macrodynamics provides a significant example of the endogenous business cycle approach" (Arena and Raybaut 2001: 113). To understand this, consider Minsky's determinants of investment. It is premised on the existence of two prices: P_K, or the demand price of capital, and P_I, or the supply price. The former is that which the firm is willing to pay for a unit of capital and the latter is that at which one will be supplied. At first estimation, the former is a horizontal line whose position in space is determined by the firm's estimation of potential profit (see Figure A.4). Assuming this to be at least initially above P_I, positive investment results. The supply price will eventually rise as producers of capital goods use equipment more intensely and find costs increasing. As a consequence, investment takes place up to the point where the two curves intersect.

But this is far from the whole story. As Minsky writes:

> The above figure however has no place for financing: presumably the amount of investment designated by the intersection will be ordered independently of the financing arrangements. This is palpable nonsense. The investment producers will not undertake their activity unless there is some guarantee that the final purchaser will be able to pay for the completed investment good (Minsky 2008: 210).

Production takes time and financing is therefore central: "A decision to invest – to acquire capital assets – is always a decision about a liability structure" (Minsky 2008: 192).

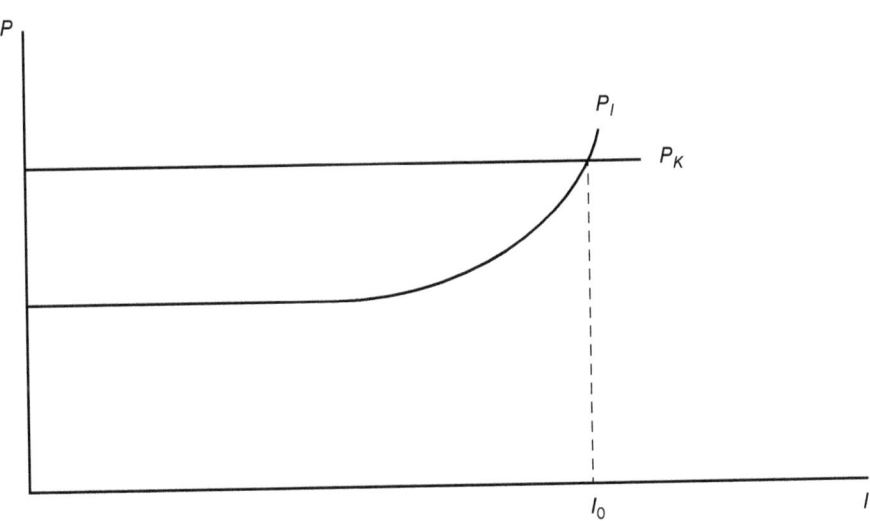

FIGURE A.4 Minsky's investment without financing

Firms have a number of choices in this regard, but these can be reduced to using existing and anticipated internal funds and borrowing. Consideration of the former is reflected in Q on Figure A.5. It is downward sloping because as I rises, the ability to fund out of expected retained earnings declines. To invest past I_i, "it is necessary either to run down holdings of financial assets that are superfluous to operations or to engage in external finance" (Minsky 2008: 213). In either event, this reduces the firm's margin of safety and this creates both lender's risk and borrower's risk. The former is the chance the lender is taking that the borrower will be unable to repay, while the latter is the borrower's worry about the same thing. Because the latter essentially lowers the expected profit from investment, it creates the dashed portion of P_K (and it makes the solid line thereafter irrelevant). This portion of P_K slopes down as the volume of investment increases, representing the fact that the borrower's worry increases. Were this the whole story (lender's risk will be saved for Figure A.6), total investment would be I' with I_i funded internally and $I'-I_i$ externally.

This leaves only lender's risk, which is shown on Figure A.6 (along with all the equilibria). This adds an implicit and potentially explicit cost (the latter in terms of the interest rate the borrower must pay or conditions she must meet), creating the dashed line P_I' above P_I (of increasing slope since the ratio of debt to income would be rising). It is not costless to finance a \$5 million purchase capital goods, meaning that the firm may have to settle for borrowing only \$4.5 million. Current investment is thus determined by the intersection of P_K' and P_I' (point a). The actual cost per unit is P_{Io}, since this is what they would be charged by the producer of investment goods (point b). Total funding required

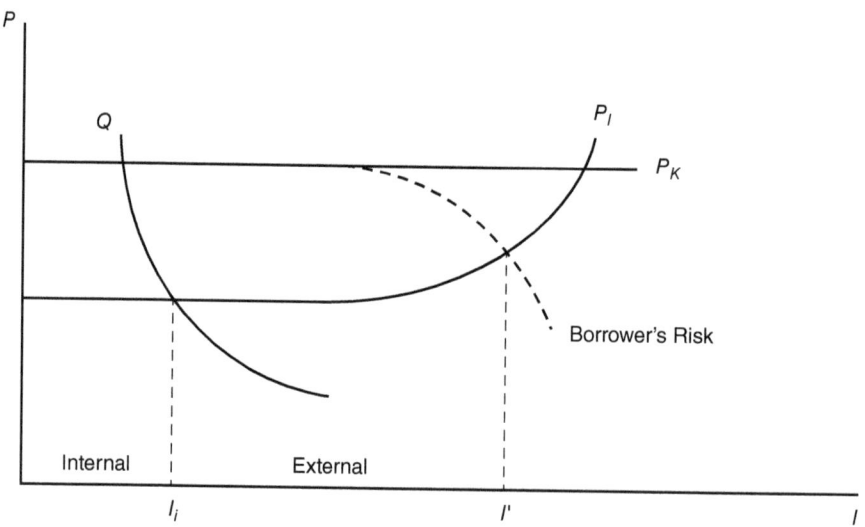

FIGURE A.5 Minsky's investment including internal financing and borrower's risk

Appendix: Critical Survey of Business Cycle Theories

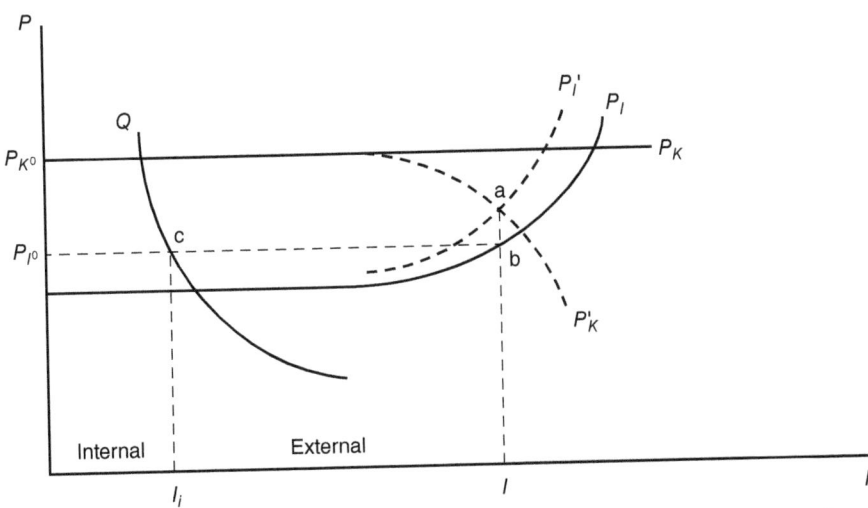

FIGURE A.6 Minsky's investment with financing and borrower's and lender's risk

is $(I \times P_{I0})$, of which $(I_i \times P_{I0})$ is internal (point c) and the remainder is external. The gap between P_{K0} and P_{I0} is a direct function of the margin of safety jointly determined by the borrower and lender (De Antoni 2008: 9). Note how a decline in either borrower's or lender's perception of risk would shift points a and b to the right, thereby lowering this margin.

The key to Minsky's business cycle is contained in the last sentence above. For, during good times, both firms and banks reduce their estimates of risk. This puts both in an increasingly precarious position, which alone may be sufficient to bring on a decline since it makes it increasingly likely that any given shock could bring on default and disaster. On top of that, however, Minsky forecast that expansions lead to a rise in short-term interest rates:

> For a variety of reasons – the limited equity base of banks, internal and foreign drains of bank reserves, and, in modern times, central bank (Federal Reserve) actions to restrain the money supply – the supply of finance from banks eventually becomes less than infinitely elastic. This means that after favorable conditions for investment are sustained for some time, the cost of financing investment as it is being produced increases. Furthermore, the supply of finance can become very inelastic because of policy decisions or the internal processes of the banking and financial system. This means that short-term interest rates can become very high quite rapidly (Minsky 2008: 217).

The consequence is that some hedge units (those which could meet all contractual obligations out of cash flow) become speculative ones (those able to cover interest payments, but not principle, out of cash flow) and some speculative units become Ponzi ones (those for whom it is necessary to continue borrowing even to meet interest payments). The last group will find it necessary to liquidate assets and those sales will cause the rate of increase in asset prices (which naturally accompanied the investment boom) to slow if not reverse. This has repercussions throughout the economy, with more Ponzi units being created and erstwhile liquid assets becoming illiquid. Capital-to-asset ratios of even conservative firms and banks become suspect. "The asset market becomes flooded and the euphoria becomes a panic, the boom becomes a slump" (Keen 1995: 612–13).

Returning to the question of whether Minsky's business cycle theory was an endogenous one, there are certainly elements of this above and there is no question that his followers have built models based on this assumption. But there is also a "and-then-something-happened" aspect in that he argues that the decline in margins of safety over booms leave us more vulnerable to "anything" that might happen. Probably the most accurate thing to say, however, is that he was not trying to create a business cycle theory in the first place, but an explanation of longer-term institutional change (Arena and Raybaut 2001). While the former clearly has an important and perhaps even vital role to play, it is the evolution of the financial system over time, especially its ability to continually find new means of liquidity creation and risk taking, that is the real story in Minsky.

A.1.5 Paul Davidson (1930–2024)

The cofounder of the *Journal of Post Keynesian Economics*, Davidson played a central role in the development of Post Keynesian economics. Among his many contributions is a graphical analysis of the investment decision introduced in *Money and the Real World* (1978). His model begins with a specification for the demand for physical capital:

$$D_k = f(p_k, i, \Phi, E) \qquad (A.9)$$
$$-\ \ -\ +\ +$$

where D_k is the quantity of capital demanded, p_k is the price of capital goods, i is the rate of discount used by entrepreneurs in considering the present value of expected future profits, Φ is the expected growth in demand for the products produced by the capital in question, and E is the number of investors able to obtain finance for their projects. Note that, though it is less detailed than Minsky's, Davidson explicitly includes a role for financing.

Figure A.7 shows this function placed in p_k and quantity of capital space. The effect of changes in p_k on the demand for capital are reflected in the slope, while changes in i, Φ, or E will cause shifts in the function in the directions implied by the signs of their partial derivatives. Figure A.8 adds a supply side in the form of the vertical line, S_k, which shows the current stock of capital. Where S_k and D_k intersect is the demand price for capital (p_s in Davidson's original), or that "necessary to allocate the stock without remainder among demanders" (Davidson 2011: 68). It is the price entrepreneurs are *willing* to pay.

The demand price is half of the story. In order to determine the current level of investment, it is necessary to compare it to the supply price, or what

Appendix: Critical Survey of Business Cycle Theories

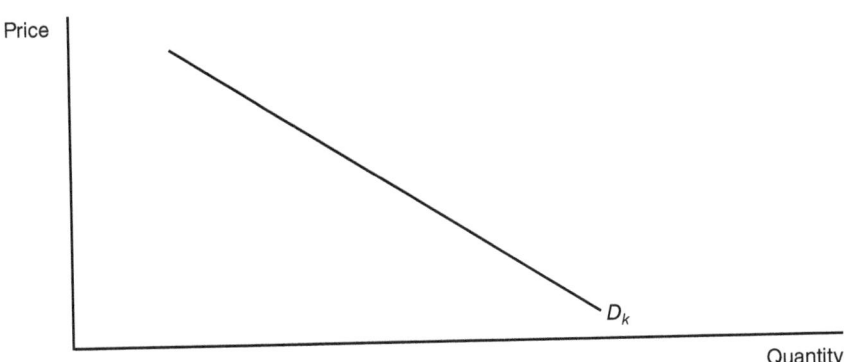

FIGURE A.7 Demand for capital curve

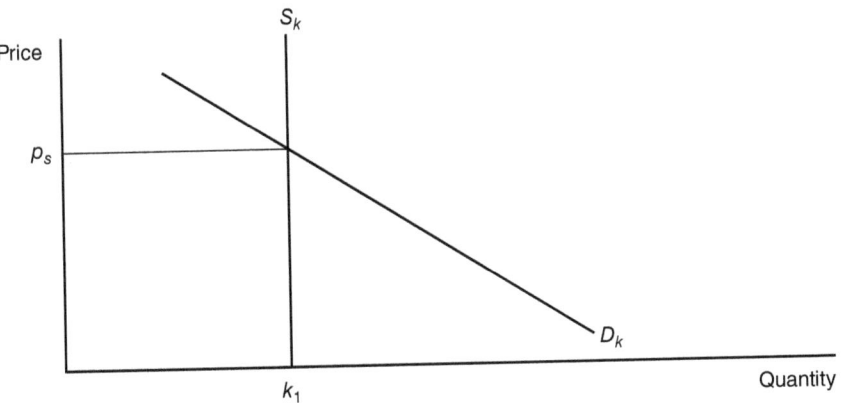

FIGURE A.8 The determination of the spot price

entrepreneurs *must actually* pay to purchase capital. The calculation of the latter requires two additional concepts: new production and depreciation. New production is represented by s_k which, as shown in Figure A.9, begins at p_m. This is the minimum price at which producers of capital will sell one unit. Above that, the curve is positively sloped on the assumption that the costs of construction will increase. Since k_1 units of capital already exist, the s_k curve is added to the S_k one as shown in Figure A.9. $(S_k + s_k)$ therefore represents existing stock supply (S_k) plus the flow resulting from building (s_k). Depreciation is represented by d_k, which is the gap between D_k and $(D_k + d_k)$. Firms must add at least that much capital or the existing stock will shrink.

Since $(S_k + s_k)$ represents the total supply of capital (both that already in existence and that which can be built) and $(D_k + d_k)$ the total demand (for new plus upkeep), their intersection must yield the supply price (p_f), or the price at which the market is willing to supply a unit of capital. Because the supply price lies below the demand price in Figure A.9, this means that agents are willing to pay more than they actually must and so the stock of capital will increase.

Note the implicit dynamic in Davidson's model: It is clear that next period, S_k will be k_2 and not k_1. Indeed, the entire S_k and $(S_k + s_k)$ apparatus will shift right. The supply and demand prices, p_s and p_f, will move closer together as firms reach targeted levels of capacity, a process that will continue until $p_s = p_f$ and net investment $= 0$. Note further that it does not matter if we begin with a scenario in which $p_s < p_f$ as in Figure A.10. Under these circumstances, net investment is negative and the S_k and $(S_k + s_k)$ apparatus shifts left. But, again, it is moving inexorably toward a steady state equilibrium where net investment is zero and firms have reached targeted capacity. Their only subsequent investment is to replace depreciation.

This, of course, does not describe a cycle. One can be created, however, by including a factor thus far largely ignored: demand. There is no reason to

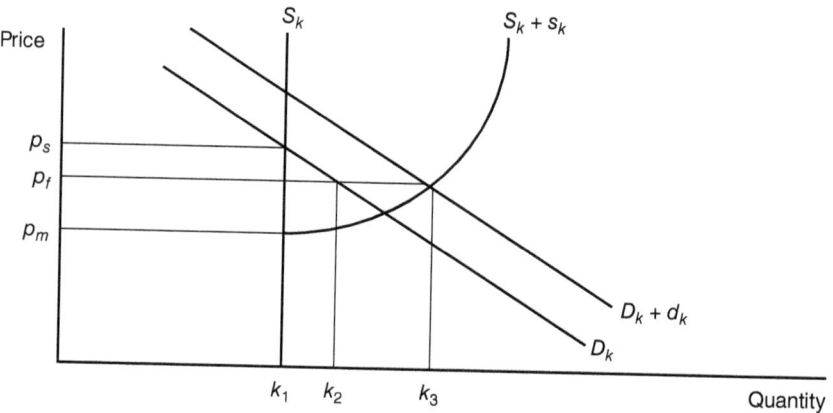

FIGURE A.9 Complete demand for and supply of capital

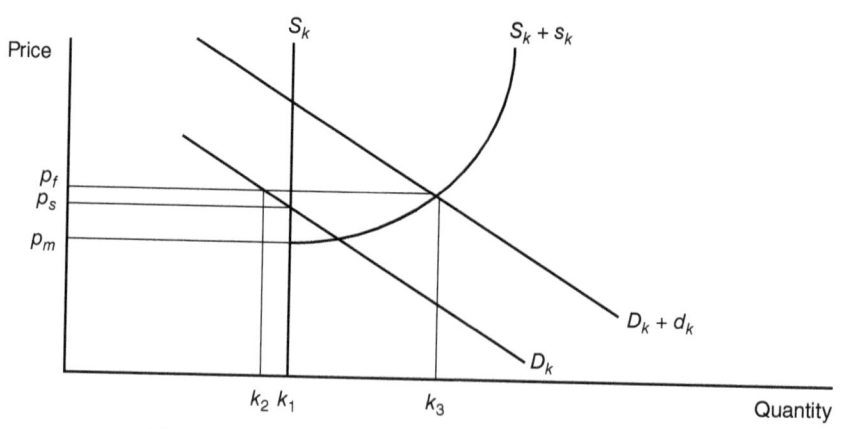

FIGURE A.10 Negative net investment

Appendix: Critical Survey of Business Cycle Theories

expect D_k and $(D_k + d_k)$ to remain stationary. Far from it, the overreactions described by Keynes – a function of fundamental *uncertainty*, animal spirits, and the high cost, long time horizon, and irreversibility of investment – create a predictable and familiar pattern. Consider first early expansion. Through the recession, low demand and dampened expectations will have led firms to delay even replacement investment. Not only can they not ignore depreciation indefinitely, but bad memories fade. Investment begins to recover – which means that profits recover.

This comes as a pleasant surprise and is greeted as a sign that the downturn has ended. As a consequence, D_k and $(D_k + d_k)$ shift right (due particularly to the rise in Φ from Eq. (A.9)) and do so sufficiently to offset any rightward movement of S_k and $(S_k + s_k)$. Early expansion becomes mid expansion, with p_s well above p_f and the stock of capital rising toward entrepreneurs' target levels. But, it will not reach them, the reason being that while agents' optimism remains high, buoyed by the high levels of investment and profit, S_k and $(S_k + s_k)$ are slowly shifting right. On the one hand, the latter is their goal; on the other, this means that as p_s approaches p_f in late expansion, investment and profits decelerate and fall. Instead of a positive surprise driving D_k and $(D_k + d_k)$ to the right, this is a negative one pushing them left. The combination of rising S_k and $(S_k + s_k)$ and falling D_k and $(D_k + d_k)$ leads to recession. This completes the cycle and sets the stage for the next one (see Harvey 2014b for an extensive explanation of Davidson's business cycle model).

A.2 ORTHODOX THEORIES

While this volume is based on the assumption that orthodox theories have fallen well short of a reasonable explanation of the business cycle, they are nevertheless described here so that the reader can be armed in the manner suggested by Joan Robinson: "The purpose of studying economics is not to acquire a set of ready-made answers to economic questions, but to learn how to avoid being deceived by economists" (Robinson 1978: 75). Four Neoclassical approaches are explained, along with an Austrian one. With one notable and quite dated exception, orthodox (plus Austrian) business cycle theories assume that fluctuations in the level of economic activity are entirely exogenous. Undisturbed, we could stay at full employment indefinitely. Apart from the belief that policy errors or inefficiencies and frictions play a key role, one sees very little consistency among the explanations. The reason for the inclusion of the Austrian Business Cycle Theory is that it not only shares several key premises with the orthodox, but it enjoyed a resurgence in popularity after the Financial Crisis of 2007–2008.

A.2.1 Interest-Rate Induced

While not really a single, identifiable body of theory in the same sense as Real Business Cycles or Monetarism, the idea that business cycles may be related to changes in interest rates is an old one in orthodoxy. Irving Fisher's early twentieth century formulation, arguing that the differential reactions of prices and interest rates create the observed patterns of expansion and recession, is representative. Initially, prices rise faster than interest rates, creating profit opportunities for businesses (who represent the largest share of borrowers). Firms may therefore borrow too much and overinvest so that when interest rates inevitably catch up (due to the rising ratio of loans to bank reserves), profits are squeezed and recession results (Fisher 1910: 176). Fisher writes, "Had the previous rate of interest been high enough, they would never have overinvested" (Fisher 1910: 177).[2]

That this is an endogenous theory of cycles makes it unique for an orthodox model. What keeps it firmly in that camp, however, is the identification of overinvestment as the culprit. The economy is pushed away from full employment not because demand is lacking or agents' expectations are disappointed, but as a result of interest rates being sticky. This causes a misallocation of resources during the expansion. The price is paid during the corrective downturn – but it is simply corrective and not a symptom of a serious systemic problem.

As suggested by the citations, this theory was popular pre-Great Depression. The more common variant of the Interest-Rate Induced approach today views central bank policy as the villain. That said, these roots also go back many years. Simon Kuznets notes (quoting from a German source, Budge 1925):

> Experience shows that within the limits of their discretion the central banks also are inclined to a too generous granting of credits. Also for them the granting of credits is a profitable business. Furthermore, with the central banks, it is a certain conservatism which accounts for the fact that they cannot decide upon a raise in the discount rate at the proper moment.
>
> In such a mistimed rise of the discount rate during expansion, i.e., in a too generous extension of capital credit, not justified by circumstances, is to be found the true cause of the cycles (Kuznets 1930: v152).[3]

Both of the above perspectives fit neatly with the widely held orthodox opinion that interest rates have a powerful impact in any context (Mishkin 1995). This is reflected in Rudiger Dornbusch's famous statement, "None of the U.S. expansions of the past 40 years died in bed of old age; every one was murdered by the Federal Reserve" (quoted in Temin 1998: 1). And while the most recent literature has become more varied (especially since the Financial Crisis of 2007–2008), it was observed at the forty-second annual conference of the Federal Reserve Bank of Boston that "Most participants agreed that

---

[2] Similar theories have been forwarded more recently, albeit with the source of the endogenous fluctuations being based on Neoclassical micro-foundational factors like search costs (Dong, Wang, and Wen 2016) and asymmetric information (Bigio 2015).

[3] This is very similar to the Austrian view to be covered later and, in fact, Kuznets, references both Friedrich Hayek and Ludwig von Mises.

Appendix: Critical Survey of Business Cycle Theories 151

the Fed played a significant role in causing many of the recessions of the past century, largely in the pursuit of its goal of long-run price stability" (Fuhrer and Schuh 1998: 3). Indeed, one of Paul Romer's goals in his attack on modern macroeconomics is to place monetary policy and interest rates back at the center of the assumed determinants of economic fluctuations (Romer 2016: 1–4).

It is interesting to note that the endogenous version of this approach is rarely heard today. While this is no doubt partly due to the very public role central banks now play it targeting interest rates, it is also likely that today's orthodox economist would argue that "rational" entrepreneurs would compensate for the lagging interest rate adjustment during the upturn, thus avoiding what in their conception would be an entirely foreseeable episode of overinvestment. In addition, the de-emphasis of the endogenous version is entirely consistent with the overall shift toward models that view deviations from full employment as ephemeral and a function of shocks.

A.2.2 Neoclassical/New Keynesian and Stop-Go

This section, like the previous one, combines related approaches. While Neoclassical Keynesian and New Keynesian are different iterations of the same tradition, they are close enough in this context to not warrant separate treatment. In addition, though Stop-Go is only one application of Neoclassical Keynesianism, it was so dominant for several decades that it was very nearly the only orthodox game in town. It therefore receives special attention here.

The Neoclassical Keynesian (and eventually New Keynesian) focus has evolved considerably over the years. For the first few decades after World War II, the primary story was one derivative of the fine-tuning concept where it was assumed that the government could, with reasonable precision, place the economy at whatever point was desired (so long as there was a corresponding position on the Phillips Curve). The Stop-Go theory of cycles is consistent with this framework. It has similarities to the monetary-policy version of the Interest-Rate Induced perspective described above, except that (a) it also includes fiscal policy and (b) it excludes errors. This is not to say that they do not think errors are possible, but that cycles related to Stop-Go policies are premeditated and intentional.

In short, the idea is that the primary source of cycles is government policy (fiscal and monetary) shifting between unemployment reduction ("Go") and inflation control ("Stop"). On the assumption that these problems are inversely related, periods of Go aim to lower unemployment at the cost of raising inflation, while periods of Stop target inflation reduction but tend to increase unemployment. Because of the negative side effects of each and assuming that the government may tend to overshoot targets, they must follow one another in order to clean up the problems left behind by the previous one. An American Economic Review article from 1962 on European business cycles provides an excellent example (where "post-Keynesian" is meant to imply a world where Keynesian policies are employed):

As to the recession of 1958, it was an entirely different affair from that of 1952 because it did not have its origins in any shock event, like the outbreak of the Korean War. One may say, therefore, that it was the first normal recession of post-Keynesian Europe. How and why did it come about?

The years 1953, 1954, and 1955 were years of exceptional economic expansion; the rise in the real GNP for the OEEC [Organisation for European Economic Co-operation] averaged 5 ½ per cent and in 1955 it was over 6 per cent. In the course of this expansion all the industrial countries, except Italy, reached a position of excessive total demand and overfull employment, which produced inflationary pressures and, in many cases, balance-of-payments difficulties. The recession came about through the gradual efforts of the authorities to curb this excess demand situation by shifting from a policy of stimulation to one of restraint (emphasis added; Gilbert 1962: 97).

Consistent with the Stop-Go understanding of the business cycle, Gilbert goes on to say "I assume that the authorities will continue to aim actively at maintaining full employment by appropriately managing the level of total demand" and "Experience shows that they [bouts of extreme inflation] are always caused by excessive deficits in the public finances" (Gilbert 1962: 101 and 102).

The literature is filled with examples of this sort. Duncan Foley writes in his review of a book by Arthur Burns that the latter encourages us to avoid "excessive prosperity" not only because it may lead to depression (a position Foley argues that Burns never really effectively supports), but it may cause inflation (Foley 1970). A theme in *Are Business Cycles Obsolete?*, edited by Martin Bronfenbrenner following an international conference in 1967, was whether or not Keynesianism had solved the basic problem and it only remained to not get carried away with the upturns (Bronfenbrenner 1969).

The New Classical counterrevolution put this approach on hold to an extent, with Monetarism, rational expectations, and the Lucas Critique taking center stage in the late 1970s and 1980s. But Keynesian business cycle articles still appeared, though with decreasing focus on Stop-Go aspects. Fischer (1977), for example, argued that the relevant "Keynesian" imperfection leading to fluctuations was wage contracting, while McCallum (1986) raised serious objections to Lucas' approach and built an alternative based on sticky product prices.

In the 1990s, Keynesianism did not die but tended to drift even further away from Keynes as researchers continued to try to reconcile it with the new approaches. Roger Farmer writes,

The model that I describe in this paper is a fully articulated rational expectations market clearing model. In this sense it is 'classical'. However the model is capable of replicating the price responses that one observes in the data. In this sense it is 'Keynesian'. I hope to persuade the reader that more elaborate models of this kind will provide an explanation of business fluctuations that represents a viable middle ground between real business cycle theory and the 'neo-Keynesian' agenda (Farmer 1991: 1369).

This effort continued with papers shedding even more doubt on Lucas' characterization. Eventually, this line of micro-foundational, rational-expectations

Appendix: Critical Survey of Business Cycle Theories 153

based models with various imperfections and rigidities became known as New Keynesian economics and the focus shifted even more decisively toward shocks rather than Stop-Go policies. History no doubt played a role in this transformation. The long noninflationary expansion of the 1990s called into question the need to encourage a "stop," while the fact that the Financial Crisis of 2007–2008 did not coincide with a Federal Reserve interest rate hike suggested, at least from the standpoint of their theory, a non-policy exogenous event.

Interestingly, the fact that these positions are far more "Keynesian" than "Keynes" is often lost on the authors. James Holmes and Patricia Hutton, for example, take on New Classical economics, but do so by trying to prove that Keynes was right about something he did not say:

This paper has demonstrated that Keynesian involuntary unemployment and sticky wages can be the outcome of optimising decisions of rational economic agents. It has done so based upon the intertemporal optimisation decisions of monopsonistic firms which form rational expectations of the uncertain price they will receive for their product at the time they post wages, after which employment decisions are made ... When unemployment occurs, all of the defining characteristics of Keynesian involuntary unemployment are satisfied (Holmes and Hutton 1996: 1581–2).

They support this labor-market-frictions story with quotes from the General Theory!

Throughout its postwar evolution, Neoclassical (or New) Keynesian theory has become increasingly classical in its rejection of systemic instability. One might expect Keynesian Christina Romer, once Chair of Democratic President Barack Obama's Council of Economic Advisers, to think otherwise in the aftermath of the worst recession since the Great Depression. But, as shown in Chapters 1 and 2, she believes: "Just as there is no regularity in the timing of business cycles, there is no reason why cycles have to occur at all. The prevailing view among economists is that there is a level of economic activity, often referred to as full employment, at which the economy could stay forever (Romer 2008)."

Hence, any fluctuations must necessarily be exogenous in origin.

A.2.3 Monetarist

One can identify a number of similarities between the approaches outlined in the first two sections. Though not identical, the Interest-Rate Induced and Neoclassical Keynesian models, especially the Stop-Go version of the latter, show considerable overlap. Monetarism, however, is quite distinct (though still Neoclassical).

While Keynesianism dominated theory and policy in the 1950s and 1960s, Milton Friedman and like-minded economists were arguing even then for a return to more classical principles. The inflationary problems of the 1970s gave them traction so that it is not surprising to find that Monetarism's relative peak popularity in business cycle research appears in the 1980s. The aspect of Monetarism explained here represents yet another approach to the same problem: how to explain economic fluctuations with a model that assumes systemic stability? While the answer will once again be related to policy, the transmission mechanism is very different.

Central to their model are the following:

(1) Prices and wages are perfectly flexible. However, perfect information does not exist.
(2) Changes in aggregate demand do not affect real output in the long run, but they do affect real output in the short run.
(3) Fluctuations in the money supply drive fluctuations in aggregate demand and are responsible for business cycles (emphasis added; Knoop 2010, 56–57).

To understand their business cycle theory, start with the quantity theory of money:

$$MV = Py, \tag{A.10}$$

where M is the money supply, V the velocity of money, P the price level, and y real output. Taking natural logs, it becomes:

$$lnM + lnV = lnP + lny. \tag{A.11}$$

A key premise of the Monetarist approach is that there exists a natural rate of growth of output, lny^*, that "is determined by real factors including technological growth, the growth of the labor supply, the rate of real investment, and institutional arrangements" (Hall 1990, 69). Though lny can be pushed away from lny^* in the short run, it is continually drawn back over the long run (which may represent up to ten years; Knoop 2010: 60). It strays when workers' expectations of the price level or rate of inflation are incorrect, which would only occur as a result of erratic (and therefore unpredictable, perhaps even irresponsible) changes in the money supply.

Say, for example, that the central bank suddenly and without warning raises lnM. Assuming no change in lnV, this will increase lnP and lead firms to want to expand output. In order to attract the necessary labor, they will raise the rate of increase of nominal wages (lnW). Herein lies the key, for workers, since they must keep track of many more prices than firms and lack in-house accountants, are unaware of the fact that today's lnP is higher than yesterday's. Thus, the $\uparrow lnW$ necessary to attract the needed workers is lower than the corresponding $\uparrow lnP$, meaning that firms are paying higher nominal wages but lower real ones. Workers come rushing back to the factory because of the perceived increase in compensation while firms are happy to hire them because they are actually paying less. The rise in employment causes lny to at least temporarily exceed lny^*. Eventually, however, workers come to understand that lnP has accelerated, forcing firms to raise lnW by the same proportion.

Employment returns to the natural rate, as does output growth. An analogous situation results when there is an unexpected fall in prices. Firms then lower lnW but workers, perceiving this as a cut in real wages, quit. Employment falls as does lny – at least until workers catch on once again.

It is easy to construct their business cycle from the above: unexpected fluctuations in lnM lead to temporary movements of lny above and below lny^*. While the market will immediately begin to adjust and pull growth back toward the natural rate, not only can this process take many years but other shocks can appear in the meantime. In other words,

> The Monetarist model asserts that economic fluctuations are largely the result of unanticipated changes in the money supply that lead to fluctuations in aggregate demand. Expectation stickiness, not price stickiness like in the Keynesian model, means that changes in aggregate demand have real effects on output and unemployment. Recessionary periods in which output growth is below the natural rate are the result of money growth being lower than anticipated. Expansions, where output growth is above the natural rate, are caused by higher than anticipated money growth (Knoop 2010: 60).

It follows logically from this that, "The monetarists' proposal to reduce the amplitude of the business cycle is to maintain stable, sustained growth of the money supply which, they contend, would minimize deviations in nominal aggregate demand and being about a higher degree of economic stability than we have actually experienced (Hall 1990: 84)."

Note, incidentally, that the above assumes that all changes in unemployment are voluntary. This was not true of the first two orthodox approaches described.

In summary, Monetarism uses imperfect information combined with unstable monetary policy to explain how fluctuations can occur within a model that assumes long-run-full-employment equilibrium. This is very different from either of the above approaches and it held sway for some time, to the point of driving Federal Reserve monetary policy from October 1979 to September 1982 (Hakes and Rose 1992). It has largely fallen out of favor, however, in no small part due to declining empirical support. Theoretical developments have also played a role in the sense that those originally subscribing to this view have evolved into Real Business Cycle theorists. That approach is explained next and it is quite distinct yet again from anything explained so far.

A.2.4 Real Business Cycles

Real business cycle theory views fluctuations as a consequence of external shocks. This, by itself, is not unique. What is, however, is the assumption that short-term fluctuations are simply a rational reaction to long-term adjustments, usually described as changes in productivity. As one proponent writes:

> For example, one percent permanent (once and for all) change in labor productivity in the long run leads to a one percent permanent increase in the level of capital stock,

consumption, output and investment once the transitory dynamics have been dissipated. These transitory dynamics are important for understanding fluctuations. They are initiated by the requirement that the economy must move to a permanently higher capital stock. To get there requires substantial increases in investment in the near term that taper off to a new higher steady state level as the economy converges to the higher capital stock. There will also be gradual increases in consumption and output towards their respective higher steady state levels. Work effort will also be temporarily high along the transition path. While wealth has increased, which discourages current work effort, productivity is also higher which encourages work effort. Productivity is higher because the desired or steady capital stock has risen. Thus in the near term real interest rates rise, which induces intertemporal substitution of current for future work effort. The responses, and thus the fluctuations that are present in the model, are the result of the same factors that generate economic growth. The Real Business Cycle model, therefore, provides an integrated approach to the theory of growth and fluctuations (Plosser 1989: 60).

The bottom line is that employment surges when there is a jump in productivity (because this will boost wages, making it rational to work now) and it falls when there is a decline (because this will lower wages, making leisure more attractive). These exogenous shocks lead to the adjustments we view as expansions and recession.

Real Business Cycles is viewed as a continuation of the return to Classical economic principles started by Monetarism. Among its premises are that markets are perfectly competitive, agents have perfect information, and the natural rate of output growth holds over the long and even short run (Knoop 2010: 85). The last is particularly significant as it breaks from earlier natural rate-based theories in not arguing that deviations from the short-run value are inevitably drawn toward the long-run. Rather, the former's fluctuations are instrumental in causing permanent adjustments in the latter – permanent, that is, until a new deviation occurs.[4] These deviations are a result of a result of exogenous shocks to productivity, which in turn occur as a result of a change in the price of an important input, changes in technology, changes in government taxation and regulation, wars and natural disasters, and demographics (Knoop 2010: 87–9).

These create a business cycle as follows. First, labor markets operate perfectly and all unemployment is voluntary. The latter is justified on the premise that "involuntary" unemployment exists only because out of work corporate CEOs are unwilling to take a job as a greeter at WalMart. Jobs exist, but people may voluntarily choose not to take them (Knoop 2010: 90). Second, wages are a direct function of labor productivity. Hence, any shock to the latter caused by one of the above will also change wages. When wages fall, unemployment

---

[4] Note that though the economy may be growing at the same long-run rate in numerical terms, it is doing so from a higher base. In other words, if the long-run rate is 3.5% and we suddenly accelerate to 4.5%, we should not expect to see a decline to 2.5% to compensate. Rather, we may drop back to 3.5%, but with the lasting benefit of the momentary burst (Hall 1990: 124).

Appendix: Critical Survey of Business Cycle Theories 157

rises as people exit the labor force. When wages rise, unemployment falls. In short, exogenous shocks to productivity cause the business cycle. These do not appear to be totally random to us because (a) even a random coin toss will yield series of heads or tails and (b) a single shock can take time to work through the economy as firms adjustments are made in capital and some firms go bankrupt while others start up (Hall 1990: 124–5).

In all of this, demand is totally irrelevant. All real fluctuations originate in the supply side of the economy. This, as suggested above, is a return to Classical economics, and an even more significant one than reflected in Monetarism or New Classicism. One important difference from earlier models is the focus on very specific, modern microfoundations:

> What makes these macroeconomic models and not simply well-specified microeconomic models is the assumption of representational agents, or the assumption that all individuals have the same preferences and act alike in every way. Likewise, all firms face the same production functions, cost curves, and budget constraints. As a result, macroeconomics behavior becomes a simply summation of microeconomic behavior (Knoop 2010: 87).

While it would be fair to say that this view has become less popular, it nevertheless remains a force to the point that it is the primary target of the Romer attack cited above (Romer 2016). What makes it particularly of interest here is the fact that it is yet another entirely distinct method of introducing cyclical fluctuations into a model that assumes systemic stability. It adds to the list of orthodox approaches that now includes: (1) lagged interest-rate responses leading to overinvestment, (2) central bank-induced recession (intentional or not), (3) premeditated contractionary fiscal and monetary policy aimed at alternately controlling unemployment and inflation, and (4) workers' money illusion leading to fluctuations around the natural rates of output and employment.

A.2.5 Austrian Business Cycle Theory

Though not strictly an orthodox contribution, Austrian Business Cycle Theory is included here because it faces the same essential problem as Neoclassicism: How to explain fluctuations with a model that assumes systemic stability. Also making it of interest is the fact that it experienced something of a resurgence in popularity after the Financial Crisis of 2007–2008. The Austrian approach bears some superficial similarities to those premised on the idea that central banks cause the business cycle. However, the monetary authority does so not by raising interest rates but by lowering them. Many Austrians view it as one of their most significant contributions. Robert Batemarco suggests that it is:

> an altogether different kind of theory. Derived using the method Ludwig von Mises dubbed praxeology, it is the logical consequence of the axiom of human action in conjunction with its corollaries of time preference, interest, the vertical structure of

production and capital complementarity, and the nature of the institution of central banking. Praxeology dispenses with mathematical tools, restricts aggregation to within individual stages of production and refrains from proffering predictions of either timing or magnitude (Batemarco 1994: 216).

These are extremely important and unique distinctions. Austrians are suspicious of aggregated statistics because they view economic behavior as being inescapably individualistic in nature. That and the fact that those individuals possess free will leads them to believe that mathematical generalizations are inappropriate. One may wonder how they can possibly explain the business cycle while omitting much of what the rest of the discipline considers essential.

As Batemarco indicates, their solution is what they consider to be the proper specification of individual preferences alongside a more accurate understanding of the capital-formation process. Begin with a seemingly innocuous statement: individuals generally prefer consumption today to consumption tomorrow. Because of this, they will only undertake the latter if they are offered some reward. This is why banks pay interest to attract the savings they hope to subsequently loan at a profit to investors. Ceteris paribus, the more unwilling are households to postpone consumption, the more interest banks must offer.

Note the deeper significance of this. If one of our goals is to make sure that our limited resources are properly allocated between consumption goods (the present) and investment goods (the future), all we have to do is make sure that we do not interfere with the rate of interest set by market forces. If people want to consume today, this will drive up interest rates and thereby lower investment; if they would prefer to consume tomorrow, interest rates will fall and investment rises. No government authority has to decree this, banks do not have to survey their depositors, and firms are not forced to ask their potential customers what they want. Instead, say Austrians, the free interaction of millions of individuals, each of whom doing no more than pursuing their own limited goals, creates the appropriate signal, incentive, and outcome.

Unfortunately, say Austrians, central banks are often not content to sit back and simply allow market forces to drive interest rates, and therein lies the problem. What if, for example, the monetary authorities decide to "help" by printing money/lowering interest rates? This encourages additional investment to take place without increased household saving or a change in household time preferences. Assuming full employment (which Hayek insists is necessary for a systematic explanation: Repapis 2011: 701), pressures are created such that:

Eventually, claims on actual goods for consumption or investment reach a point in which the economic agents start to compete for insufficient available present goods. That is the moment in which the upturn side of the cycle crests. In order to have access to the scarce present goods available in the economy, economic agents involved in more roundabout forms of production start to bid for capital, that is, for the supposedly saved resources available to be invested in the production of future goods. In a

Appendix: Critical Survey of Business Cycle Theories

monetary economy, the way in which the bidding is done is by demanding financial instruments representative of those supposedly saved real resources that would allow their possessors to have access to all available goods in the economy, that is, the generally accepted medium of exchange usually known as money (Zelmanovitz 2011: 27).

This, of course, drives interest rates back up meaning that those investment projects that should never have been undertaken in the first place are faced with rising costs of financing and start to fail. This creates something ranging from concern to panic in the financial market and there is a rush to liquidity. Credit conditions become even more strained, adding fuel to the downturn. Once a depression is underway, Austrian economists have stated that the best policy is to avoid artificial stimulus and let the economy remove the bankrupt enterprises. It will then recover on its own.

The basic lesson is that government interference with the market mechanism, regardless of its intent, is bound to skew outcomes in a way that eventually causes more harm than good. As Angel Martin Oro writes of the recent crisis:

In our previous analysis, we have tried to show that monetary policies, along with the inherent nature of our current fiat money system, are the ultimate causes of the boom-and-bust cycle we are now witnessing. It should also be clear that the institutional structure of the financial world has little in common with that of the free market.

Free markets therefore cannot be blamed for the current meltdown. Instead of being a failure of the free market, it has been a failure of regulation and monetary central-planning.

It is our contention that in a free, gold-based monetary system, the instabilities and expansionary monetary policies of the banking system would be severely limited. The return to sound money and free markets is the only path towards true economic stability and sustainable prosperity (Oro 2010: 88).

The Austrians are not unique in blaming the business cycle on easy monetary policy, but their near-exclusive focus on this line of causation is, as is their approach to modeling. Their insistence on framing the issue as one that can be – indeed, must be – explained at the level of individual preferences sets them apart, as does their characterization of the underlying problem being the fact that government policy has frustrated those preferences. It represents yet one more disparate approach to explaining booms and busts while using a model that assumes systemic stability.

A.3 CONCLUSIONS

The reason for this appendix is to both give readers a deeper understanding of the theory developed in the Chapters 2 and 3 and to substantiate two key contentions driving this volume:

1. Institutionalist/Post Keynesian explanations of the business cycle are mutually supportive and complementary; and

2. Orthodox explanations of the business cycle vary widely and are based on premises that often stretch credulity (all unemployment is voluntary, fluctuations are caused by confusion over the actual rate of inflation, etc.).

One possible interpretation of this is that while the Institutionalist/Post Keynesian approach has generated numerous fruitful lines of investigation, the mainstream has struggled to come up with a single useful model and has instead struck out (in more ways than one) in multiple, barren directions. It is certainly mine.

References

AAA Staff. 2021. "What It Costs to Drive a New Car in 2021," *American Automobile Association*. Available: www.ace.aaa.com/automotive/advocacy/cost-of-driving.html. Accessed February 22, 2023.

Alexander, R. 2013. "Reinhart, Rogoff … and Herndon: The Student Who Caught Out the Profs," *BBC Online*. Available: www.bbc.com/news/magazine-22223190. Accessed April 17, 2024.

Allen, P. 2011. "No Chance of Default, US Can Print Money: Greenspan," *CNBC*. Available: www.cnbc.com/2011/08/07/no-chance-of-default-us-can-print-money-greenspan.html. Accessed March 26, 2024.

Arena, R. and Raybaut, A. 2001. "On the Foundations of Minsky's Business Cycle Theory: An Interpretation," in *Financial Fragility and Investment in the Capitalist Economy*, R. Bellofiore and P. Ferri, editors. Cheltenham, UK and Northampton: Edward Elgar, pp. 113–132.

Arnone, M. and Iden, G. R. 2003. "Primary Dealers in Government Securities: Policy Issues and Selected Countries Experience," *International Monetary Fund, IMF Working Papers*: 03/45.

Aron-Dine, A., Stone, C. and Kogan, R. 2008. "How Robust Was the 2001–2007 Economic Expansion?" *Center on Budget and Policy Priorities*. Available: www.cbpp.org/sites/default/files/archive/8-9-05bud.htm. Accessed April 17, 2024.

Arthur, W. B. 1989. "Competing Technologies, Increasing Returns, and Lock-In by Historical Events," *The Economic Journal*, 99(394), pp. 116–131.

Baba, C. and Lee, M. J. 2022. "Second-Round Effects of Oil Price Shocks – Implications for Europe's Inflation Outlook," *International Monetary Fund*. Available: www.imf.org/en/Publications/WP/Issues/2022/09/06/Second-Round-Effects-of-Oil-Price-Shocks-Implications-for-Europes-Inflation-Outlook-523201. Accessed March 2, 2023.

Backhouse, R. E. 2017. "From Business Cycle Theory to the Theory of Employment: Alvin Hansen and Paul Samuelson," *Journal of the History of Economic Thought*, 39(1), pp. 89–99.

Baker, M. and Wurgler, J. 2007. "Investor Sentiment in the Stock Market," *Journal of Economic Perspectives*, 21(2), pp. 129–151.

Ball, L. M. 2016. "The Fed and Lehman Brothers: Introduction and Summary," *National Bureau of Economic Research*, Cambridge, MA, Working Paper No. 22410. Available: www.nber.org/papers/w22410. Accessed October 4, 2024.

Batemarco, R. J. 1994. "Austrian Business Cycle Theory," in *The Elgar Companion to Austrian Economics*, P. J. Boettke, editor. Aldershot, UK: Edward Elgar, pp. 216–223.

Batten, D. S. 1981. "Inflation: The Cost-Push Myth," *Review, Federal Reserve Bank of St. Louis*, June/July 1981, pp. 20–26.

Bauer, L., Liu, P., Moss, E., Nunn, R. and Shambaugh, J. 2019. "All School and No Work Becoming the Norm for American Teens," *The Brookings Institution*. Available: www.brookings.edu/articles/all-school-and-no-work-becoming-the-norm-for-american-teens/. Accessed March 1, 2023.

Bell, S. 1998. "Can Taxes and Bonds Finance Government Spending?" *Levy Economics Institute* Working Paper No. 244. Available: www.levyinstitute.org/pubs/wp244.pdf. Accessed October 3, 2022.

Bellofiore, R. 1999. "Schumpeter's Theory of Innovation, Development, and Cycles," in *Encyclopedia of Political Economy*, Phillip Anthony O'Hara, editor. London: Routledge, pp. 1010–1013.

Betterton, R. 2023. "Current Car Loan Interest Rates," *BankRate.com*. Available: www.bankrate.com/loans/auto-loans/current-auto-loan-interest-rates/. Accessed February 22, 2023.

Biden, J. 2023. "State of the Union Address," *The White House*. Available: www.whitehouse.gov/briefing-room/speeches-remarks/2023/02/07/remarks-of-president-joe-biden-state-of-the-union-address-as-prepared-for-delivery/. Accessed March 1, 2023.

Bigio, S. 2015. "Endogenous Liquidity and the Business Cycle," *American Economic Review*, 105(6), pp. 1883–1927.

Bischoff, C., Kokkelenberg, E. and Terregrossa, R. 1991. "Tax Policy and Business Fixed Investment during the Reagan Era," in *The Economic Legacy of the Reagan Years: Euphoria or Chaos?* A. P. Sahu and R. L. Tracy, editors. Westport, CT, and London: Greenwood, Praeger, pp. 21–39.

Bivens, J. 2023. "Recent Banking Failures Add Another Reason to Halt Interest Rate Hikes," *Economic Policy Institute*. Working Economics Blog. Available: www.epi.org/blog/recent-banking-failures-add-another-reason-to-halt-interest-rate-hikes/. Accessed April 1, 2024.

Blackley, J. 2023. "This Is the Average Price of a Used Car in Each State," *ISeeCars.com*. Available: www.iseecars.com/used-car-prices-by-state-study. Accessed February 22, 2023.

BLS (Bureau of Labor Statistics). 1967. "CPI Reports, Various Issues."

BLS (Bureau of Labor Statistics). 2021. "Characteristics of Minimum Wage Workers, 2020," *Bureau of Labor Statistics*. Available: www.bls.gov/opub/reports/minimum-wage/2020/home.htm. Accessed February 24, 2023.

BLS (Bureau of Labor Statistics). 2023. "Consumer Expenditures in 2022," *Bureau of Labor Statistics*. Available: www.bls.gov/opub/reports/consumer-expenditures/2022/home.htm. Accessed April 1, 2024.

Boettke, P. 1991. "The Reagan Regulatory Regime – Reality vs. Rhetoric: Comment," in *The Economic Legacy of the Reagan Years: Euphoria or Chaos?* A. P. Sahu and R. L. Tracy, editors. Westport, CT, and London: Greenwood, Praeger, pp. 117–123.

References

Bordo, M. D. and Eichengreen, B. 2008. "Bretton Woods and the Great Inflation," *National Bureau of Economic Research*. Conference on the Great Inflation. Available: www.nber.org/system/files/chapters/c9174/revisions/c9174.revo.pdf. Accessed April 6, 2022.

Boyer, R. 2005. "From Shareholder Value to CEO Power: The Paradox of the 1990s," *Competition and Change*, 9(1), pp. 7–47.

Bronfenbrenner, M. 1969. *Is the Business Cycle Obsolete?* New York: Wiley-Interscience.

Brown, M. A. and Ahmadi, M. 2019. "Would a Green New Deal Add or Kill Jobs?" *Scientific American*. Available: www.scientificamerican.com/article/would-a-green-new-deal-add-or-kill-jobs1/. Accessed February 27, 2023.

Brown-Collier, E. K. 1998. "Johnson's Great Society: Its Legacy in the 1990s," *Review of Social Economy*, 56(3), pp. 259–276.

Budge, S. 1925. *Grundzüge der Theoretischen Nationalökonomie*, Jena: Fischer.

Bureau of Labor Statistics. 1967. "CPI Reports," *December 1967*.

Bureau of Labor Statistics. 1968. "CPI Reports," *December 1968*.

Bureau of Labor Statistics. 1969. "CPI Reports," *December 1967*.

Bureau of Labor Statistics. 1974. "CPI Reports," *December 1974*

Burns, A. F. 1951. "Mitchell on What Happens during Business Cycles," *Conference on Business Cycles, National Bureau of Economic Research*. Available: www.nber.org/system/files/chapters/c4759/c4759.pdf. Accessed October 1, 2020.

Burtless, G. 1991. "The Supply-side Legacy of the Reagan Years – Effects on Labor Supply," in *The Economic Legacy of the Reagan Years: Euphoria or Chaos?* A. P. Sahu and R. L. Tracy, editors. Westport, CT, and London: Greenwood, Praeger, pp. 43–66.

Byrne, P. A. and Hudson-Edwards, K. A. 2018. "Three Ways Making a Smartphone Can Harm the Environment," *The Conversation Trust*. Available: https://theconversation.com/three-ways-making-a-smartphone-can-harm-the-environment-102148. Accessed February 27, 2023.

Callen, T. 2007. "IMF Survey: IMF Forecasts Slower World Growth in 2008," *International Monetary Fund*. Available: www.imf.org/en/News/Articles/2015/09/28/04/53/sores1017b. Accessed November 16, 2022.

Calmes, J. 2009. "House Passes Stimulus Plan with No GOP Votes," *New York Times*. Available: www.nytimes.com/2009/01/29/us/politics/29obama.html. Accessed April 1, 2024.

Campagna, A. S. 1994. *The Economy in the Reagan Years*, New York: Bloomsbury Publishing.

CBC Staff. 2006. "Hurricanes Push U.S. Inflation to 5.4 Per Cent in 2005," *Canadian Broadcasting Corporation*. Available: www.cbc.ca/news/business/hurricanes-push-u-s-inflation-to-5-4-per-cent-in-2005-1.580205. Accessed April 17, 2024.

CFI Team. 2022. "Black Monday: The Stock Market Crash of 1987," *Corporate Finance Institute* Available: https://corporatefinanceinstitute.com/resources/equities/black-Monday/. Accessed November 4, 2022.

Child Care Aware. 2021. "Demanding Change: Repairing Our Child Care System," *Child Care Aware of America*. Available: https://info.childcareaware.org/hubfs/FINAL-Demanding%20Change%20Report-020322.pdf. Accessed February 27, 2023.

Clinton, H. 2023. "An Economy That Works For Everyone," *HillaryClinton.com*. Available: www.hillaryclinton.com/issues/an-economy-that-works-for-everyone/. Accessed March 1, 2023.

Colander, D. 2005. "The Making of an Economist Redux," *Journal of Economic Perspectives*, 19(1), pp. 175–198.

Davidson, P. 1978. *Money and the Real World*, Springer.

Davidson, P. 2011. *Post Keynesian Macroeconomic Theory, Second Edition: A Foundation for Successful Economic Policies for the Twenty-First Century*, Cheltenham, UK: Edward Elgar.

Davis, A. M. 1901. "Currency and Banking in the Province of the Massachusetts-Bay," *Publications of the American Economic Association*, 2(2), pp. 1–332.

Davis, J. and Lehn, K. 1991. "Securities Regulation during the Reagan Administration – Corporate Takeovers and the 1987 Stock Market Crash," in *The Economic Legacy of the Reagan Years: Euphoria or Chaos?* A. P. Sahu and R. L. Tracy, editors. Westport, CT, and London: Greenwood, Praeger, pp. 129–146.

De Antoni, E. 2008. "Minsky's Upward Instability: The Not-Too-Keynesian Optimism of a Financial Cassandra," in *Computable, Constructive and Behavioural Economic Dynamics*, Stefano Zambelli, editor. London: Routledge, pp. 462–484.

De Loecker, J., Eeckhout, J. and Unger, G. 2020. "The Rise of Market Power and the Macroeconomic Implications," *Quarterly Journal of Economics*, 135(2), pp. 561–644.

Democratic Party. 2020. "2020 Democratic Party Platform," *Democratic Party*. Available: https://democrats.org/wp-content/uploads/2020/08/2020-Democratic-Party-Platform.pdf. Accessed February 28, 2023.

Deranty, J. 2019. "Work Is a Fundamental Part of Being Human. Robots Won't Stop Us Doing It," *The Conversation*. Available: https://theconversation.com/work-is-a-fundamental-part-of-being-human-robots-wont-stop-us-doing-it-127925. Accessed March 25, 2024.

Dong, F., Wang, P. and Wen, Y. 2016. "Credit Search and Credit Cycles," *Economic Theory*, 61(2), pp. 215–239.

Dotsey, M., Fujita, S. and Rudanko, L. 2017. "Where Is Everybody? The Shrinking Labor Force Participation Rate," in *Economic Insights*, Federal Reserve Bank of Philadelphia, pp. 17–24. https://en.wikipedia.org/wiki/Economic_Insights.

Druat, T. and Silva, J. 2003. "Borrowing to Make Ends Meet: The Growth of Credit Card Debt in the '90s," *Demos: A Network for Ideas and Action*. Available: www.demos.org/sites/default/files/publications/borrowing_to_make_ends_meet.pdf. Accessed November 11, 2022.

Economic Report of the President. 1956. *Transmitted to the Congress Together with the Annual Report of the Council of Economic Advisors*, Council of Economic Advisers.

Economic Report of the President. 1957. *Transmitted to the Congress Together with the Annual Report of the Council of Economic Advisors*, Council of Economic Advisers.

Economic Report of the President. 1958. *Transmitted to the Congress Together with the Annual Report of the Council of Economic Advisors*, Council of Economic Advisers.

Economic Report of the President. 1959. *Transmitted to the Congress Together with the Annual Report of the Council of Economic Advisors*, Council of Economic Advisers.

Economic Report of the President. 1961. *Transmitted to the Congress Together with the Annual Report of the Council of Economic Advisors*, Council of Economic Advisers.

Economic Report of the President. 1962. *Transmitted to the Congress Together with the Annual Report of the Council of Economic Advisors*, Council of Economic Advisers.

Economic Report of the President. 1963. *Transmitted to the Congress Together with the Annual Report of the Council of Economic Advisors*, Council of Economic Advisers.

References

Economic Report of the President. 1966. *Transmitted to the Congress Together with the Annual Report of the Council of Economic Advisors*, Council of Economic Advisers.
Economic Report of the President. 1968. *Transmitted to the Congress Together with the Annual Report of the Council of Economic Advisors*, Council of Economic Advisers.
Economic Report of the President. 1971. *Transmitted to the Congress Together with the Annual Report of the Council of Economic Advisors*, Council of Economic Advisers.
Economic Report of the President. 1972. *Transmitted to the Congress Together with the Annual Report of the Council of Economic Advisors*, Council of Economic Advisers.
Economic Report of the President. 1975. *Transmitted to the Congress Together with the Annual Report of the Council of Economic Advisors*, Council of Economic Advisers.
Economic Report of the President. 1976. *Transmitted to the Congress Together with the Annual Report of the Council of Economic Advisors*, Council of Economic Advisers.
Economic Report of the President. 1977. *Transmitted to the Congress Together with the Annual Report of the Council of Economic Advisors*, Council of Economic Advisers.
Economic Report of the President. 1979. *Transmitted to the Congress Together with the Annual Report of the Council of Economic Advisors*, Council of Economic Advisers.
Economic Report of the President. 1980. *Transmitted to the Congress Together with the Annual Report of the Council of Economic Advisors*, Council of Economic Advisers.
Economic Report of the President. 1982. *Transmitted to the Congress Together with the Annual Report of the Council of Economic Advisors*, Council of Economic Advisers.
Economic Report of the President. 1983. *Transmitted to the Congress Together with the Annual Report of the Council of Economic Advisors*, Council of Economic Advisers.
Economic Report of the President. 1984. *Transmitted to the Congress Together with the Annual Report of the Council of Economic Advisors*, Council of Economic Advisers.
Economic Report of the President. 1988. *Transmitted to the Congress Together with the Annual Report of the Council of Economic Advisors*, Council of Economic Advisers.
Economic Report of the President. 1990. *Transmitted to the Congress Together with the Annual Report of the Council of Economic Advisors*, Council of Economic Advisers.
Economic Report of the President. 1993. *Transmitted to the Congress Together with the Annual Report of the Council of Economic Advisors*, Council of Economic Advisers.
Economic Report of the President. 1995. *Transmitted to the Congress Together with the Annual Report of the Council of Economic Advisors*, Council of Economic Advisers.
Economic Report of the President. 1996. *Transmitted to the Congress Together with the Annual Report of the Council of Economic Advisors*, Council of Economic Advisers.
Economic Report of the President. 2001. *Transmitted to the Congress Together with the Annual Report of the Council of Economic Advisors*, Council of Economic Advisers.
Economic Report of the President. 2002. *Transmitted to the Congress Together with the Annual Report of the Council of Economic Advisors*, Council of Economic Advisers.
Economic Report of the President. 2003. *Transmitted to the Congress Together with the Annual Report of the Council of Economic Advisors*, Council of Economic Advisers.
Economic Report of the President. 2004. *Transmitted to the Congress Together with the Annual Report of the Council of Economic Advisors*, Council of Economic Advisers.
Economic Report of the President. 2005. *Transmitted to the Congress Together with the Annual Report of the Council of Economic Advisors*, Council of Economic Advisers.
Economic Report of the President. 2006. *Transmitted to the Congress Together with the Annual Report of the Council of Economic Advisors*, Council of Economic Advisers.
Economic Report of the President. 2007. *Transmitted to the Congress Together with the Annual Report of the Council of Economic Advisors*, Council of Economic Advisers.

Economic Report of the President. 2010. *Transmitted to the Congress Together with the Annual Report of the Council of Economic Advisors*, Council of Economic Advisers.

Eggertsson, G. B. and Krugman, P. 2012. "Debt, Deleveraging, and the Liquidity Trap: A Fisher-Minsky-Koo Approach," *The Quarterly Journal of Economics*, 127(3), pp. 1469–1513.

Farmer, Rorger E. A. 1991. "Sticky Prices," *The Economic Journal*, 101, pp. 1369–1379.

Farre, L., Fasani, F. and Mueller, H. 2018. "Feeling Useless: The Effect of Unemployment on Mental Health in the Great Recession," *IZA Journal of Labor Economics*, 7(1), pp. 1–34.

Fawley, B. W. and Juvenal, L. 2011. "Why Health Care Matters and the Current Debt Does Not," *The Regional Economist*, 19(4), pp. 4–5.

Federal Reserve Board. 2006. "Economic and Financial Developments in 2006 and Early 2007," *Federal Reserve Board*. Available: www.federalreserve.gov/boarddocs/rptcongress/annual06/sec1/c2.htm. Accessed November 16, 2022.

Federal Reserve Bulletin. 1979. Board of Governors of the Federal Reserve System.

Feyrer, J. and Sacerdote, B. 2011. "Did the Stimulus Stimulate? Real Time Estimates of the Effects of the American Recovery and Reinvestment Act," *National Bureau of Economic Research*. Available: www.nber.org/papers/w16759. Accessed January 20, 2023.

Fischer, S. 1977. "Long-Term Contracts, Rational Expectations, and the Optimal Money Supply Rule," *Journal of Political Economy*, 85(1), pp. 191–205.

Fisher, I. 1910. *Introduction to Economic Science*, New York: The Macmillan Company.

Foley, D. K. 1970. "Review of Arthur Burns' the Business Cycle in a Changing World," *Journal of Finance*, 25(4), pp. 954.

Frank, J. 2013. *Ike and Dick*, Riverside: Simon and Schuster.

Friedman, M. 1969. *The Optimum Quantity of Money and Other Essays*, Chicago: Aldine Publishing Company.

Frumkin, N. 2010. *Recession Prevention Handbook*, Armonk, NY: Sharpe.

Fu, F., Huang, S. and Wang, R. 2022. "Why Do U.S. Firms Invest Less Over Time?" *Journal of Empirical Finance*, 69, pp. 15–42.

Fuhrer, J. C. and Schuh, S. 1998. "Beyond Shocks: What Causes Business Cycles? An Overview," *New England Economic Review*, pp. 3–24.

Fullwiler, S. T. 2016. "The Debt Ratio and Sustainable Macroeconomic Policy," *World Economic Review*, 7, pp. 12–42.

Fulton, B. D. 2017. "Health Care Market Concentration Trends In The United States: Evidence And Policy Responses," *Health Affairs*, 36(9), pp. 1530–1538.

Furman, J. 2015. "Business Investment in the United States: Facts, Explanations, Puzzles, and Policies," *Progressive Policy Institute*. Available: www.progressivepolicy.org/wp-content/uploads/2015/09/2015.09.30-Jason-Furman_Business-Investment-in-US-Facts-Explanations-Puzzles-Policies.pdf. Accessed April 15, 2024.

Galbraith, J. K. 2023. "In Defense of Low Interest Rates," *Levy Economics Institute* Policy Note 2023/3. Available: www.levyinstitute.org/pubs/pn_23-3.pdf. Accessed April 1, 2024.

Galbraith, J. K. and Hale, T. 2004. "Income Distribution and the Information Technology Bubble," *University of Texas Inequality Project*. Available: http://utip.gov.utexas.edu/papers/utip_27.pdf. Accessed August 15, 2010.

Galvani, A. P. and Fitzpatrick, M. C. 2020. "Cost-Effectiveness of Transitional Us Plans for Universal Health Care," *The Lancet*, 395(10238), pp. 1692–1693.

Geier, B. 2015. "What Did We Learn From the Dotcom Stock Bubble of 2000?" *Time Magazine*. Available: https://time.com/3741681/2000-dotcom-stock-bust/. Accessed April 17, 2024.

Gilbert, M. 1962. "The Postwar Business Cycle in Western Europe," *American Economic Review*, 52, pp. 93–109.

Giles, C. 2017. "Central Bankers Face a Crisis of Confidence As Models Fail," *Financial Times*, Oct 11, 2017. Available: www.ft.com/content/333b3406-acd5-11e7-beba-5521c713abf4. Accessed February 22, 2023.

Godley, Wynne. 1999. "Seven Unsustainable Processes: Medium-Term Prospects and Policies for the United States and the World," *Levy Economics Institute*, Special Report. Available: www.levyinstitute.org/pubs/SA_1999_Godley.pdf. Accessed October 4, 2024.

Gordon, Robert J. 2016. "Perspectives on the Rise and Fall of American Growth," *The American Economic Review*, 106(5), pp. 72–76.

Goutsmedt, A. 2022. "How the Phillips Curve Shaped Full Employment Policy in the 1970s: The Debates on the Humphrey-Hawkins Act," *History of Political Economy*, 54(4), pp. 619–653.

Greenspan, A. 1997. "Remarks by Alan Greenspan at the Catholic University Leuven, Leuven, Belgium," *Federal Reserve Board*. Available: www.federalreserve.gov/boarddocs/speeches/1997/19970114.htm. Accessed March 26, 2024.

Greider, W. 1989. *Secrets of the Temple: How the Federal Reserve Runs the Country*, Simon and Schuster.

Gutiérrez, G. and Philippon, T. 2016. "Investment-less Growth: An Empirical Investigation," *National Bureau of Economic Research*. Available: www.nber.org/papers/w22897. Accessed April 20, 2023.

Hakes, D. R. and Rose, D. C. 1992. "The 1979–1982 Monetary Policy Experiment: Monetarist, Anti-Monetarist, or Quasi-Monetarist?" *Journal of Post Keynesian Economics*, 15(2), pp. 281–288.

Hall, T. E. 1990. *Business Cycles: The Nature and Causes of Economic Fluctuations*, Westport, CA: Greenwood, Praeger.

Harris, M. and Jamroz, D. 1976. "Evaluating the Leading Indicators," *Federal Reserve Bank of New York*. Available: www.newyorkfed.org/medialibrary/media/research/monthly_review/1976_pdf/06_4_76.pdf. Accessed February 12, 2024.

Harvey, J. T. 2002. "Keynes' Chapter 22: A System Dynamics Model," *Journal of Economic Issues*, 36(2), pp. 373–81.

Harvey, J. T. 2009. *Currencies, Capital Flows and Crises: A Post Keynesian Analysis of Exchange Rate Determination*, London: Routledge.

Harvey, J. T. 2010. "Modeling Financial Crises: A Schematic Approach," *Journal of Post Keynesian Economics*, 33(1), pp. 61–82.

Harvey, J. T. 2011. "United States Business Cycles from 1971 through 2010: A Post Keynesian Explanation," *Journal of Economic Issues*, 45(2), pp. 381–390.

Harvey, J. T. 2014a. "Using the General Theory to Explain the U.S. Business Cycle, 1950–2009," *Journal of Post Keynesian Economics*, 36(3), pp. 391–414.

Harvey, J. T. 2014b. "Teaching Keynes's Business Cycle: An Extension of Paul Davidson's Capital Market Model," *Journal of Post Keynesian Economics*, 36(4), pp 589–606.

Harvey, J. T. 2020a. *Contending Perspectives in Economics: A Guide to Contemporary Schools of Thought*, Cheltenham, UK: Edward Elgar Publishing, 2nd edition.

Harvey, J. T. 2020b. "Getting the Financial Crisis Wrong: The Dead End that is Neoclassical Macro Modeling," in *Contemporary Issues in Heterodox Economics*, Arturo Hermann and Simon Mouatt, editors. London: Routledge, pp. 160–168.

Harvey, J. T. 2022. "Testing Keynes' Aggregate Investment Function," *Journal of Post Keynesian Economics*, 45(2), pp. 246–262.

Harvey, J. T. and Pham, Khanh. 2024. "Austrian vs Post Keynesian Explanations of the Business Cycle: An Empirical Examination." *Journal of Post Keynesian Economics*, 47(2), pp. 419–441.

Hickel, J. 2019. "Degrowth: A Theory of Radical Abundance," *Real-World Economics Review*, 87(19), pp. 54–68.

High, S. 2021. "Deindustrialization and Its Consequences," in *Routledge International Handbook of Working-Class Studies*, Michele Fazio, Christie Launius, and Tim Strangleman, editors, London: Routledge, pp. 169–179.

Holmes, J. M. and Hutton, P. A. 1996. "Keynesian Involuntary Unemployment and Sticky Nominal Wages," *The Economic Journal*, 106(439), pp. 1564–1585.

Hornstein, A., Kudlyak, M., Meisenbacher, B., and Ramachandran, David A. 2023. "How Far Is Labor Force Participation from Its Trend?" *Federal Reserve Bank of San Francisco*. Available: www.frbsf.org/research-and-insights/publications/economic-letter/2023/08/how-far-is-labor-force-participation-from-its-trend/. Accessed April 17, 2024.

Horowitz, Juliana M., Igielnik, R. and Kochhar, R. 2020. "Trends in Income and Wealth Inequality," *Pew Research*. Available: www.pewresearch.org/social-trends/2020/01/09/trends-in-income-and-wealth-inequality/. Accessed April 17, 2024.

Isaacs, J. B. and Lovell, P. 2010. "Families of the Recession: Unemployed Parents and Their Children," *Brookings Institution First Focus Campaign for Children*. Available: www.brookings.edu/research/families-of-the-recession-unemployed-parents-their-children/. Accessed February 27, 2023.

Jacobs, D. and Myers, L. 2014. "Union Strength, Neoliberalism, and Inequality: Contingent Political Analyses of US Income Differences since 1950," *American Sociological Review*, 79(4), pp. 752–774.

Joffe-Walt, Chana. undated. "UNFIT FOR WORK: The Startling Rise of Disability in America," *National Public Radio*. Available: https://apps.npr.org/unfit-for-work/. Accessed April 17, 2024.

Jorgenson, D. W. 2001. "Information Technology and the U.S. Economy," *American Economic Review*, 91(1), pp. 1–32.

Jorgenson, D. W., Ho, M. S., Samuels, J. D. and Stiroh, K. J. 2007. "Industry Origins of the American Productivity Resurgence," *Economic Systems Research*, 19(3), pp. 229–252.

JPMorgan. 2023. "Supply Chain Issues and Autos: When Will the Chip Shortage End?" *JP Morgan Global Research*, Available: www.jpmorgan.com/insights/research/supply-chain-chip-shortage. Accessed April 1, 2024.

Kaldor, N. 1940. "A Model of the Trade Cycle," *The Economic Journal*, 50(197), pp. 78–92.

Kalecki, M. 1937. "A Theory of the Business Cycle," *The Review of Economic Studies*, 4(2), pp. 77–97.

Kalecki, M. 1939. *Essays in the Theory of Economic Fluctuations*, London: Allen and Unwin.

References

Kara, S. 2018. "Is Your Phone Tainted by the Misery of the 35,000 Children in Congo's Mines?" *The Guardian*. Available: www.theguardian.com/global-development/2018/oct/12/phone-misery-children-congo-cobalt-mines-drc. Accessed February 27, 2023.

Keen, S. 1995. "Finance and Economic Breakdown: Modeling Minsky's 'Financial Instability Hypothesis,'" *Journal of Post Keynesian Economics*, 17(4), pp. 607–635.

Keen, S. 2011. *Debunking Economics: The Naked Emperor Dethroned?*, Zed Books Ltd.

Kelton, S. 2020. *The Deficit Myth: Modern Monetary Theory and the Birth of the People's Economy*, PublicAffairs.

Keynes, J. M. 1920. *The Economic Consequences of the Peace*, New York: Harcourt, Brace.

Keynes, J. M. 1936. *The General Theory of Employment, Interest and Money*, New York: Harcourt, Brace.

Keynes, J. M. 1937a. "The General Theory of Employment," *The Quarterly Journal of Economics*, 51(2), pp. 209–223.

Keynes, J. M. 1937b. "The 'ex-ante' Theory of the Rate of Interest," *The Economic Journal*, 47(188), pp. 663–669.

Kliesen, K. and Wheelock, D. 2021. "Managing a New Policy Framework: Paul Volcker, the St. Louis Fed, and the 1979–82 War on Inflation," *Federal Reserve Bank of St. Louis Review*, 103(1), pp. 71–97.

Knoop, T. A. 2010. *Recessions and Depressions: Understanding Business Cycles*, 2nd ed. Santa Barbara, CA, and Oxford: ABC-CLIO, Praeger.

Komlos, J. 2018. "Reaganomics: A Historical Watershed," *Center for Economic Studies and iFo Institute*, Working Paper 7301. Available: www.cesifo.org/en/publications/2018/working-paper/reaganomics-historical-watershed. Accessed March 12, 2023.

Kuznets, S. 1930. "Monetary Business Cycle Theory in Germany," *Journal of Political Economy*, 38, pp. 125–163.

Lindsey, D. E., Orphanides, A. and Rasche, R. H. 2005. "The Reform of October 1979: How It Happened and Why," *Federal Reserve Bank of St. Louis Review*, 87(2), pp. 187–235.

Long, H. and Luhby, T. 2016. "Yes, This Is the Slowest U.S. Recovery since WWII," *CNN Business*. Available: https://money.cnn.com/2016/10/05/news/economy/us-recovery-slowest-since-wwii/index.html. Accessed February 5, 2023.

López G. J. and Assous, M. 2010. *Michal Kalecki, Great Thinkers in Economics Series*, Basingstoke, UK: Palgrave Macmillan.

Maas, S. 2017. "Explaining Low Investment Spending," *The National Bureau of Economic Research Digest*. Available: www.nber.org/digest/feb17/explaining-low-investment-spending. Accessed July 12, 2023.

Mahe, E. 2011. "Wake Up SandP: The US Can't Default on Its Debt," *Seeking Alpha*. Available: https://seekingalpha.com/article/264717-wake-up-s-and-p-the-u-s-cant-default-on-its-debt. Accessed March 26, 2024.

May, A. M. 1990. "President Eisenhower, Economic Policy, and the 1960 Presidential Election," *The Journal of Economic History*, 50(2), pp. 417–427.

McCallum, B. T. 1986. "On 'Real' and 'Sticky-Price' Theories of the Business Cycle," *Journal of Money, Credit, and Banking*, 18(4), pp. 397–414.

Mills, D. Quinn. 2001. "Who's to Blame for the Bubble?" *Harvard Business Review*, Available: https://hbr.org/2001/05/whos-to-blame-for-the-bubble. Accessed May 2001.

Millstone, C. 2018. "Why Economic 'Degrowth' Is an Ethical Imperative," *GreenBiz*. Available: www.greenbiz.com/article/why-economic-degrowth-ethical-imperative Accessed January 13, 2020.

Milner, A., Page, A. and LaMontagne, A. D. 2014. "Cause and Effect in Studies on Unemployment, Mental Health and Suicide: A Meta-analytic and Conceptual Review," *Psychological Medicine*, 44(5), pp. 909–917.

Minchin, T. J. 2023. "'A Gallant Fight': The UAW and the 1970 General Motors Strike," *International Review of Social History*, 68(1), pp. 41–73.

Minsky, H. 1942. Notes Taken by Minsky on Oscar Lange's class "Business Cycle Theory." Available: http://digitalcommons.bard.edu/hm_archive/482. Accessed April 1, 2020.

Minsky, H. 1954a. The Use of Stochastic Processes in Business Cycle Analysis. Available: http://digitalcommons.bard.edu/hm_archive/249. Accessed April 1, 2020.

Minsky, H. 1954b. The Use of Stochastic Assumption in Accelerator-Multiplier Business Cycle Theory. Available: http://digitalcommons.bard.edu/hm_archive/252. Accessed April 1, 2020.

Minsky, H. 1954c. Alternative Non-Linear Formulation of Business Cycle Models. Available: http://digitalcommons.bard.edu/hm_archive/110. Accessed April 1, 2020.

Minsky, H. 1959. On Animal Spirits and the Lure of a Bonanza. Available: http://digitalcommons.bard.edu/hm_archive/259. Accessed April 1, 2020.

Minsky, H. 1982. *Can "It" Happen Again?: Essays on Instability and Finance*. M.E. Sharpe.

Minsky, H. 2008 (1st ed 1986). *Stabilizing an Unstable Economy*, 1st ed. 1986. New York: McGraw Hill.

Minsky, H., Friend, I. and Andrews, V. L. 1960. Financial Crisis, Financial Systems, and the Performance of the Economy. Available: http://digitalcommons.bard.edu/hm_archive/232. Accessed April 1, 2020.

Mishkin, F. S. 1995. "Symposium on the Monetary Transmission Mechanism," *Journal of Economic Perspectives*, 9(4), pp. 3–10.

Mitchell, W. C. 1913. *Business Cycles*, University of California Press.

Moe, A. 2022. "The Crisis Facing Nursing Homes, Assisted Living and Home Care for America's Elderly," *Politico*. Available: www.politico.com/news/magazine/2022/07/28/elder-care-worker-shortage-immigration-crisis-00047454. Accessed February 24, 2023.

Morath, E. 2016. "Seven Years Later, Recovery Remains the Weakest of the Post-World War II Era," *Wall Street Journal*. Available: www.wsj.com/articles/BL-REB-36300. Accessed February 5, 2023.

Murphy, J. M. 2004. "The Language of the Liberal Consensus: John F. Kennedy, Technical Reason, and the 'New Economics' at Yale University," *The Quarterly Journal of Speech*, 90(2), pp. 133–162.

Murray, M. J. 2013. "Effective Demand, Technological Change, and The Job Guarantee Program," in *The Job Guarantee: Toward True Full Employment*, Michael J. Murray and Mathew Forstater, editors. Springer, pp. 95–124.

NASA. 2020. "Scientific Consensus: Earth's Climate is Warming," *Earth Science Communications Team at NASA's Jet Propulsion Laboratory*, California Institute of Technology. Available: https://climate.nasa.gov/consensus/. Accessed January 28, 2020.

Nelson, J. A. 1995. "Feminism and economics," *Journal of Economic Perspectives*, 9(2), pp. 131–148.

References

Nguyen, J. 2021. "The Economics of Nursing Homes (and Paying for One)," *Marketplace*. Available: www.marketplace.org/2021/02/11/the-economics-of-nursing-homes-and-paying-for-one/. Accessed February 24, 2023.

Nichols, J. 2013. "Gotta Sequester? Or Was Cheney Right That 'Deficits Don't Matter'?" *The Nation*. Available: www.thenation.com/article/archive/gotta-sequester-or-was-cheney-right-deficits-dont-matter/. Accessed March 26, 2024.

Norgaard, R. 2015. "The Church of Economism and Its Discontents," *Great Transition Initiative: Toward a Transformative Vision and Praxis*. Available: https://greattransition.org/publication/the-church-of-economism-and-its-discontents. Accessed February 27, 2023.

Obama, B. 2016. "State of the Union Address," *The White House*. Available: https://obamawhitehouse.archives.gov/the-press-office/2016/01/12/remarks-president-barack-obama-%E2%80%93-prepared-delivery-state-union-address. Accessed February 28, 2023.

Oro, A. M. 2010. "Why Free Markets Should Not Be Blamed for the Current Recession," *Economic Affairs*, 30(3), pp. 86–89.

Palley, T. 2007. "Financialization: What It Is and Why It Matters," *Levy Economics Institute*, Working Paper No. 525. Available: www.levyinstitute.org/pubs/wp_525.pdf. Accessed August 15, 2010.

Papadimitriou, D. B. and Wray, L. Randall. 1998. "What to Do with the Surplus: Fiscal Policy and the Coming Recession," *Levy Economics Institute*, Policy Note 1998/6. Available: www.levyinstitute.org/pubs/pn98_6.pdf. Accessed August 15, 2010.

Papadimitriou, D. B., Hannsgen, G. and Zezza, G. 2007. "Cracks in the Foundations of Growth: What Will the Housing Debacle Mean for the US Economy?" *Levy Economics Institute*, Public Policy Brief No. 90. Available: www.levyinstitute.org/pubs/ppb_90.pdf. Accessed November 16, 2022.

Papadimitriou, D. B., Nikiforos, M., Zezza, G. and Hannsgen, G. 2014. "Is Rising Inequality a Hindrance to the US Economic Recovery?" *Levy Economics Institute* Strategic Analysis April 2014. Available: www.levyinstitute.org/pubs/sa_apr_14.pdf. Accessed February 5, 2023.

Pappas, S. 2020. "The Toll of Job Loss," *Monitor on Psychology*, 51(7), pp. 51–61.

Parenteau, R. W. 2006. "U.S. Household Deficit Spending: A Rendezvous with Reality," *Levy Economics Institute*, Public Policy Brief No. 88. Available: www.levyinstitute.org/pubs/ppb_88.pdf. Accessed November 16, 2022.

Peterson, Wallace. 1994. *Silent Depression: Twenty-Five Years of Wage Squeeze and Middle Class Decline*, New York: Norton.

Plosser, C. I. 1989. "Understanding Real Business Cycles," *Journal of Economic Perspectives*, 3(3), pp. 51–77.

Rasmus, J. 2020. *The Scourge of Neoliberalism: US Economic Policy from Reagan to Trump*, Atlanta, GA: Clarity Press, Inc.

Repapis, Constantinos. 2011. "Hayek's Business Cycle Theory during the 1930s: A Critical Account of its Development," *History of Political Economy*, 43 (4), pp. 699–742.

Roberts, Lily, Ives-Rublee, Mia and Khattar, Rose. 2022. "COVID-19 Likely Resulted in 1.2 Million More Disabled People by the End of 2021 – Workplaces and Policy Will Need to Adapt," *Center for American Progress*. Available: www.americanprogress.org/article/covid-19-likely-resulted-in-1-2-million-more-disabled-people-by-the-end-of-2021-workplaces-and-policy-will-need-to-adapt/. Accessed April 17, 2024.

Robinson, J. 1978. *Contributions to Modern Economics*, New York: Academic Press.
Romer, C. and Romer, D. 2002. "The Evolution of Economic Understanding and Postwar Stabilization Policy," *National Bureau of Economic Research*, Working Paper 9274. Available: www.nber.org/papers/w9274. Accessed November 12, 2024.
Romer, C. D. 2008. "Business Cycles," *Library of Economics and Liberty*, Liberty Fund, Inc. Available: www.econlib.org/library/Enc1/BusinessCycles.html. Accessed November 16, 2022.
Romer, P. 2016. "The Trouble with Macroeconomics," Available: https://faculty.sites.iastate.edu/tesfatsi/archive/tesfatsi/TheTroubleWithMacro.PRomer2016.pdf. Accessed November 16, 2022.
Rosenfeld, J. 2019. "The Consequences of Union Decline," in *The Cambridge Handbook of U.S. Labor Law for the Twenty-First Century*, Richard Bales and Charlotte Garden, editors. Cambridge: Cambridge University Press, pp. 12–22.
Rubin, A. 2003. "The Double-Edged Crisis: OPEC and the Outbreak of the Iran-Iraq War," *Middle East*, 7(4), pp. 1–14.
Rudd, J. 2022. "The Anatomy of Single-Digit Inflation in the 1960s," in *Finance and Economics Discussion Series 2022–029*, Washington: Board of Governors of the Federal Reserve System. Available: www.federalreserve.gov/econres/feds/files/2022029pap.pdf. Accessed October 1, 2023.
Ruml, B. 1946. "Taxes for Revenue Are Obsolete," *American Affairs*, 8(1), pp. 35–39.
Sablik, T. 2013. "Recession of 1981–82," Federal Reserve History, *Federal Reserve System*. Available: www.federalreservehistory.org/essays/recession-of-1981-82. Accessed October 31, 2022.
Sahu, A. P. and Tracy, R. L., editors. 1991. *The Economic Legacy of the Reagan Years: Euphoria or Chaos?* New York City: Praeger.
Salvucci, J. 2023. "What Was the Dot-Com Bubble and Why Did It Burst?" *The Street*. Available: www.thestreet.com/dictionary/dot-com-bubble-and-burst. Accessed April 16, 2024.
Samuelson, P. A. 1987. "Evaluating Reaganomics," *Challenge*, 30, pp. 58–65.
Sawyer, W. C. and Sprinkle, R. L. 1996. "The Demand for Imports and Exports in the US: A Survey," *Journal of Economics and Finance*, 20(1), pp. 147–178.
Schmidt, R. H. 1983. "Effects of Natural Gas Deregulation on the Distribution of Income," *Federal Reserve Bank of Dallas Economic Review*, pp. 1–12. Available: https://fraser.stlouisfed.org/files/docs/publications/frbdalreview/frbdal_er8305.pdf. Accessed October 1, 2024.
Seegert, L. 2017. "U.S. Ranks Worse in Elder Care vs. Other Wealthy Nations," *Association of Health Care Journalists*. Available: https://healthjournalism.org/blog/2017/11/u-s-ranks-worse-in-elder-care-vs-other-wealthy-nations/. Accessed February 24, 2023.
Senate 2006. "The Role of Market Speculation in Rising Oil and Gas Prices: A Need to Put the Cop Back on the Beat," in Staff Report Prepared by the *Permanent Subcommittee on Investigations on the Committee on Homeland Security and Governmental Affairs*. United States Senate. Available: www.govinfo.gov/content/pkg/CPRT-109SPRT28640/html/CPRT-109SPRT28640.htm. Accessed November 1, 2023.
Sharpe, S. A. and Suarez, G. 2013. "The Insensitivity of Investment to Interest Rates: Evidence from a Survey of CFOs," *Finance and Economics Discussion Series*, Federal

Reserve Board, Washington, DC. Available: www.federalreserve.gov/pubs/feds/2014/201402/201402pap.pdf. Accessed November 11, 2023.

Smart, T. 2021. "Who Owns Stocks in America? Mostly, It's the Wealthy and White," *US News and World Report*, Available: www.usnews.com/news/national-news/articles/2021-03-15/who-owns-stocks-in-america-mostly-its-the-wealthy-and-white. Accessed April 1, 2024.

Sterman, J. 2000. *Business Dynamics*, Irwin/McGraw-Hill, c2000.

Stewart, L. A. and Atkinson, R. D. 2013. "The Greater Stagnation: The Decline in Capital Investment is the Real Threat to US Economic Growth," *The Information Technology and Innovation Foundation*. Available: www2.itif.org/2013-the-greater-stagnation.pdf. Accessed October 15, 2023.

Stillman, J. 2020. "For 95 Percent of Human History, People Worked 15 Hours a Week. Could We Do It Again?" *Inc.com*. Available: www.inc.com/jessica-stillman/for-95-percent-of-human-history-people-worked-15-hours-a-week-could-we-do-it-again.html. Accessed February 24, 2023.

Strandh, M., Winefield, A., Nilsson, K. and Hammarström, A. 2014. "Unemployment and Mental Health Scarring During the Life Course," *The European Journal of Public Health*, 24(3), pp. 440–445.

STRATFOR Worldview. 2011. "Default Is Absolutely Impossible While the Dollar Is the Global Currency," *Business Insider*. Available: www.businessinsider.com/default-is-absolutely-impossible-while-the-dollar-is-the-global-currency-2011-4. Accessed March 26, 2024.

Strauss, William A. and Engel, Emily A. 2008. "Economic Outlook Symposium: Summary of 2007 Results and Forecasts for 2008," *Chicago Fed*. Available: www.chicagofed.org/-/media/publications/chicago-fed-letter/2008/cflfebruary2008-247-pdf.pdf. Accessed November 16, 2022.

Survey of Current Business. 1957a, *US Department of Commerce*, Bureau of Foreign and Domestic Commerce, January 1957.

Survey of Current Business. 1957b, *US Department of Commerce*, Bureau of Foreign and Domestic Commerce, October 1957.

Survey of Current Business. 1958a, *US Department of Commerce*, Bureau of Foreign and Domestic Commerce, March 1958.

Survey of Current Business. 1958b, *US Department of Commerce*, Bureau of Foreign and Domestic Commerce, May 1958.

Survey of Current Business. 1960a, *US Department of Commerce*, Bureau of Foreign and Domestic Commerce, August 1960.

Survey of Current Business. 1960b, *US Department of Commerce*, Bureau of Foreign and Domestic Commerce, December 1960.

Survey of Current Business. 1961, *US Department of Commerce*, Bureau of Foreign and Domestic Commerce, March 1961.

Survey of Current Business. 1966, *US Department of Commerce*, Bureau of Foreign and Domestic Commerce, December 1966.

Survey of Current Business. 1967a, *US Department of Commerce*, Bureau of Foreign and Domestic Commerce, January 1967.

Survey of Current Business. 1967b, *US Department of Commerce*, Bureau of Foreign and Domestic Commerce, July 1967.

Survey of Current Business. 1971, *US Department of Commerce*, Bureau of Foreign and Domestic Commerce, April 1971.

Survey of Current Business. 1977, *US Department of Commerce*, Bureau of Foreign and Domestic Commerce, October 1977.

Survey of Current Business. 1983, *US Department of Commerce*, Bureau of Foreign and Domestic Commerce, December 1983.

Survey of Current Business. 1991, *US Department of Commerce*, Bureau of Foreign and Domestic Commerce, April 1991.

Survey of Current Business. 1995a, *US Department of Commerce*, Bureau of Foreign and Domestic Commerce, April 1995.

Survey of Current Business. 1995b, *US Department of Commerce*, Bureau of Foreign and Domestic Commerce, August 1995.

Survey of Current Business. 2004, *US Department of Commerce*, Bureau of Foreign and Domestic Commerce, March 2004.

Sylvester, B. 2019. "Fact Check: Are There More than 633,000 Homeless People and 13.9 Million Vacant Homes in the US?" *CheckYourFact.com*. Available: https://checkyourfact.com/2019/12/24/fact-check-633000-homeless-million-vacant-homes/. Accessed March 3, 2023.

Tahmassebi, H. 1986. "The Impact of the Iran-Iraq War on the World Oil Market," *Energy* (Oxford), 11(4), pp. 409–411.

Tcherneva, P. R. 2009. "Obama's Job Creation Promise: A Modest Proposal to Guarantee That He Meets and Exceeds Expectations," *Levy Economics Institute*. Policy Note 2009/1. Available: www.levyinstitute.org/pubs/pn_09_01.pdf. Accessed March 25, 2024.

Tcherneva, P. R. 2012. "Inflationary and Distributional Effects of Alternative Fiscal Policies: An Augmented Minskyan-Kaleckian Model," *Levy Economics Institute*. Working Paper No. 706. Available: www.levyinstitute.org/pubs/wp_706.pdf. Accessed January 20, 2020.

Tcherneva, P. R. 2014. "Reorienting Fiscal Policy: A Bottom-Up Approach," *Journal of Post Keynesian Economics*, 37(1), pp. 43–66.

Tcherneva, P. R. 2017a. "Unemployment: The Silent Epidemic," *Levy Economics Institute*. Economics Working Paper No. 895. Available: www.levyinstitute.org/pubs/wp_895.pdf. Accessed November 3, 2020.

Tcherneva, P. R. 2017b. "Unemployment: The Silent Epidemic," *Levy Economics Institute*. Working Papers Series no. 895. Available: www.levyinstitute.org/pubs/wp_895.pdf. Accessed April 3, 2023.

Tcherneva, P. R. 2018. "The Job Guarantee: Design, Jobs, and Implementation," *Levy Economics Institute*. Economics Working Paper No. 902. Available: www.levyinstitute.org/pubs/wp_902.pdf. Accessed November 3, 2020.

Tcherneva, P. R. 2020. *The Case for a Job Guarantee*, John Wiley and Sons.

Temin, P. 1998a. "The Causes of American Business Cycles: An Essay in Economic Historiography," *National Bureau of Economic Research*. Working Paper 6692, Cambridge, MA. Available: www.nber.org/papers/w6692. Accessed November 1, 2022.

Temin, P. 1998b. *The Causes of American Business Cycles: An Essay in Economic Historiography*, Cambridge, MA: National Bureau of Economic Research.

Tevlin, S. and Whelan, K. 2003. "Explaining the Investment Boom of the 1990s," *Journal of Money, Credit, and Banking*, 35(1), pp. 1–22.

Texas McCombs. 2021. "Housing Speculators Could Bring on Repeat Crash," *Medium.com*. Available: https://medium.com/texas-mccombs/housing-speculators-could-bring-on-repeat-crash-cb906225115f. Accessed March 15, 2023.

References

Trebing, Harry M. 2008. "A Critical Assessment of Electricity and Natural Gas Deregulation." *Journal of Economic Issues*, 42(2), pp. 469–77.

Tussing, A. 1983. "An OPEC Obituary," *National Affairs* (61). Available: www.nationalaffairs.com/public_interest/detail/an-opec-obituary. Accessed September 12, 2023.

Tymoigne, E. 2014. "Modern Money Theory and Interrelations between the Treasury and the Central Bank: The Case of the United States," *Levy Economics Institute* Economics Working Paper No. 788. Available: www.levyinstitute.org/pubs/wp_788.pdf. Accessed June 3, 2023.

Tymoigne, E. 2022. "Secular Stagnation and the Age of Ultra-Low Interest Rates," in *Handbook of Economic Stagnation*, L. Randall and Flavia Dantas Wray, editors. Elsevier Inc., pp. 321–340.

UN. undated. "Causes and Effects of Climate Change," *United Nations*. Available: www.un.org/en/climatechange/science/causes-effects-climate-change. Accessed February 27, 2023.

Vaghul, K., Fenelon, Kelley-F. and Glasmeier, Amy K. 2022. "What a Living Wage Is and Why Businesses Should Use It as a Benchmark," *JustCapital.com*. Available: https://justcapital.com/reports/living-wage-guide-for-business-just-jobs-explained/. Accessed February 27, 2023.

Voth, Hans-J. 2020. "Roots of War: Hitler's Rise to Power," in *The Economics of the Second World War: Seventy-Five Years On*, Stephen Broadberry and Mark Harrison, editors. London: Centre for Economic Policy Research, pp. 9–17. Available: https://kclpure.kcl.ac.uk/ws/portalfiles/portal/128186764/The_Economics_of_the_Second_World_War_Seventy_Five_Years_On_.pdf. Accessed October 31, 2024.

Wager, E., McGough, M., Rakshit, S., Amin, K., and Cox, C. 2024. "How Does Health Spending in the U.S. Compare to Other Countries?" *The Peterson Center on Healthcare and KFF*. Available: www.healthsystemtracker.org/chart-collection/health-spending-u-s-compare-countries/. Accessed March 25, 2024.

Wallerstein, I. 1999. "Cycles and Trends in the World Capitalist Economy," in *Encyclopedia of Political Economy*, Phillip Anthony O'Hara, editor. London: Routledge, pp. 177–179.

Weatherford, M. S. 1987. "The Interplay of Ideology and Advice in Economic Policy-Making: The Case of Political Business Cycles," *The Journal of Politics*, 49(4), pp. 925–952.

Weinberg, D. H. 1996. "A Brief Look at Postwar US Income Inequality," *Bureau of the Census*, Economics and Statistics Administration. Available: www.census.gov/hhes/www/img/p60-191.pdf. Accessed August 15, 2010.

Weller, C. 2002. "Learning Lessons from the 1990s: Long-term Growth Prospects for the US," *Economic Policy Institute*. Available: www.epi.org/publication/webfeatures_viewpoints_l-t_growth_lessons/. Accessed November 9, 2022.

Weller, C. and Helppie, B. 2005. "Biting the Hand That Fed It: Did the Stock Market Boom of the Late 1990s Impede Investment in Manufacturing?," *Journal of Economics and Finance*, 29(3), pp. 359–381.

Welsh, C. 2024. "Russia, Ukraine, and Global Food Security: A Two-Year Assessment," *Center for Strategic and International Studies*. Available: www.csis.org/analysis/russia-ukraine-and-global-food-security-two-year-assessment. Accessed April 5, 2024.

Weltman, B. 2023. "10 Years after the Financial Crisis: The Impact on Small Business," *Investopedia*. Available: www.investopedia.com/small-business/10-years-after-financial-crisis-impact-small-business/. Accessed April 1, 2024.

Werner, R. A. 2014. "How Do Banks Create Money, and Why Can Other Firms Not Do the Same? An Explanation for the Coexistence of Lending and Deposit-Taking," *International Review of Financial Analysis*, 36, pp. 71–77.

Whalen, C. J. 2007. "The US Credit Crunch of 2007: A Minsky Moment," Levy Economics Institute Public Policy Brief No. 92. Available: www.levyinstitute.org/pubs/ppb_92.pdf. Accessed November 16, 2022.

Williamson, O. E. 1996. "Revisiting Legal Realism: The Law, Economics, and Organization Perspective," *Industrial and Corporate Change*, 5(2), pp. 383–420.

Woodham, D. M. 1984. "Autumn-Last Update, Are the Leading Indicators Signaling a Recession?" Federal Reserve Bank of New York Quarterly Review (Autumn 1984). Available: www.newyorkfed.org/medialibrary/media/research/quarterly_review/1984v9/v9n3article8.pdf. Accessed October 3, 2022.

Wray, L. R. 1998a. "Goldilocks and the Three Bears," *Levy Economics Institute* Policy Note 1998/7. Available: www.levyinstitute.org/pubs/pn98_7.pdf. Accessed August 15, 2010.

Wray, L. R. 1998b. *Understanding Modern Money: The Key to Full Employment and Price Stability*, Cheltenham, UK: Edward Elgar.

Wray, L. R. 2008. "Demand Constraints and Big Government," *Journal of Economic Issues*, 42(1), pp. 153–173.

Wray, L. R. 2011. "Ignore the Raters," *New York Times*. Available: www.nytimes.com/roomfordebate/2011/04/18/is-anyone-listening-to-the-standard-poors/ignore-the-raters. Accessed March 26, 2024.

Wray, L. R. 2015. *Why Minsky Matters: An Introduction to the Work of a Maverick Economist*, Princeton and Oxford: Princeton University Press.

Wray, L. R. 2023. *Money for Beginners: An Illustrated Guide*, John Wiley and Sons.

Wray, L. R., Dantas, F., Fullwiler, S., Tcherneva, Pavlina R. and Kelton, Stephanie A. 2018. "Public Service Employment: A Path to Full Employment," *Levy Economics Institute*. Research Project Report. Available: www.levyinstitute.org/pubs/rpr_4_18.pdf. Accessed March 25, 2024.

Zelmanovitz, L. 2011. "The Austrian Business Cycle Theory and the Recent Financial Crisis," *Revista Criterio Libre*, 9(15), pp. 24–57.

Index

Afghanistan, 95
American Economic Association
    Mitchell's role, 129
American Recovery and Reinvestment
    Act, 49, 100–102, 107, 109–110, 123
animal spirits, 16–18, 29, 149
    binary nature, 16–17
    in Keynes' theory, 133, 135
Arab–Israeli War, 70, 72
assets, 32, 121, 125
    Ike I cycle, 59
    and liabilities approach. *See* finance, assets and liabilities approach
    in Minsky's theory, 143–146
    Oil Shock I cycle, 72
    September 11 cycle, 91
austerity
    COVID-Cycle, 102
Austrian economics, 34, 135, 149
    business cycle theory, 157–159
automatic stabilizers. *See* government spending, automatic stabilizers

balance-of-payments. *See* international trade
banking, 32, 40, 46, 50, 121, 124–125
    assets and liabilities approach. *See* finance, assets and liabilities approach
    Austrian theory, 157–159
    central banking. *See* central bank
    investment
        September 11 cycle, 90
        in Minsky's theory, 145–146

    in Mitchell's theory, 130–132
    Neoclassical theory, 150
    Oil Shock II cycle, 77
    September 11 cycle, 91
    Subprime Crisis cycle, 94, 97
bankruptcy
    in Austrian theory, 159
    in Real Business Cycle theory, 157
    September 11 cycle, 91
barriers to entry, 4, 42–43
Bretton Woods, 70, 73
Bush, George H. W., 83, 87–88, 118
Bush, George W., 88, 92, 94, 97
business cycle
    definition, 9
    endogeneity, 8–9
    long-term, 7–8
    Minsky's definition, 142
    Mitchell's definition, 130
    types, 6–8
business cycle theory, 6–25
    Austrian. *See* Austrian economics, business cycle theory
    Davidson. *See* Davidson, Paul, business cycle theory
    Interest-Rate Induced. *See* Interest-Rate Induced business cycle
    Kalecki. *See* Kalecki, Michal, business cycle theory
    Keynes. *See* Keynes, John Maynard, business cycle theory
    Minsky. *See* Minsky, Hyman, business cycle theory

177

business cycle theory (cont.)
  Mitchell. *See* Mitchell, Wesley Clair, business cycle theory
  Monetarist. *See* Monetarism, business cycle theory
  Neoclassical. *See* Neoclassical economics, business cycle theory
  New Keynesian. *See* New Keynesian business cycle theory
  Real Business Cycle. *See* Real Business Cycle theory
  Stop-Go. *See* Stop-Go business cycle theory
business cycles in US
  COVID, 100–105
  Desert Storm, 83–87
  Ike I, 57–61
  Ike II, 61–63
  Oil Shock I, 71–74
  Oil Shock II, 75–78
  September 11, 88–93
  Subprime Crisis, 94–99
  Vietnam, 64–70
  Volcker, 79–82

capacity. *See* productive capacity
capital
  equipment. *See* productive capacity
  financial. *See* finance
  physical. *See* productive capacity
capitalist class
  in Kalecki's theory, 135–137
capital-to-asset ratio. *See* net worth-to-asset ratio
CARES Act. *See* Coronavirus Aid, Relief, and Economic Security Act
Carter, Jimmy, 75, 79
central bank, 32, 40, 46–48, 82, 93, 121, 145, 150–151
  in Austrian theory, 157–158
  Federal Reserve, 9, 26–27, 47, 69, 77, 79, 85
    Monetarist experiment, 77–78, 80, 86, 155
    Neoclassical theory, 150, 153
    Volcker cycle, 80–81
  inflation policy. *See* inflation, Federal Reserve policy
  in Interest-Rate Induced theory, 150
  interest-rate targeting, 27–28, 46, 77, 125, 151
  Modern Monetary Theory explanation. *See* government spending, deficit financing
  in Monetarist theory, 152
  Neoclassical theory, 157
  open market operations, 28, 46, 48

  policy. *See* policy, monetary
  regulation by, 47
child care, 108, 115, 118–119
Civil Rights Act, 66
class
  in Kalecki's theory, 135–137
climate change, 5, 105, 114, 118, 120, 127
Clinton, Bill, 87–88, 92, 102–103, 122
Clinton, Hillary, 128
COLA. *See* cost of living adjustments
Cold War, 57–58
computer
  chips, 39–40
  investment in
    September 11 cycle, 89–90, 92–93
    Subprime Crisis cycle, 95
confidence, 16, 23, 31, 99
  forecast. *See* forecast, confidence
  overall versus investment. *See* forecast, confidence, overall versus investment
  September 11 cycle, 93
consumer. *See* consumption
consumer class
  in Kalecki's theory, 135–137
consumption, 11, 21, 37–46, 64, 69, 102, 116, 135
  in Austrian theory, 158
  COVID cycle, 104
  Desert Storm cycle, 84
  GDP component, 10–11
  Ike I cycle, 58, 60
  Ike II cycle, 61–62
  Mitchell's theory, 132
  Oil Shock I cycle, 72
  Oil Shock II cycle, 75
  in Real Business Cycle theory, 156
  September 11 cycle, 89, 91–93
  Subprime Crisis cycle, 94–99
  Vietnam cycle, 66, 68
contracts
  in Mitchell's theory, 131
Coronavirus Aid, Relief, and Economic Security Act, 49
cost of living adjustments
  Vietnam cycle, 69
  Volcker cycle, 81
costs
  in Mitchell's theory, 131
COVID, xii, 1, 6, 12, 27, 40, 42–43, 56, 81–82, 98, 104, 111, 114, 117
  relief program, 11, 49
  supply chain issues, 39–40
crisis, 18, 32, 110

Index

in Keynes' theory, 133
in Mitchell's theory, 130, 132

Davidson, Paul
 business cycle theory, 146–149
debt
 Neoclassical treatment, 9
 private sector, 29, 92, 99
  COVID cycle, 102
  Ike I cycle, 60
  in Minsky's theory, 141–146
  September 11 cycle, 88, 91–93
  Subprime Crisis cycle, 97, 99
 public sector. See government spending, debt default
decision making
 confidence. See forecast, confidence
 investment costs and benefits, 14
 optimism. See forecast, optimism
 steps, 18–19
 under risk, 14–15
 under uncertainty, 15–16
  disillusion, 21
  volatility, 21
defense spending, 87, 112, 119
 Oil Shock I cycle, 71
 September 11 cycle, 88
degrowth, 114–115
deindustrialization, 91
demand, 109
 in Davidson's theory, 148
 in Mitchell's theory, 132
 in Monetarist theory, 154
 in Neoclassical theory, 152
 in Real Business Cycle theory, 157
deregulation, 98
 Desert Storm cycle, 87
 Volcker cycle, 79, 81–82
Desert Storm, 81
dot-com. See computer, investment in
Dow Jones Industrial Average, 85
durable goods, 18
 Ike I cycle, 58–59
 Ike II cycle, 61–62
 in Keynes' theory, 134
 Mitchell's theory, 132
 September 11 cycle, 89
 Vietnam cycle, 64, 66, 68

economism, 126–128
Eisenhower, Dwight David, 57, 60–61, 63
elder care, 114, 118
employment, 109

full, 47, 51
 in Austrian theory, 158
 in Neoclassical theory, 152
 in Mitchell's theory, 130
 Oil Shock II cycle, 75
 in Real Business Cycle theory, 156
 unemployment. See unemployment
energy, 36, 42
 Oil Shock I cycle, 73–74
 Oil Shock II cycle, 76
 prices
  Oil Shock I cycle, 73
  Oil Shock II cycle, 77
  Volcker cycle, 82
 Subprime Crisis cycle, 96
entrepreneurial class
 in Kalecki's theory, 135–137
equilibrium, 1, 141
 full-employment
  in Minsky's theory, 143
  in Monetarist theory, 155
  in Kalecki's theory, 138
 stable
  in Davidson's theory, 148
  in Kalecki's theory, 140
euphoria, 29–30, 90
 in Keynes' theory, 134
 in Minsky's theory, 146
exchange rate
 effect on inflation. See inflation, currency depreciation
 Volcker cycle, 79
expansion
 COVID cycle, 100–104
 Desert Storm cycle, 86
 Ike I cycle, 57–59
 Ike II cycle, 61–62
 Oil Shock I cycle, 71–73
 Oil Shock II cycle, 75–77
 September 11 cycle, 88–92
 Subprime Crisis cycle, 94–98
 Vietnam cycle, 64–69
 Volcker cycle, 80
expectations. See forecast
exports, 10–12, 24–25, 43–44, 58, 102, 122–123, 135
 COVID cycle, 104
 Desert Storm cycle, 84
 Ike I cycle, 60

Federal Deposit Insurance Corporation, 26
Federal Reserve. See central bank, Federal Reserve

finance
  assets and liabilities approach, 25–30
  business
    in Austrian theory, 159
    Ike I cycle, 59–60
    Ike II cycle, 62
    Vietnam cycle, 67
    in Davidson's theory, 146
  stock market. *See* stock market
financial crisis, 9
  Minsky's theory, 142
Financial Crisis of 2007–2008, 1, 6, 9, 12–13, 30, 47, 49–50, 52, 95, 102, 105, 110, 122, 149, 157
  Neoclassical theory, 150, 153
financial instability hypothesis. *See* Minsky, Hyman, financial instability hypothesis
financialization, 98–99
fiscal policy. *See* policy, fiscal
food, 43
  climate change effect on, 114
  desert, 113
  Ike II cycle, 61
  inflation
    Oil Shock II cycle, 76
    Vietnam cycle, 69
  inflation example, 40
  living wage allowance, 115–116
  Vietnam cycle, 68
Ford, Gerald, 71, 73, 75
forecast
  confidence, 17–21
  overall versus investment, 17–21
  in Davidson's theory, 149
  Ike I cycle, 60
  in Kalecki's theory, 141
  in Keynes' theory, 133–134
  in Mitchell's theory, 132
  Oil Shock II cycle, 77
  optimism, 17–21
    overall versus investment, 17–21
  Subprime Crisis cycle, 98
  Vietnam cycle, 67
foreign currency. *See* exchange rate
Friedman, Milton, 47–49, 153
Full Employment Act of 1946, 64–65, 78

GDP. *See* gross domestic product
General Motors, 70–71
Glass-Steagall, 27, 29–30
GM. *See* General Motors
gold, 131
  in Austrian theory, 159
  Oil Shock I cycle, 71–72
government spending, 10, 49, 51, 109
  automatic stabilizers, 23–24, 49, 54, 70, 105, 110, 112
  September 11 cycle, 88
  Vietnam cycle, 66, 70
  COVID cycle, 104
  debt, 102, 124, 128
    Desert Storm cycle, 83
  debt default, 49, 51, 88, 120–121
  deficit, 24, 88
    COVID cycle, 100
    Desert Storm cycle, 83–84
    expansionary effect, 49, 56
    Ike I cycle, 57, 60, 65
    Ike II cycle, 61–62
    Oil Shock II cycle, 77
    Vietnam cycle, 66–67, 70
    Volcker cycle, 79
  deficit financing, 49, 123–125
    Desert Storm cycle, 84–87
  discretionary, 49
    Ike I cycle, 58, 60
    Ike II cycle, 62
  interest payments, 126
  primary dealer system, 124–125
  Subprime Crisis cycle, 95
  surplus, 121–123
    September 11 cycle, 93
    Vietnam cycle, 66
  tax, 11, 41, 49, 111
    Desert Storm cycle, 83, 87
    Oil Shock I cycle, 73
    Oil Shock II cycle, 75, 77
    September 11 cycle, 90
    Subprime Crisis cycle, 95
    Vietnam cycle, 65, 68
    Volcker cycle, 79
Great Depression, 36, 110
  COVID cycle, 103
  in Interest-Rate Induced theory, 150
  in Neoclassical theory, 153
  Volcker cycle, 80–81
Great Society Program, 66
Green New Deal, 114, 128
gross domestic product, 50, 57
  COVID cycle, 100, 104
  Desert Storm cycle, 85–86
  determinants of, 10–12
  Ike I cycle, 57–58, 60
  Ike II cycle, 61

Index

investment as key driver. *See* investment, as key driver of GDP
  Oil Shock I cycle, 71–73
  Oil Shock II cycle, 77
  September 11 cycle, 88–89, 92–93
  Subprime Crisis cycle, 94, 96, 98–99
  Vietnam cycle, 64, 66–67, 70
Gulf of Tonkin incident, 66

health care, 42, 91–92, 108, 111, 118–119
hedge unit
  in Minsky's theory, 145
homeless, 126
housing market, 13
  contribution to inflation. *See* inflation, examples
  costs, 116
    September 11 cycle, 91
  mortgage
    in Mitchell's theory, 131
    Subprime Crisis cycle, 95–97, 99
    Vietnam cycle, 68–69
  Subprime Crisis cycle, 95–97
Humphrey–Hawkins bill, 78
hurricane, 40
  Subprime Crisis cycle, 96

imports, 11, 44–45
  Oil Shock I cycle, 72
  September 11 crisis, 89
income, 81–82, 87, 91, 99, 102
  Desert Storm cycle, 84
  distribution, 51, 87, 99
    Ike I cycle, 57
    in Kalecki's theory, 135
    September 11 cycle, 88, 92
    Subprime Crisis cycle, 99
  as equal to output and sales, 10
  Ike I cycle, 57
  in Kalecki's theory, 135–137
  in Minsky's theory, 141
  Oil Shock II cycle, 75
  September 11 cycle, 93
  Subprime Crisis cycle, 94, 96–97
Index of Leading Indicators
  Desert Storm cycle, 84
  Mitchell's role, 129
  Vietnam cycle, 67
inflation
  cost-push/market power, 42–43
  cost-push/supply shock, 43
  COVID cycle, 104
  currency depreciation, 44–45
    Oil Shock II cycle, 76
  demand-pull, 41
  demand-pull/labor market, 41–42
  demographic housing boom example, 37–38
  Desert Storm cycle, 83–84
  examples, 37–41
  expectations driving, 47
    Volcker cycle, 80–81
  Federal Reserve policy, 35–36, 38, 40, 42–43, 46
    Oil Shock II cycle, 78
    Vietnam cycle, 67
    Volcker cycle, 81
  food cost example, 40
  as incentive to entrepreneurs, 37
  money growth. *See* money, growth as inflationary
  in Neoclassical theory, 152
  Oil Shock I cycle, 72–73
  Oil Shock II cycle, 77
  redistribution of income, 37
  sectoral nature, 36
  September 11 cycle, 88
  speculative, 43–44
  speculative housing boom example, 38–39
  Subprime Crisis cycle, 96
  summary of causes, 45–46
  supply chain example, 39–40
  unemployment tradeoff. *See* unemployment, inflation tradeoff
  Vietnam cycle, 68–70
  Volcker recession, 80
  World War II, 41
injections-leakages approach, 10–12
Institutionalism, 129
interest rate, 31–32, 46–47
  in Austrian theory, 157–159
  Desert Storm cycle, 83–85
  Ike I cycle, 60
  Ike II cycle, 62
  in Interest-Rate Induced business cycle, 149–151
  in Minsky's theory, 145
  in Mitchell's theory, 131–132
  Oil Shock II cycle, 77
  in Real Business Cycle theory, 156
  September 11 cycle, 90
  Vietnam cycle, 67–68
  Volcker cycle, 80–81
Interest-Rate Induced business cycle, 149–151

international trade, 10
  exports. *See* exports
  imports. *See* imports
  Oil Shock I cycle, 72
  Oil Shock II cycle, 77
inventory investment. *See* investment, inventory investment
investment, 9–10, 22, 33, 50–51, 57, 107
  in Austrian theory, 158–159
  components of, 13–14
    fixed investment, 13
    gross investment, 13
    inventory investment, 13
    net investment, 13
    replacement investment, 13
    residential investment, 13
  COVID cycle, 102, 104
  in Davidson's theory, 146–149
  decision, 18–22
  depreciation
    in Davidson's theory, 147–149
  Desert Storm cycle, 83–86
  financing, 25–30
  gestation period, 33
    in Kalecki's theory, 137
  Ike I cycle, 57–60
  Ike II cycle, 61–63
  inventory, 57
    Ike II cycle, 61–62
    Oil Shock I cycle, 71
    September 11 cycle, 92
    Subprime Crisis cycle, 96
    Vietnam cycle, 70
    Volcker cycle, 80
  in Kalecki's theory, 135–141
  as key driver of GDP, 12–13
  in Keynes' theory, 134–135
  in Minsky's theory, 143–146
  Oil Shock I cycle, 71–73
  Oil Shock II cycle, 75–77
  in Real Business Cycle theory, 156
  replacement
    in Mitchell's theory, 131
  residential
    Ike II cycle, 61
    Oil Shock II cycle, 76
    Subprime Crisis cycle, 96–97
  secular decline
    COVID cycle, 103
  September 11 cycle, 92–93
  Subprime Crisis cycle, 94–96, 98–99
  Vietnam cycle, 64–65, 67, 70

volatility, 12
Volcker cycle, 80
Iran, 77, 82
Iran–Iraq War, 82
Iraq, 82, 86, 95

Job Guarantee
  benefits, 109–112
  coercion, 117–118
  cost, 118–120
  criticisms, 115–118
  funding, 120–126
  inflation caused by, 116–117
  job training, 108
  popularity, 128
  structure, 108–109
  types of jobs, 112–115
job program. *See* Job Guarantee
jobless recovery, 86
Johnson, Lyndon Baines, 64, 66, 70
Journal of Post Keynesian Economics, 146
journal ranking system, 4

Kalecki, Michal
  business cycle theory, 135–141
  profit equation, 136–137
Keen, Steve, 97–98, 146
Kennedy, John F., 61, 63–67
Keynes, John Maynard
  business cycle theory, 132–135
Korean War, 57, 152

labor
  as a cost to be minimized, 109
  in Mitchell's theory, 130–131
labor force participation, 65
  COVID cycle, 103–104
Lehman Brothers, 29–30
liquidity preference, 32
  in Keynes' theory, 133

margin of safety, 47
  in Minsky's theory, 141–142, 146
  in Mitchell's theory, 132
marginal efficiency of capital, 18, 32, 133
  in Keynes' theory, 133
marginal propensity to consume, 99
  in Keynes' theory, 133–134
method
  Keynes', 3
  Neoclassical, 2–3
Mexican financial crisis, 89
minimum wage, 112, 115, 117

Index

Minsky, Hyman, 29, 33
  business cycle theory, 141–146
  financial instability hypothesis, 8, 141–146
Mitchell, Wesley Clair
  business cycle theory, 129–132
Monetarism
  business cycle theory, 153–155
monetary policy. *See* policy, monetary
money
  excess supply of, 48
  growth as inflationary
    in Monetarist theory, 154–155
    rejection, 47–49
    Vietnam cycle, 68
    Volcker cycle, 80
  quantity theory
    in Monetarist theory, 154
  supply, 46
    in Monetarist theory, 154
  taxation as anchor of value, 123–124
money illusion
  in Monetarist theory, 155
money-manager capitalism, 51–52
mortgage, 31
  Vietnam cycle, 68
multiplier effect, 110
  Desert Storm cycle, 84
  in Minsky's theory, 142
  in Mitchell's theory, 131
muppet, 90

National Bureau of Economic Research, 53, 92
  Mitchell's role, 2, 129
natural rate
  in Monetarist theory, 154–155
  in Real Business Cycle theory, 156
NBER. *See* National Bureau of Economic Research
Neoclassical economics
  business cycle theory, 151–153
  unpopularity with students, 3–4
net worth, 26, 28–30
net worth-to-asset ratio, 28–31, 47, 50
  in Minsky's theory, 146
New Deal, xiv, 87
New Economy, 92
New Keynesian business cycle theory, 151–153
Nixon, Richard M., 63–64, 71, 73

Obama, Barack, 1, 94, 100–104, 111, 127, 153
OPEC, 23, 36–37, 39, 42–43, 56, 58, 72, 80, 82

optimism, 10, 16, 22–23, 31, 33, 54, 56, 90
  in Davidson's theory, 149
  forecast. *See* forecast, optimism
  Ike I cycle, 59–60
  Ike II cycle, 63
  in Kalecki's theory, 138, 141
  in Keynes' theory, 133–134
  in Minsky's theory, 141
  in Mitchell's theory, 130–132
  Oil Shock I cycle, 74
  overall versus investment. *See* forecast, optimism, overall versus investment
  Subprime Crisis cycle, 97, 99
  Volcker cycle, 80
output
  as equal to income and sales. *See* income, as equal to output and sales
  in Mitchell's theory, 130–131
  in Monetarist theory, 154
  in Real Business Cycle theory, 156
overhead
  in Mitchell's theory, 131
overinvestment, 34
  in Interest-Rate Induced theory, 150
  in Keynes' theory, 133, 135
  in Neoclassical theory, 151
  in Real Business Cycle theory, 157

panic, 15, 18, 29–30, 32, 54, 85, 90
  in Austrian theory, 159
  in Keynes' theory, 134
  in Minsky's theory, 146
pessimism, 16, 21, 23, 31, 56
  in Keynes' theory, 134
  Subprime Crisis cycle, 97
  Volcker cycle, 80
Phillip's Curve, 78
PMI. *See* Purchasing Managers' Index
policy
  fine tuning
    in Neoclassical theory, 151
  fiscal, 48–49
    COVID cycle, 101, 104
    in Neoclassical theory, 151
    Oil Shock I cycle, 72–73
    Oil Shock II cycle, 77
    Vietnam cycle, 64
  monetary, 46–49
    in Austrian theory, 159
    in Monetarist theory, 153
    September 11 cycle, 93
    Vietnam cycle, 64, 67–68
    Volcker cycle, 80–82
    Subprime Crisis cycle, 95

Ponzi unit
  in Minsky's theory, 145–146
poverty, 112–114, 127
prices
  elasticity of demand, 39–40, 45
  in Interest-Rate Induced theory, 150
  in Mitchell's theory, 130–132
  in Monetarist theory, 154
  principle of increasing risk, 33–34,
    140–141
  productive capacity, 9–10, 13–14, 20–21,
    23, 34, 47, 51, 54–55, 93, 107, 117,
    125
  in Davidson's theory, 146–149
  Ike I cycle, 59
  Ike II cycle, 62
  Kalecki's theory, 141
  in Mitchell's theory, 131–132
  Oil Shock I cycle, 73
  in Real Business Cycle theory, 155
  saturation of demand for, 10, 21–22, 31
    in Keynes' theory, 134
  September 11 cycle, 91–92
  Subprime Crisis cycle, 95
  Vietnam cycle, 67
productivity, 51
  job-destroying nature, 104–105
  in Real Business Cycle theory, 155–156
  September 11 cycle, 88–89, 92
profit, 22, 32–33
  Desert Storm cycle, 84–86
  Ike I cycle, 59
  Ike II cycle, 63
  in Kalecki's theory, 135–141
  in Keynes' theory, 134
  in Mitchell's theory, 130–132
  Oil Shock II cycle, 76–77
  September 11 cycle, 92–93
  versus social benefit, 112
  Subprime Crisis cycle, 97–98
  Vietnam cycle, 67
  Volcker cycle, 80
Purchasing Managers' Index
  COVID cycle, 104
  definition, 23
  Desert Storm cycle, 83–84, 86
  Ike I cycle, 58–59
  Oil Shock I cycle, 72
  Oil Shock II cycle, 76
  September 11 cycle, 92–93
  Subprime Crisis cycle, 97–99
  Vietnam cycle, 65, 67
  Volcker cycle, 80

rationality, 15, 30, 98
  in Neoclassical theory, 151
rational expectations
  in Neoclassical theory, 153
  in Real Business Cycle theory, 155
Reagan, Ronald, 79, 81, 83, 87, 92, 103, 121
  negative economic consequences of, 87
Real Business Cycle theory, 4, 149, 152,
  155–157
recession, 57
  COVID, 104
  Desert Storm cycle, 86
  Ike I cycle, 59–60
  Ike II cycle, 62
  Oil Shock I cycle, 73–74
  Oil Shock II cycle, 77
  September 11 cycle, 92–93
  Subprime Crisis cycle, 98
  Vietnam cycle, 70
  Volcker cycle, 80
risk, 14
  borrower's
    in Minsky's theory, 144–146
  decision making under. See decision making,
    under risk
  Keynes' approach
    definition, 14
  lender's
    in Minsky's theory, 144–146
Rogoff and Reinhart controversy, 102
Romer, Christina, 1, 6–7, 153
Romer, Paul, 2–4, 12–13, 151, 157
Russian invasion of Ukraine, 40, 43, 82

S&P 500 Index, 85
sales
  as equal to income and output. See income,
    as equal to output and sales
  in Kalecki's theory, 135–137
  in Mitchell's theory, 131
saving, 11
  in Austrian theory, 158
  September 11 cycle, 91
sectoral balances approach, 121–123
secular stagnation, 51–52
securities. See stock market
September 11 terrorist attacks, 93
shocks to the economy, 1, 4, 7, 22, 53, 60, 86,
  105, 111
  Oil Shock I, 74
  in Real Business Cycle theory, 155–157
  September 11 cycle, 93
Social Security, xiv, 119

Index

speculation, 38–39, 43–44, 46–47, 117
speculative unit
  in Minsky's theory, 145
stock market
  boom
    Desert Storm cycle, 84
    September 11 cycle, 90, 93
  circuit breaker
    Desert Storm cycle, 85
  computerized trading
    Desert Storm cycle, 85
  crash
    Desert Storm cycle, 84
    September 11 cycle, 90–92
    in Mitchell's theory, 131
  securities, 50–51
  Vietnam cycle, 65
Stop-Go business cycle theory, 151–153
strike
  Ike II cycle, 61–62
  Oil Shock I cycle, 71
  Oil Shock II cycle, 76
  Vietnam cycle, 70

tax. *See* government spending, tax
Treasury Bills, 26–29, 46, 48
  Ike I cycle, 60
  Ike II cycle, 62
  Modern Monetary Theory explanation, 123–125
Trump, Donald, 87, 100–101, 103–104
twin deficits
  Desert Storm cycle, 85

uncertainty, 95
  binary nature, 16
  decision making under. *See* decision making, under uncertainty
  Keynes' approach, 29, 50, 90, 97, 132–133, 135, 149

unemployment, 1, 109
  COVID cycle, 103–104
  Desert Storm cycle, 83–86
  inflation tradeoff, 9, 47
    in Neoclassical theory, 151–153
  involuntary
    in Neoclassical theory, 153
  Oil Shock I cycle, 72–73
  Oil Shock II cycle, 75–77
  in Real Business Cycle theory, 157
  September 11 cycle, 92–93
  Subprime Crisis cycle, 95
  Vietnam cycle, 64, 66, 68
  voluntary
    in Monetarist theory, 155
    in Real Business Cycle theory, 156
unions, 71, 92
  Volcker cycle, 81
universal basic income, 118

Vietnam War, 66, 70
Volcker, Paul, 36, 77–78, 81

wage, 41
  in Kalecki's theory, 135–137
  living, 108, 115–116
  in Monetarist theory, 154
  in Neoclassical theory, 152
  Oil Shock II cycle, 76, 78
  in Real Business Cycle theory, 156–157
  September 11 cycle, 91
  Volcker cycle, 81
wage and price controls, 42, 70
  Oil Shock I cycle, 72
worker
  in Kalecki's theory, 135–137
World War II, xi, 6, 49, 68, 96, 99–100, 119, 151

For EU product safety concerns, contact us at Calle de José Abascal, 56–1°,
28003 Madrid, Spain or eugpsr@cambridge.org.

www.ingramcontent.com/pod-product-compliance
Ingram Content Group UK Ltd.
Pitfield, Milton Keynes, MK11 3LW, UK
UKHW020053040426
469672UK00019B/421